Meridians feminism, race, transnationalism

VOLUME 18 · NUMBER 2 · OCTOBER 2019

Ginetta E. B. Candelario

Editor's Introduction

In the mid-1990s a small group of feminist faculty from women's studies, Latin American studies, and Afro-American studies at Smith College came together to discuss the troubling lacunae in each of their respective fields.[1] Because each interdisciplinary field had a foundational mission to address the biases and assumptions of traditional disciplines that had overlooked—or worse, distorted—the experiences of its particular oppressed and/or exploited community, the fields prioritized one locus of discrimination and generally glossed over others. This paradigmatic weakness extended to each field's otherwise innovative curricula, scholarship, and pedagogy. As a group of Black feminist scholars put it in the title of their groundbreaking anthology more than a decade earlier, within women's studies and race and ethnicity studies it seemed that *All the Women Are White, All the Blacks Are Men, But Some of Us Are Brave* (Hull, Scott, and Smith [1982] 2015). Thus, one of the signature pieces of the *Brave* collection—the Combahee River Collective Statement—argued that gender, race, class, and sexuality are mutually constitutive systems that must be considered and addressed together as a critical corrective to single-issue agendas and paradigms. Just as these systems of oppression were co-constitutive of what another Black feminist called a "matrix of domination," so too would their dismantling require an "intersectional" strategy in law and society (Collins 1990, 21; Crenshaw 1989, 140). Yet, despite the Combahee Collective's critique of U.S. imperialism and its celebration of Third World/Internationalist affinities—not to mention the long history

MERIDIANS · feminism, race, transnationalism   18:2 October 2019
DOI: 10.1215/15366936-7775608 © 2019 Smith College

of Black internationalism in the United States—their radical intervention was still largely U.S. centric, as was the *Brave* anthology itself.

Likewise, given area studies's origins in the Cold War U.S. anti-communist intelligence community, early Latin American studies scholars (who were predominantly white men) invested minimally in studying race, even less in studying women and gender, and little to nothing in understanding the region's diasporas and its historic presence in North America. This was the case despite the concurrent rise and establishment of Chicano/Mexican American, Puerto Rican, and/or Latino studies. Unlike their contemporary Latin Americanist colleagues, these early Latino studies scholars did articulate what are now called "transnational" analyses and political concerns, including with race and gender, as systems produced by and productive of *both* geopolitics *and* domestic power structures. Nonetheless, Latino studies also largely shared with Afro-American studies a U.S. mainland analytical focus on civil rights matters. Similarly, Latina feminists joined Black feminists in insisting on intersectional analyses, but it was the more radical collectives such as Third World Women's Alliance that produced an analysis of the links between U.S. imperialism, European colonialism, and oppressive conditions for Black and brown women around the world.

So it was that although the word *trans-nationalism* was first coined by U.S. ethnic pluralist Randolph S. Bourne in his 1916 critique of the era's nativism, the term's meaning was radically transformed because of the facts on the ground of the late twentieth century U.S. academy and broader society. The end of fifty years of restrictions on immigration from Latin America, the Caribbean, and Asia following the passage of the 1965 Immigration and Naturalization Act meant that the turn of the twenty-first century saw tremendous growth in non-European heritage populations. These changing demographics forced a reconsideration of conventional (im)migrant assimilation and acculturation axioms. For example, by 1990 the anthropologist Eugenia Georges argued that Dominicans in the Dominican Republic and the United States should be studied together, as part of a unified social field that transcended national boundaries (Georges 1990). From there it was but a short step to the argument that intersectionality and transnationalism *together* offered a powerful corrective to the particular paradigms of earlier race and ethnic studies, area studies, and women's studies (Candelario 2017: 236–39).

It was within this historic context that professors Ann Arnett Ferguson, Nancy Saporta Sternbach, and Susan Van Dyne decided to establish *Meridians: feminism, race, transnationalism* at Smith College. They did so in order to center knowledges produced by and about women of color who critically integrated and interrogated feminist, racial, and transnational concerns. Serendipitously, Ruth Simmons, who in 1995 had become Smith College's first Black president and was committed to supporting innovation and equity at our historically white-serving women's college, responded enthusiastically to this intellectual and political project. With Simmons's generous support, *Meridians* published its first issue in fall 2000.

Thus, as we gear up to celebrate our twentieth anniversary in 2020, *Meridians; feminism,race,transnationalism* is particularly pleased to presage that milestone with this fall 2019 special issue on "Radical Transnational Feminisms," guest edited by highly regarded transnational feminist scholars Laura Briggs and Robyn C. Spencer. As Briggs and Spencer note in their introduction to this issue, in specifying that theirs is a "radical" transnational feminist commitment, they want to signal "an alliance with political movements that work to undo the nation and its violences, including imperialism, racisms, and colonialisms" while also "allow[ing] for certain types of solidarities to take root"(255). Accordingly, the texts in this issue call for consideration of a range of transnational feminist alliances, solidarities, and complicities. These various terms reflect related ideas, and perhaps are even considered synonyms by some. However, as a closer reading of this issue shows, each term signals divergent political responsibilities and possibilities. I encourage our readers to note where, when, and how *alliance*, *solidarity*, and *complicity* are used in the collection, and to consider how these terms both reveal and obscure the tensions within transnational feminisms.

Lastly, I take this opportunity to dedicate this issue to Professor Nancy Saporta Sternbach, who retired from Smith this year. During her thirty-five years on the faculty Nancy was not only a central member of the *Meridians* founding and subsequent editorial collective, she continued to serve on the journal's editorial advisory board in the decades that followed.[2] An outspoken transnational feminist, Nancy also labored ceaselessly to introduce, incorporate, and institutionalize Latin American and Latin@ studies at Smith and the Five Colleges. She taught thousands of students that Latin American peoples, languages, literatures, cultures, and social movements are central to understanding global history. As important, Nancy published some of the earliest English-language scholarship on Latin American, Caribbean, and Latina feminisms and women's movements, a commitment sparked when she was one of a handful of U.S. women in attendance at the first Latin American and Caribbean Feminists *Encuentro* held in Bogotá, Colombia in 1980. In the edited volumes, book chapters, journal articles, and college courses that followed, Nancy documented the long, illustrious, and complicated histories of feminism and women's movements in Latin America, the Caribbean, and the United States (Horno-Delgado et al. 1988; Sternbach 1991: 91–102; Sternbach et al. 1992: 393–434). In doing so she was part of small group of U.S.-based feminist scholars working to correct the distorted and incomplete historical record typically relied upon by the U.S. scholarly and activist communities. In other words, Nancy Saporta Sternbach modeled radical transnational feminism in her politics, pedagogy, and scholarship well before it was safe to do so; she is one of those who were brave. I know all this because I had the good fortune to have been one of her undergraduate students when she first joined the Smith faculty in 1985, her faculty colleague from 1999 to 2019, and now part of her legacy at *Meridians*. *Gracias profesora, por todo.*

Notes

1   Today these units at Smith are called Study of Women and Gender Program, Latin American and Latin@ Studies, and Africana Studies. However, I have used the monikers in place at the time of their activism.
2   The names of our founding editorial collective members can be found on our masthead.

Works Cited

Candelario, Ginetta E. B. 2017. "Transnationalism." In *Keywords in Latino Studies*, edited by Nancy R. Mirabal, Larry Lafontaine Stokes, and Debra Vargas, 236–39. New York: Routledge.

Collins, Patricia Hill. 1990. *Black Feminist Thought: Knowledge, Consciousness, and the Politics of Empowerment*. Boston: Unwin Hyman.

Crenshaw, Kimberle. 1989. "Demarginalizing the Intersection of Race and Sex: A Black Feminist Critique of Antidiscrimination Doctrine, Feminist Theory and Antiracist Politics." *University of Chicago Legal Forum* 140: 139–68.

Georges, Eugenia. 1990. *The Making of a Transnational Community: Migration, Development, and Cultural Change in the Dominican Republic*. New York: Columbia University Press.

Horno-Delgado, Asuncíon, Eliana Ortega, Nina M. Scott, and Nancy Saporta Sternbach, eds. 1988. *Breaking Boundaries: Latina Writings and Critical Readings*. Amherst: University of Massachusetts Press.

Hull, Akasha (Gloria T.), Patricia Bell Scott, and Barbara Smith, eds. (1982) 2015. *All the Women Are White, All the Blacks Are Men, But Some of Us Are Brave: Black Women's Studies*. 2nd ed. New York: The Feminist Press at CUNY.

Sternbach, Nancy Saporta. 1991. "Re-membering the Dead: Latin American Women's 'Testimonial' Discourse." *Latin American Perspectives* 18, no. 3: 91–102.

Sternbach, Nancy Saporta, Marysa Navarro-Aranguren, Patricia Chuchryk, and Sonia E. Alvarez. 1992. "Feminisms in Latin America: From Bogota to San Bernado." *Signs: Journal of Women in Culture and Society* 17, no. 2: 393–434.

Laura Briggs and Robyn C. Spencer

Introduction

Our Intellectual Coming Together

This special issue began as a set of overlapping conversations among an interdisciplinary group of feminist scholars whose work centered political economy and performance; postcoloniality and empire; racialization and indigeneity; as well as traversed borders of nation, ideology, space, and time. Our intellectual praxis unfolded at the intersections of transnationalism and feminisms, yet the field of "transnational feminism" as it has been defined and institutionalized in the academy in the 1990s conjured frameworks and definitions that were ill-suited to contain the scope of our inquiries. Many of the questions we asked individually and collectively— How did transnational feminism relate to women of color and black feminist genealogies? Could transnational feminism decenter the Global North as a touchstone or default comparative for women's experiences worldwide and include geographies that were Pacific, African, Latin American, and Caribbean? What was the potential of transnational feminism to shed light on ongoing settler colonialism in North America?—stretched the boundaries of transnational feminism. Our conversations grew as new people from graduate students to activists to senior scholars from a multiplicity of places and fields brought new questions from different sites of engagement.

We came together in multiple configurations, trying to engage multiple networks of scholars and pull in new people at every turn, yet ever conscious of all the intellectuals inside and especially outside the United

MERIDIANS · feminism, race, transnationalism   18:2 October 2019
DOI: 10.1215/15366936-7775619 © 2019 Smith College

States who were missing, to think together about how to productively destabilize transnational feminist frameworks. At the Ohio State University, some of us worked to put together a "Thinking Transnational Feminisms Summer Institute" in 2014, defining transnational feminism as a "quickly growing but contested field" fraught with "potentialities and continued erasures." Eighty participants collaborated and engaged in dialogue for a week in this feminist summer camp.[1] A special issue of *Frontiers: A Journal of Women Studies* grew out of this initiative.[2] Some of us worked to establish a Transnational Feminisms Caucus at the National Women's Studies Association Conference. At the University of Michigan, some of us crafted a collaborative research seminar on Radical Transnational Feminisms, sponsored by the Institute for Research on Women and Gender. Under the umbrella of the University of California Research Institute some of us designed a research cluster called Rethinking Transnational Feminism with the goal of attending to labor, centering Africa and the Americas, borderlands and indigeneity, as well as examining the "transformative impact of activism on transnational feminist scholarship." The effort has included a symposium and will potentially result in an edited volume.[3] These burgeoning networks have coalesced publicly on social media in the Thinking Transnational Feminisms Facebook group, a robust and international space where hundreds of scholars and activists share calls for papers, articles on contemporary politics, and publication announcements.[4] This special issue is part of this intellectual ecosystem.

The work in this volume adopts a critical stance in relation to the "nation" in transnational feminism. From the outset, we have sought to center Indigenous Studies and Native feminisms as crucial to the solidarities and politics we are interested in, and that inevitably makes the whole Westphalian "nations" framework that grounds "transnationalisms" deeply problematic. Whether we are thinking about the Americas or a great many other places, starting with Native feminism reminds us that the violence of the settler colonial project is at the heart of the nation. Thinking of "transnationalism" as kinds of solidarity across tribal nations, or conceiving of the United States as a nation of nations only uneasily resolves this problem. Further, for those of us interested in the island-territories that make up regions in the Pacific or the Caribbean, places whose legal status has names like Department, Commonwealth, Land, Territory, Municipality—anything but colony, even when they are under the administration of sovereign nations, often far away—speaking of the "transnational" makes only the most limited kind of sense.

Our understanding of transnational feminism rejects imperial feminisms and neoliberal constructs, and remains attuned to the nuances of power and privilege that shape political exchanges and can obscure non-EuroAmerican axes of knowledge. We see the potential of a *radical* transnational feminist framework to foreground the global solidarities that can transform everything from international regimes of debt and austerity, to the macro and micro politics of social reproduction. *Radical* transnational feminism can demonstrate the impact of globalization and the scope of racial capitalism. A *radical* transnational feminist framework allows for the juxtaposition of fields like Diasporic Black Studies and TransPacific World Studies. The modifier *radical* ("at the root") signals an alliance with political movements that work to undo the nation and its violences, including imperialism, racisms, and colonialisms. It allows us to take up the most productive areas of potential in transnational feminist frameworks.

The modifier *radical* does analytical work that is unsettled, reflecting the dynamic ongoing conversations that continue to unite our group. We are delving into the potential of radical transnational feminism to shed light on decolonization and postcolonial movements, including racial formations, settler colonialism, colonialism, military bases, racial capitalism, antisemitism, slavery and its afterlives, sex work and the sexual violence of militaries and empires, political movements, migration and anti-immigrant sentiment, and all the other ways that we know racism and misogyny to be spacialized and to materialize their violence in ways that rely on national borders. We are less interested in pinning down a final definition of a radical transnational politic outright and are more comfortable letting the essays, interviews, poetry, field reports, and primary source analyses contained in this special issue lay out the scope of inquiry and the ways in which we leaned into the contradictions and negotiated the tensions between what transnational feminism obscures and what it reveals. As scholars and activists we have taught, read widely, or published in the field and are in conversation with the foundational literature even as we gesture beyond definitions.[5] We seek, throughout, to specify the analytical and political work that needs to be done in diverse spaces to sediment the contradictions and allow for certain types of solidarities to take root.

Inside the Issue

Transnational feminist frameworks have grappled with the role of women and formal political power. What are the radical possibilities and the potential limitations for transformation using this framework? Judy Tzu-Chun Wu's essay on Patsy Mink, the Japanese American, feminist, and liberal Democratic U.S. representative from Hawaii, analyzes how Mink embodied both feminism and antimilitarism in the Pacific. The paper explores Mink's worldview and the role of "life, land, and water" in her conceptualization of the Pacific world. It also sheds light on her advocacy of an end to nuclear weapon testing in the Pacific, including the Marshall Islands and Hawaii's Kahoʻolawe. Mink worked alongside Native Hawaiians but also fundamentally in conflict with them, as she sought better terms of inclusion in the United States and they sought sovereignty. Mink's worldview and activism speak to the political fissures in projects that were transnational yet not ideologically aligned, and Wu's essay offers a thick reading of formal politics as a site of feminist engagement with the U.S. state.

Settler colonialism is increasingly used as an analytical tool to describe processes of dispossession and violence in a variety of academic fields. Maile Arvin's article asks readers to reconsider the knowledge production of indigenous women, feminist, and queer theorists who center gender and sexuality in their political analyses, like scholar-activist Haunani-Kay Trask. How can this perspective inform a critique of Asian settler colonialism faced by Native Hawaiians? Her article looks at the relationship between "white mainstream feminisms," indigenous feminisms, and transnational feminisms, and attends to the politics of citation that often erase indigenous scholars from the very geographies and histories in which they are rooted while making them hypervisible for "neoliberal diversity" work in academia. Considering the Women's March in Honolulu in 2017, Arvin's essay offers timely lessons for the politics of solidarity.

Radical transnational feminism demands an epistemological shift. Rosamond S. King's essay pushes the border of transnational feminist inquiry by using the radical interdisciplinarity of poetry, creative arts, and biography to flesh out the stories of jamette women in Trinidad in the face of archival silences. By expanding the boundaries of scholarly writing to include knowledge traditions that are organically intellectual and rooted outside of the academy, King centers activism as historical reconstruction and feminist methodology. Global south genealogies of transnational feminism knowledge production are attended to in Stanlie James's essay, which reinserts African feminists into a longer tradition of publishing manifestos. James analyzes the text of the Charter of Feminist Principles for African Feminists, productively comparing it to the Combahee River Collective manifesto. How do concepts like interlocking oppression, methodologies like radical collectivity, and the praxis of feminist alliance building resonate in different racialized geographies? How does the recovery of African feminist intellectual traditions shift the embedded hierarchies in the notion of the transnational? Readers are offered the full text of the document following James's comments, with this juxtaposition literally expanding the archives of feminist struggle.

Deema Kaedbey and Nadine Naber model collaborative research and embodied praxis in their reflections on research in Lebanon. Their essay centers a regional, Middle Eastern feminism, and asks what it would look like to think through the female participation in anti-authoritarian movements across the region as a kind of transnational feminism. They analyze the mobilization in Beirut in response to the state's refusal to pick up garbage in relation to the Tahrir Square protests and to queer and feminist activism. While anti-authoritarian mobilizations in Beirut and Egypt were often criticized for not being feminist, Kaedbey and Naber use oral histories to demonstrate the extensive participation of women and feminists in left mobilizations as well as the South-South transnational solidarities between and among feminists in the Middle East and North Africa region.

Elisabeth Armstrong's essay on the 1949 Asian Women's Conference suggests that an earlier generation struggled with similar issues, and that they too nested the politics of women's liberation within their work in decolonization movements. As women in Africa, Asia, and Latin America took up arms in anticolonial wars, they called on women in Western Europe and the United States to oppose imperial counterinsurgent violence and the neo-imperialism of Wall Street. As difficult as these kinds of solidarities were, Armstrong argues that they were centered in a formation that linked women's liberation, antiracism, and anti-imperialism as a unified politics.

The power of language to shift the terms of transnational engagement onto decolonial ground is laid bare in Neda Maghbouleh, Laila Omar, Melissa A. Milkie, and Ito Peng's essay on conducting community-based research in Arabic among Syrian women in Canada. Their analysis encompasses translation as transnational feminist praxis, the role that language plays in disciplining knowledge, and participants' agency in shaping research studies. Tara Daly uses a feminist reading of Peruvian pop art by Claudia Coca to disentangle the term *chola* from its liminal framing and recast it as a site of potential transnational feminist mobilization and anticolonial critique. Her essay explores the transnational resonance of art that illuminates wars both historical and psychic; and the power of alternative imaginaries to gesture toward the possibility of a woman-led politics of solidarity.

The history of transnational solidarity work by women of color is captured in the primary sources featured in this issue. "Salvadoran Women: In Search of Peace and Justice" by Miriam Louie and Vicki Alexander details the work of *Somos Hermanas* and the Alliance Against Women's Oppression. The position paper chronicles the nationwide, multi-issue, and intersectional work undertaken by multiracial organizations during the Reagan era and the long timeline of U.S.-backed dictatorships in Latin America. It takes readers to the front lines of movements for human rights, exploring the plight of women political prisoners and the activism of women in trade unions. The second primary source, "Pan Pacific and Southeast Asia Women's Association of the United States of America Discussion Group," during the chill of the Cold War in the 1950s, chronicles the discussions between five Asian and five American women whose work in United Nations projects and agencies made them coalesce under the umbrella of "Southeast Asia and the United Nations." These highly educated women operated transnationally as UN representatives and their discussions demonstrate the potentials and restraints of UN frameworks.

Brooke Lober's interview with Aurora Levins Morales, a Puerto Rican and Jewish writer, poet, and storyteller who authored key texts in the woman of color feminist intellectual tradition and remains active in disability justice and anti-imperialist and feminist struggles, weaves together a rich tapestry from a life in struggle. From Morales's family history, to the impact of Hurricane Maria on Puerto Rico in 2017, to the importance of the seminal *This Bridge Called My Back: Writing by Radical Women of Color* edited by Cherríe Moraga and Gloria Anzaldúa, this interview embodies the landscape of radical transnational concerns with justice.

Pedagogical Synergies

The analyses in this issue unfold in thematic, chronological, and geographical registers. This broad approach makes this issue uniquely suited for traditional and nontraditional classroom use. In particular, essays engage oral history, ethnography, and embodied research in ways that critically interrogate the power dynamics of the process and engage a variety of sites and disciplinary perspectives. Settler colonialism is understood as an ongoing event that animates the study of the Pacific and unsettles contemporary experiences of immigration in the United States. Solidarity and the possibility and problematics of shared struggle are explored in almost all of the essays. Readers encounter interviews with poets, scholars using poetry as methodology, and the urgent provocations in poems and creative writing by Ching-In Chen, Nancy Kang, Evelyne Trouillot, Nathan H. Dize, and Maylei Blackwell, which punctuate the issue not as sidebars but as illuminations of transnational feminist concerns.

Laura Briggs is Professor of Women, Gender, Sexuality Studies at the University of Massachusetts Amherst. She is a scholar of reproductive politics and U.S. empire, and the author of three books, most recently *How All Politics Became Reproductive Politics: From Welfare Reform to Foreclosure to Trump* (2017).

Robyn C. Spencer is a historian who studies Black social protest after World War II, urban and working-class radicalism, and gender. She teaches at Lehman College, CUNY and is the author of *The Revolution Has Come: Black Power, Gender, and the Black Panther Party in Oakland* (2016).

Notes

1   "Thinking Transnational Feminisms Summer Institute 2014," Ohio State University, accessed March 20, 2019. https://frontiers.osu.edu/tfsi.
2   *Frontiers: A Journal of Women Studies* 36, no. 3 (2015).
3   "Rethinking Transnational Feminisms," accessed April 9, 2019. https://uchri .org/awards/rethinking-transnational-feminisms/.
4   "Thinking Transnational Feminisms," accessed March 20, 2019. https://www .facebook.com/groups/tfsinstitute/.
5   Some of our collective engagement with issues of transnationalism and feminism are reflected in these writings: Nixon and King 2013; Naber 2016; Blackwell 2014; Briggs 2002; Arvin 2019; and Wu 2013.

Works Cited

Arvin, Maile. 2019. *Possessing Polynesians: The Science of Settler Colonial Whiteness in Hawai'i and Oceania.* Durham, NC: Duke University Press.
Blackwell, Maylei. 2014. "Translenguas: Mapping the Possibilities and Challenges of Transnational Women's Organizing across Geographies of Difference." In *Translocalities/Translocalidades: Feminist Politics of Translation in the Latin/a Américas,* edited by Sonia E. Alvarez, 299–320. Durham, NC: Duke University Press.

Briggs, Laura. 2002. *Reproducing Empire: Race, Sex, Science, and the U.S. Imperial Project in Puerto Rico*. Berkeley: University of California Press.

Naber, Nadine. 2016. "Arab and Black Feminisms: Joint Struggle and Transnational Anti-Imperialist Activism." *Departures in Critical Qualitative Research* 5, no. 3: 116–25.

Nixon, Angelique, and Rosamond S. King. 2013. "Embodied Theories: Local Knowledge(s), Community Organizing, and Feminist Methodologies in Caribbean Sexuality Studies." *Caribbean Review of Gender Studies* 7: 1–15.

Wu, Judy Tzu-Chun. 2013. *Radicals on the Road: Internationalism, Orientalism, and Feminism during the Vietnam Era*. Ithaca, NY: Cornell University Press.

Elisabeth Armstrong

. . . .

Peace and the Barrel of the Gun in the Internationalist Women's Movement, 1945–49

Abstract: In 1949, at a conference instigated by the Women's International Democratic Federation (WIDF) held in Beijing, China, the Asian Women's Conference solidified an anticolonial, antifascist, and antiracist theory for organizing women transnationally. This transnational feminist praxis drew its movement demands and strategies from the masses of women in antico-lonial movements, both rural and urban poor women. It also framed a two-fold theory of women's organizing: it delineated one platform for women fighting imperialism within colonized countries, and another platform for women fighting imperialism within aggressor nations. This transnational feminism supported an explicitly pro-socialist vision for the future.

Colonialism is dead, and it only remains for the corpse to be buried.
—Asian Women's Conference

Asian Women's Conference, Beijing, 1949

The air was cold in December of 1949, and delegates of the Asian Women's Conference (AWC) stayed bundled up at their seats in the Winter Palace in Beijing, People's Republic of China. Banners hung on the walls that celebrated their historic gathering of anti-imperialist women activists, a conference hosted by the Women's International Democratic Federation

MERIDIANS · feminism, race, transnationalism   18:2 October 2019
DOI: 10.1215/15366936-7775685 © 2019 Smith College

(WIDF) and the All China Women's Federation (ACWF). Delegates from fourteen Asian countries and thirty-three fraternal delegates from around the world listened to speeches and country reports, danced the Korean lindy hop and listened to experimental, pan-Asian musical performances; many also toured Shanghai and Huairou factories and art institutes after the conference ended (Millard Papers; Ramelson Notes).

The celebrations did not mask the seriousness of their political moment, however. Delegate after delegate described the horrendous conditions faced by women, children, and men under Dutch, French, and British rule in Asian and African colonies. They spoke of planned starvation, forced labor, and conscription into colonial armies. They condemned the military occupations that gave lie to the Western rhetoric of democracy, let alone freedom. They built the sinews of a mass-based transnational women's movement: one that fought systems of colonialism, fascism, racism, and patriarchy simultaneously.

Delegates attending the AWC lauded the bravery of peasant women as the militant backbone to their anticolonial struggles for independence and women's emancipation from oppressive customs. These rural women primarily fought battles against feudal landowners and old forms of subjugation based on land ownership, customary rule, and local hierarchies. As activists from the Tebhaga peasant struggles of Bengal between 1946 and 1948 described, colonial rule at it its inception yoked these systems of violence against peasant women to its own reproduction at the global level (Chakravartty 1980; Lahiri 2001; Sen 2001). Peasant women in Bengal in the Tebhaga movement fought for the rights to the crops they grew as well as for their own sexual autonomy over the demands of landed men (Armstrong 2017; Panjabi 2017). Intrinsic to these struggles, they fought and briefly won the right to live without violence in their own familial relationships, serving justice for women in violent relationships in their own courts.

As interviews of peasant activists from this period show, women particularly, but also men narrated all of these demands as integral to anticolonial struggles (Cooper 1988). Similarly, AWC delegates across Asia spoke about how anticolonialism and women's full autonomy were entwined struggles. Neither national nor social self-determination could precede the other, since both were deeply embedded economic forms of enslavement to another's gain. Colonial regimes relied on localized patriarchal relationships to secure their regional control. The demand for women's self-determination was an inseparable and mutually reinforcing struggle for regional independence. For anticolonialism to have any purchase on the future, women's full emancipation was today's work, not tomorrow's aspiration.

As ceremony, the Asian Women's Conference symbolized the truth of postwar imperialism: colonialism was over and revolutionary women had dug that grave. As politics, the conference evoked another future: of equality, of independence, of emancipation for all—patriarchy, fascism, racism, and imperialism would not be tolerated any longer. Colonialism, configured as the past, and socialism hailed as the future reverberated throughout the delegates' speeches. The most concrete gain from the gathering was one of strategy for a feminist anticolonialism that truly encompassed the aspirations of women from around the globe. The AWC successfully ratified a profound shift in strategy for women's internationalism, one that has disappeared, almost without a trace. The best place to view this anticolonial, socialist, and feminist strategy lies not in delegates' speeches at the 1949 conference, though they provide valuable clues to the interweaving of techniques developed across Asia. The clearest articulation of anticolonial feminist socialism was collectively framed in their conference appeals, and put into action the moment delegates returned home.

Women's Internationalism, 1945–49

At the 1945 inception of the leftist international women's organization called the Women's International Democratic Federation, participants from Asian and North African colonies successfully added anticolonialism to antifascism and antiracism in WIDF's platform for action. By 1949, WIDF's internationalist praxis went far beyond symbolic solidarity and called for all women's active confrontation with imperialism at home and in the world. For women in colonies, the call to action was two-fold: build a regional unity and join women's armed resistance against colonialism. For women in imperialist countries, this praxis demanded politics against the domestic economy of imperialist militarism and colonial occupation. As a praxis grounded in a Marxist analysis led by the Soviet Union and China, it emerged from the Communist International's understanding of postwar imperialism, anticolonial nationalism, and the necessity of armed struggle. Just as important, however, were the movements of rural, agricultural waged and peasant women workers who were willing to combat oppression by any means necessary. Rural and urban working women's organizing forged this internationalist strategy, largely overriding for this moment in the late 1940s, other distinctions of practice and theory among leftists around the world.

From the blunt edge of their analysis, leftist and nationalist women's movements in Asia and Africa built an anti-imperialist strategy for women of the world that linked feminism with a systemic analysis of antiracism and antifascism (Pieper Mooney 2013). They used regional ties and international gatherings in Asia to build consensus and air their differences, including the nationalist Asian Relations Conference held in New Delhi, India in 1947, the pro-Palestinian, anticolonial women's gatherings like the Arab Women's Conference held in Cairo in 1944, and the almost entirely communist gathering of the pan-Asian Women's Conference held in Beijing in 1949 (Stolte 2014; Weber 2003). By the late 1940s, however, WIDF became the central organizational means for leftist and nationalist women to debate the postwar anticolonial order, to amplify their strategies, and to build toward a pro-socialist future. Between 1945 and 1949, WIDF members debated how to understand the dynamic of imperialism in the second half of the twentieth century as territorial colonial occupation faced its violent end.

Baya Bouhoune Allaouchiche, general secretary of the Algerian Women's Union, presented a clear picture of postwar imperialism and the solidarity Algerian women practiced:

> Algeria is in fact a colony of France with political, economic and social inequalities and the crushing of national culture. War (is) being prepared before (the) eyes of people. Algerian troops have been sent to Vietnam and Algerian women have protested against this. (Ramelson Notes)

Allaouchiche details the politics of imperialism, the place of Algerian women and men, and an Algerian women's solidarity of complicity.[1] Algerian peasant women and men drove away the recruiting agents who offered cash for their sons' enlistment into the colonial military. This solidarity laid bare the colonial relations of war. Algerian soldiers were trained by the French to crush the Vietnamese independence struggle. Algerian women's solidarity assumed accountability for the mercenary actions of Algerian soldiers and thus protested the use of Algerians by the French against the Vietnamese. As anti-imperialist women, they refused to accept the colonizers' blood on their hands. In this women's movement, colonialism was shorn of its veneer of local self-governance, its promises of women's education, or its erasure of state-planned starvation and the dispossession of peasants' land. Colonialism was war. These refusals of edicts of colonialism led by rural and urban women were not simply solidarity actions of nationalism. The actions themselves demanded confrontations with gender norms of public behavior, and more broadly, the public stage for political action itself. The very possibility of refusing to allow their sons to enlist forced a confrontation with women's access to public space, public voice, and autonomy as anticolonialism. Feminism, in the leftist diction of the time, referred to women's legal and political rights shorn of any attention to (if not outright refusal to demand) the economic transformation of capitalism. The revolutionary refusals of colonialism described by delegates like Allaouchiche, however, reframed feminism and demands for women's legal and political rights as demands made meaningful *through* anticolonialism as a movement for people's self-determination and radically different world orders.

In 1948, Cai Chang, an important women's leader in the Chinese Communist Party (CCP) and vice president of WIDF, defined the terms for WIDF's internationalist activism at its second international congress held in Budapest, Hungary. Cai paraphrased Lenin for her slogan that echoed throughout many of the speeches: "A people which oppresses another cannot itself be free."[2] This slogan, heard so many times over the six days of the congress, threaded together emergent political strategies. Women across Africa and Asia demanded freedom with peace. European and American women needed to act with equal urgency, though from a distinctly different location. Cai obliquely referenced Andrei Zhdanov's two-camp theory of the postwar order: the capitalist nations' camp was imperialist, the socialist and anticolonial nations' camp was democratic.[3] This doctrine "declared that communist parties were natural leaders of the anticolonial struggle" (Efimova and McVey 2011). As such, she bridged the character of anti-imperialist internationalism for the women on the frontlines of colonialism and the women still figuring out their role in this battle. Speaking directly to women from imperialist nations, she explained:

> This must be the slogan under which the Union of French Women fights
> to strengthen the struggle against the war in Vietnam. . . . The women of
> Holland must ceaselessly demand the cessation of the colonial war, and
> the recall of the troops from Indonesia. This slogan must also be adopted
> by women of the other imperialist countries, above all those of the

United States. They must help their sisters *not only because they are moved by a sentiment of justice, but because the struggle of the women in the dependent countries against the oppressors is part of the fight for peace and democracy.* Our American sisters must demand the retreat of the American troops from South Korea. (WIDF 1948: 488; my emphasis)

Cai named women from France, Holland, and the United States to lead an anti-imperialist campaign for peace. Within the framework of a globally coordinated fight against colonialism, she described a praxis that extended the reach of Allouchiche's solidarity of complicity to women in imperialist nations. She urged women in imperialist nations to become *accomplices* in struggle, not simply allies to colonized women. This solidarity had consequences, and women paid them in full.

Imperialism and Anticolonial Nationalism in the Postwar Order

In her speech at WIDF's 1948 Budapest Congress, Cai described the growing complexity of imperialism, between the older colonial nations and the rise of an American-led financial imperialism marked by the dominance of the dollar and Wall Street. Both forms of imperialism agreed on military solutions to "wiping out every movement for national liberation" (WIDF 1948: 476). Cai reminded her audience that the United States was the true victor of World War II, gaining a hegemony won through its capital reconstruction loans to Europe and England. She linked movements in Africa, including labor struggles in the Gold Coast, to those in Asia, citing the oil workers' strikes in Iran. She spoke about the food shortages in China that led to peasant uprisings against the Guomindang, and the starvation in India that fueled peasant resistance to large landowners in Bengal. All of these struggles included women workers on the land and in factories, exploited even more intensively than men by even lower wages and even longer hours. While Cai spoke about the exploitation of both women and men, her focus on women's lives in colonialism was clear: working women's demands should ground anticolonial demands, as the floor to change the oppressive living conditions for all.

The intensity of working-class, rural, and urban organizing, alongside alliances with the progressive middle classes, finally gave the anticolonial movement around the world the strength it needed to win. Colonial powers' use of violent force to retain colonial territories continued unabated after the war, if not fiercer than before. Economies of the Netherlands, England, and France still relied upon colonies' wealth in resources, labor, and captive consumer markets—perhaps even more desperately in the war's aftermath. But brute force and bad-faith agreements to share power no longer sufficed to hold onto power. The united front from below, one that linked landless agricultural workers to small farmers and the urban proletariat to intellectuals and progressive middle-class people, created the unity that anticolonial resistance needed to win. Cai's analysis ended with three goals of women's ongoing praxis: peace, self-determination, and a democracy that eradicated poverty and starvation to provide "the freedom to live under human conditions."[4]

Women's Revolutionary Violence and Anticolonial Activism

On the international stage of the United Nations, WIDF activists reiterated that a world peace that left imperial power unchecked was an empty slogan. Armed resistance in the colonies was not synonymous with war, but necessary to gain peace. In April 1949, WIDF joined with other leftist organizations to hold the first World Peace Conference in Paris that was both antifascist and anticolonial in its demands. The harsh nature of colonial violence, including the character of counterinsurgency wars, allowed few options for nonviolent resistance in the colonies. "After the war," Cai said in 1948, "the national independence movement in the countries of Asia and Africa has won unprecedented victories. Armed struggle is at present the characteristic feature of this movement" (WIDF 1948: 479). Delegates gave their full support for Cai's unapologetic embrace of armed freedom movements as the necessary response to colonial intransigence and exploitation. Thus, in 1949, the debate among the delegates at the Asian Women's Conference was not about the violence itself, but about the supportive actions and strategies for a meaningful internationalism. At this gathering, Asian and African delegates solidified a praxis that amplified internationalist women's material solidarity for these armed struggles.

The necessity of armed struggle echoed other recent internationalist gatherings in Asia, most notably the World Federation of Democratic Youth and Students (WFDY) held in Kolkata in February, 1948. Within months of the WFDY conference, military resistance to colonialism broke out in Myanmar (March 1948), Malaysia (June 1948), and Indonesia (September 1948). By 1949, vast sections of Vietnam gained a formal independence that proved fragile in the face of French determination to hold onto the territory as its colony. The broken promises for a slow transition to full independence proffered after the end of World War II by Britain in Myanmar and Malaysia, by France in Vietnam, and by the Netherlands in Indonesia resulted in armed resistance. In 1948 and 1949, the Indonesian independence movement had taken up the few arms available to them, through channels that led from India through Myanmar and from China through Vietnam. Many rural people fought with handmade wooden weapons and explosives left over from the end of Japanese occupation. Meanwhile, the French, British, and Dutch with the active assistance of the United States colluded to support each other's military counterinsurgency assaults by lending troop regiments, arms, military ships, planes, and other equipment from the region used against the Japanese during World War II.

Anticolonial Women's Emancipation and Debates about Revolutionary Motherhood

At the Asian Women's Conference in 1949, Cai celebrated the long odds of the gathering: "Many delegates from the Asiatic countries have risked their lives to come to the Conference, crossing firing lines and outwitting the watchfulness of secret agents and detectives to arrive at their destination."[5] In a regional context of insurgency and danger, the conference crafted two appeals—one to Asian women, and the other to women from imperialist countries. The first sought Asian women's unity for the entrenched battles ahead. The second mapped what women's internationalist solidarity outside of anticolonial warfare should be. Both appeals demanded a just peace. Both supported women's increased commitment to the militant struggle to secure this peace. Asian delegates, but also the leaders who traveled from Cuba, Ivory Coast, Algeria, and Madagascar all came from movements that had put rural women at their center.[6] Their speeches and conference documents explicitly named the linkages between antiracism and antifascism to anti-imperialism. They rejected the "humanitarian" colonial consensus that dogged anti-imperialism in the United States and Western Europe (Gaiduk 2009). No colonial power's occupation could ever be kind enough to support full self-determination, women's emancipation, and a meaningful peace. Whether Algeria, Morocco, Indonesia, or Burma, it was time for the colonizers to leave.

The Asian Women's Conference culminated in two appeals. Both appeals were crafted by a movement that was peopled by rural farmers fighting guerrilla wars against wealthy, powerful forces armed to the teeth. They sought to mobilize the differential relations of solidarity to show what an internationalist resistance to colonial aggression meant. Their appeal to Asian women connected their participation in anticolonial resistance as the *means* to support their demands for full rights:

> Women of the countries of Asia! Workers, peasants, white-collar work-ers, intellectuals—remember that in unity lies our strength and the guar-antee of victory over imperialism and feudal reaction! . . . Sisters, suffer-ing under the burden of imperialism and the yoke of reaction! Unite, and in uniting, take into consideration the concrete conditions prevailing in our respective countries and adapt to them all available forms of struggle.
>
> Women militants! Take part in all the organizations comprising masses of women, help to educate them and to defend their basic rights! ("To Our Sisters" 1950: 9)

Their appeal provided focused feminist demands: for economic, politi-cal, and social rights for women. These were demands for women's education, their right to own land, and political equality—all demands embedded in their revolutionary mass organizational work in the coun-tryside, towns, and cities. They were not discrete legal demands lodged with the colonial state, since dismantling regional customs (or "concrete conditions") demanded more focused attention from organized, leftist women and men. Their central call was a regional unity to fight imperial-ism; but without feminist demands for women's political, legal, and eco-nomic rights, imperialism could easily return or, to use the term in the resolution, *adapt* to the new conditions of local or national self-rule.

The second conference appeal targeted women of the imperialist coun-tries, and named the United States, Britain, France, and Holland in par-ticular. They described the shared violence and losses of colonial wars that affected all women. But they added a special ethical imperative: "Do not allow yourselves to be accomplices of our murderers! . . . Do not permit our sons to kill each other! Stop colonial wars! Insist that your governments recall the troops from Vietnam, Indonesia, Malaya, Korea" ("To Our Sis-ters" 1950: 9). Motherhood in this appeal could not be conceived outside of war: women must refuse to raise sons who become murderers. The appeal linked home to the theater of war. Both appeals relied on a shared analysis of imperialism—and which countries were imperialist—for two powerful aims. First, they celebrated the leadership of Asian women fighting British, American, French, and Dutch colonial militarism. Second, they promoted an internationalism led by these revolutionary anticolonial women.

But there was another internationalist feminist strategy that emerged from the conference, one that was not represented in either of the 1949 AWC appeals. It sought to build a multi-class, international women's movement for peace using the language of radical motherhood. This third strategy was an alternate path that was integral to WIDF's active debates before, during, and after the 1949 conference in Beijing, which had proponents from around the world, including the Union of Soviet Socialist Republics, the United States, and Sweden. A large delegation of women from the US Congress of American Women (CAW) attended WIDF's Budapest Congress and listened to Cai's speech in 1948. Three of them—two African American, one white—also joined the Asian Women's Conference a year later: Ada Jackson, Eslanda Robeson, and Elizabeth Millard. In 1948, CAW participants expressed the difficulty of organizing around WIDF resolutions that named the United States as the central imperialist aggressor. The political context in Cold War United States, they said, would make their organization's survival impossible. However, WIDF's final resolution in 1948 did name the United States as the primary agent of postwar imperialism: "American monopolists seek to dominate the world. With the aid of the Marshall Plan, they deprive nations of their sovereignty, turning people into servants of the American warmakers" (WIDF 1948: 12). The clarity of this resolution, and the resolve of CAW to bring it to American women had the consequences they foresaw. By 1949, CAW members were charged with subversion by the House on Un-American Activities Commission (HUAC). By 1950, CAW was banned and dismantled. Yet in 1951, these same women put their bodies on the line to stop the US-led war and occupation of Korea.[7]

Anti-imperialist Appeals in Practice

The conference configured examples of how to coordinate internationalist women's activism across geopolitical borders in its speakers' reports. For example, in the case of Indonesian anti-imperialist internationalism, Lillah Suripno was the Indonesian delegate to the Asian Women's Conference and a member of the Indonesian Communist Party (PKI). Suripno spoke immediately before Maria Lips, who was the chairwoman of the Dutch Women's Movement and a communist. Together, their reports illustrated what concerted anti-imperialist solidarity should be. Suripno emphasized Indonesian women's full participation in the fight against the Dutch military attack (Suripno 1950). Indonesian women were part of all anti-imperialist resistance movements in the region, as fighters, as well as logistical support, surveillance, communication, and infrastructure (Wieringa 2002). She emphasized the role of women in these battles: "Indonesian women fight with arms in hand for national independence!" (Suripno 1950). For her part, Lips described Dutch women's opposition at the shipyards sending off arms to colonial soldiers in Indonesia.

In October 1949, at WIDF's board meeting held in Moscow six weeks before the Asian Women's Conference, the seeds of this two-fold praxis was given a pragmatic flexibility: "To work to draw all active women into active struggle, and to achieve this, it is recommended to take into account the national peculiarities of the movement in each country" (Ramelson Notes). The women's movements across the world could develop solidarity actions to coordinate their anticolonial activism in many possible forms. However, women in imperialist countries had to oppose imperialism from within its ideologies, economies, and governmental policies. Solidified between 1945 and 1949, this two-fold internationalist praxis challenged and ultimately presaged the full support for national independence movements by the previously pro-colonial wings of European communist parties, including the Dutch and French ones. Within a month of the Asian Women's Conference, Jeannette Vermeersch, a leader in WIDF and the Union of French Women as well as a French legislator, gave a scathing speech. On January 27, 1950, Vermeersch shredded the language of humanitarianism surrounding the French colonial war in Vietnam. In a speech republished and distributed around the world, she addressed the French National Assembly, a body that included Communist Party members. "The Vietnamese people are fighting a just war," she said, "a war in the defense against your aggression, a war of national liberation. You are fighting an unjust war, a colonial war, a war of aggression" (Vermeersch 1950).

The conference resolutions were carefully negotiated ones that navigated the rapidly changing context of Asian anti-imperialism. Chinese Communist Party leaders, such as Liu Shaoqi, argued against a resolution in the Asian Women's Conference that emphasized open fights for women's legal rights in Asia. Asian women who openly sought the legal rights to marriage reform, equal pay, or land rights, Shaoqi argued, would immediately be targeted by colonial regimes (Heinzig 2004). Campaigns for legal reforms in these repressive colonial contexts would lead to women activists' imprisonment or death rather than build women's multi-class unity in the region. Women's participation in Asian liberation movements was necessarily underground. Instead of legal reforms, Liu Shaoqi favored a resolution for regional unity and support for armed combat. Even these general demands, demands that were very close to the appeals of the Asian Women's Conference, had to be kept secret in order to ensure the safety of women in Asian and African anti-imperialist movements.

Shaoqi's hesitance about Asian women's open advocacy for equal rights in the colonial context was a strategic one, not one of principle. But it was still a difficult one to navigate as delegates from the Asian Women's Conference sought to nimbly guide women's struggles through their appeals and resolutions. In the 1940s, many of WIDF's international demands for women's rights assumed that women already enjoyed some forms (even if limited) of representative governance—such as demands for the right to own property and divorce at will—all aspirations shared by Asian, Latin American, and African women. However, for those under colonial occupation, women's rights were woven into the aspiration for a socialist government that affirmed their rights to exist, to take leadership, to have a voice, and to exercise self-determination. Anticolonial women's movements across the world fought for both rights and deeply representative self-determination simultaneously. As the shared platform for the internationalist women's movement, WIDF, they argued, had to accurately mirror their commitments.

The AWC conference resolutions reflected the communists' two-camp analysis of postwar alignments, as mentioned before, but these strategies for an internationalist anti-imperialist women's movement were fueled by more complex forces of power than simply negotiations among national communist parties. They also exceed the frame of the international women's organization of WIDF. World unity among women opposing imperialism developed from Asian and African women's struggle over a longer period of time than the four years after the war in Europe ended in 1945. The moment to demand the reins of self-governance emerged with the end of the European war for countries like India, Pakistan, Vietnam, and Malaysia; but the organizational strength behind this demand lay in rural organizing that began much earlier.

Starvation after Harvest: Peasant Women's Anticolonialism

Two communist women from Africa reminded Asian women of their commonalties in struggle. Gisèle Rabesahala cofounded the communist Congress Party for the Independence of Madagascar and led the Malagasy Solidarity Committee to fight for political prisoners after the French crushed the 1947 uprising against their colonial rule. She described the conditions in Madagascar, giving details of enormous profit for French, British, and American firms, and of devastation for the people of Madagascar. "In 1944," she illustrated with stark simplicity, "there were 25,000 more deaths than births" (Ramelson Notes). Célestine Ouezzin Coulibaly was one of the founders and the secretary of the African Democratic Assembly, a communist political organization that spanned French colonies across West and Equatorial Africa. Like Rabesahala, she stressed the importance of organizing dispossessed rural and urban women to the anticolonial movement she led. Coulibaly expressed her solidarity with Asian revolutionary women in racialized terms of commonality: "I have six children. They live in a country where to have a dark skin is thought to make a person less than a human being. So we all have a lot in common to discuss in Beijing" (Ramelson 1949). The colonial economy during the war years exacerbated the demands of tribute: to feed the armies on the western front, food from grain-growing colonies in Morocco, Algeria, India, and Vietnam was expropriated at a devastating rate. Whole rural populations from these countries starved, with estimates of death in the many millions.

Rural regions of Asia during the 1940s, with different degrees of success, united small landholding peasant women and landless farming women with middle-class communist and leftist organizers. In Asia, these movements developed a united front led from below rather than from above. In China, the communists described their agrarian reform policy in four parts: "Rely on the poor peasants. Unite with the middle peasants. Isolate the rich peasants. Fight the landlords" (Robeson Papers). This strategy drew from different contexts, since some nations, like India, had powerful nationalist movements dominated by the landed and industrial elite. Other polities, like Vietnam, had virtually no nationalist organizations to align with leftist worker and peasant movements. Instead, the rural organization of poor farmers and landless agricultural workers aligned on their own terms with middle-class nationalist forces from urban areas. In rural localities, they built a powerful leftist movement.

In some parts of the North, it had enough power to create autonomous zones, or soviets, led by revolutionary ideals.

In Bengal, crossing the border between India and West Pakistan, these rural organizers built autonomous regions led by the women at the forefront of the Tebhaga struggle that sought a fairer share of the crops they reaped. A number of these regions developed their own court systems to punish domestic violence, end unequal marriage traditions, and promote women's sexual and bodily autonomy (Cooper 1988). In Vietnam, these liberated zones also protected resistance units, with most women fighters in two levels of combat (regional forces and village guerrillas): "Women partisans go from village to village to oppose the French attacks. They are also given charge of launching constant and small nocturnal assault [sic] against French isolated posts, in order to harass them and reduce their number as well as lower their morale" (UVWF 1948; Post 1989). The Union of Vietnam Women in France described dozens of accounts of mass rape by French soldiers in 1947 alone. French military sadism, they wrote, was an ineffective counterinsurgency tactic, and inspired the commitment of Vietnamese women's armed resistance.

Ling Long, one of two delegates from Malaysia, spoke bluntly about their independence war led by the Malaysian workers of Chinese descent who were miners and agricultural workers. "The Chinese in Malaya are inspired by the struggle of the Chinese against Japan and Guomindang, and also by the struggle of Indonesians for their independence. . . . The people's forces work underground in towns and cities and work amongst the peasantry in the countryside, taking up arms where necessary" (Ramelson Notes). Ling reiterated that for most of the Asian delegates, particularly those from Vietnam, Indonesia, Malaysia, Myanmar, Korea, and notably the Japanese delegation barred from attending the conference by Douglas MacArthur's government, women's work in their revolutions was clandestine and life-threatening.

In the years after the Asian Women's Conference, women increasingly became the public face of revolutionary, anticolonial peace through a rhetoric of radical motherhood. Even when couched in the language of family, this praxis maintained that anticolonial struggles were won and lost by the barrel of the gun. However, this bridge between two different visions for feminist internationalism was fraught. One, represented by the 1949 AWC conference resolutions, centered the knowledge of peasant women's struggle against colonialism and landed systems of rule that preceded it. The other was a rhetorical strategy that sought to build global linkages through radical motherhood. It was a means to circumvent rising anticommunism across the West and build sympathy for women in colonial struggles in Asia, Latin America, and Africa.

In 1949, the delegates to the AWC strengthened the two-part vision for feminist, socialist internationalism. A third, largely unspoken part of this strategy was the role of women in socialist countries, most notably China and the Soviet Union, who provided material support, guidance, and inspiration. The geopolitics of capitalism bifurcated its strategy into two main parts: feminist activism outside imperial centers, and feminist activism inside those centers—as accomplices in struggle, activists in these political locations were coordinated, but not identical. Struggles and demands shaped by colonized women led both locations of activism. In rural and urban colonial territories, women's rights were a necessary kindling for colonialism. The suppression of women's rights fueled, and then congealed colonial control over occupied territories. For anticolonialism to succeed in systemically loosening the grip of imperialism on the world, in their analysis, women's rights must be at the heart of that project. At its best, internationalist feminism as women's regional anticolonial solidarity across the Third World could dig the grave for colonialism. Western women's staunch rejection of their own nations' imperialism could help bury it for good.

....

Elisabeth Armstrong is a professor in the Program for the Study of Women and Gender at Smith College. She has written two books on the praxis of organizing, one about India called *Gender and Neoliberalism: The All India Democratic Women's Association and Globalization Politics* (2013), and one about the United States called *The Retreat from Organization: US Feminism Reconceptualized* (2002). She is an executive board member of Tricontinental: Institute for Social Research based in Latin America, Africa, and South Asia. She serves on the editorial boards of *Meridians: Feminism, Race, Transnationalism* and *Kohl: A Journal for Body and Gender Research*, a queer feminist journal on gender and sexuality in the Middle East and North Africa region.

Notes

1   I have defined this term elsewhere as a form of revolutionary internationalism led by women such that "even under the conditions of colonialism women should take responsibility for atrocities carried out in their nation's name or by their nation's people" (Armstrong 2016: 311).

2   From Lenin's "Speech on the National Question," The Seventh All-Russia Conference, April 29, 1917. "No nation can be free that oppresses other nations."

3 At the founding conference of the Union of Soviet Socialist Republics' Cominform in August, 1947, Andrei Zhdanov outlined a two-camp theory of the world
order driven by the United States for the imperialist camp, and congealing
around the USSR for the democratic camp. Fascism, colonialism, imperialist
expansion, and war marked the imperialist camp, and the fight for labor,
peace, democracy, and national liberation defined the other. Andrei Zhdanov,
"Report on the International Situation to the Cominform," September 22, 1947.

4 Deng Yingchao reiterated Cai's argument a year later at the Asian Women's
Conference. "China's experiences tell us that it is only through the resolute
struggle of the armed people against armed counter-revolution that the
oppressed people in the colonies and semi-colonies may attain their freedom"
(Ramelson Notes). China's eviction of Japan from Northern China, and their
hard-fought civil war with the US-backed Guomindang proved it. Revolutionary
violence and wide nationalist coalitions were deeply linked strategies.

5 WIDF conference notes, December 21, 1949, Left Federation of Swedish
Women, Huddinge, Sweden.

6 See WIDF 1945 for a Latin American example.

7 Many of the members of CAW reconfigured as part of American Women for
Peace to maintain their activism during the McCarthy period. Their newsletter,
The Peacemaker, dedicated one issue to the WIDF contingent that toured Korea
and reported on the carnage. In "Negro G.I.s Question Korea," the authors
demanded an end to racist wars in Asia and Africa. "We think that we Negroes,
who are asked to fight wars in Asia and Europe but who are not free at home
should have our say before it is too late. If enough of us can get together, we
believe we will get our peace and freedom too." The editorial stated: "We who
are aware of the effects of these things, and who love our country look with
horror on the death and misery which has resulted from our war policy.
We cry out" ("Editorial" 1951).

Works Cited

Armstrong, Elisabeth. 2016. "Before Bandung: The Anti-imperialist Women's Movement in Asia and the Women's International Democratic Federation." Signs 41,
no. 2: 305–31.

Armstrong, Elisabeth. 2017. "Indian Peasant Women's Activism in a Hot Cold War."
In Gender, Sexuality, and the Cold War, edited by Philip Muehlenbach, 113–37. Nash-
ville, TN: Vanderbilt University Press.

Chakravartty, Renu. 1980. Communists in Indian Women's Movement. New Delhi: People's
Publishing House.

Cooper, Adrienne. 1988. Sharecropping and Sharecroppers' Struggles in Bengal, 1930–1950.
Kolkata: KP Bagchi.

"Editorial: U.S. Bankrupt Policy." 1951. The Peacemaker 2, no. 8: 3.

Efimova, Larisa, and Ruth McVey. 2011. "Stalin and the New Program for the
Communist Party of Indonesia." Indonesia, no. 91: 131–63.

Gaiduk, Ilya V. 2009. "Soviet Cold War Strategy and Prospects of Revolution in Asia."
In Connecting Histories: Decolonization and the Cold War in Southeast Asia, 1945–1962,

edited by Christopher Goscha and Christian Ostermann, 123–36. Stanford, CA: Stanford University Press.

Heinzig, Dieter. 2004. *The Soviet Union and Communist China, 1945–1950: The Arduous Road to the Alliance.* Armonk, NY: M. E. Sharpe Publishers.

Lahiri, Albani. 2001. *Postwar Revolt of the Rural Poor in Bengal: Memoirs of a Communist Activist.* Kolkata: Seagull Books.

Millard, Elizabeth. Papers. Sophia Smith Collection, Smith College.

Panjabi, Kavita. 2017. *Unclaimed Harvest: An Oral History of the Tebhaga Women's Movement.* New Delhi: Zubaan.

Pieper Mooney, Jadwiga. 2013. "Fighting Fascism and Forging New Political Activism: The Women's International Democratic Federation (WIDF) in the Cold War." In *De-centering Cold War History: Local and Global Change*, edited by Jadwiga Pieper Mooney and Fabio Lanza, 52–72. New York: Routledge.

Post, Ken. 1989. *An Interrupted Revolution.* Vol. 1 of *Revolution, Socialism, and Nationalism in Viet Nam.* 5 vols. Brookfield, VT: Dartmouth Publishing.

Ramelson, Marion. 1949. *British Woman in New China: Marion Ramelson's Report on the Asian Women's Conference, Peking.* London: British Committee, WIDF, 5.

Ramelson, Marion. Notes. Women's Bureau, Communist Party of Great Britain Collection, People's History Museum, Manchester.

Robeson, Eslanda. Papers. Moorland-Spingarn Archives, Howard University.

Sen, Manikuntala. 2001. *In Search of Freedom: An Unfinished Journey.* Kolkata: Stree.

Stolte, Carolien. 2014. "'The Asiatic hour': New perspectives on the Asian Relations Conference, New Delhi, 1947." In *The Non-aligned Movement and the Cold War: Delhi—Bandung—Belgrade*, edited by Nataša Mišković, Harald Fischer-Tiné, and Nada Boškovska, 57–75. London: Routledge.

Suripno, Lillah. 1950. "Soekarno and Hatta—Puppets of the Dutch and American Imperialists." *Information Bulletin*, no. 4: 26.

"To Our Sisters, the Women of the Countries of Asia." 1950. *Information Bulletin*, no. 4: 7.

UVWF (Union of Vietnam Women in France). 1948. *Women of Vietnam in the Struggle for the Safeguard of Independence.* Paris: Union of Vietnam Women in France.

Vermeersch, Jeannette. 1950. *The Trial of French Colonialism.* Rangoon, Burma: Vietnam News Service.

Weber, Charlotte. 2003. "Making Common Cause? Western and Middle Eastern Feminists in the International Women's Movement, 1911–1948." PhD diss., Ohio State University.

WIDF (Women's International Democratic Federation). 1948. *Second Women's International Congress Proceedings.* Communism Collection, Sophia Smith Collection, Smith College.

WIDF (Women's International Democratic Federation) and Acción Femenina Peruana. 1945. *Contra el fascismo; Por la paz, la democracia y la defensa de los derechos de la mujer.* Lima, Peru: Acción Femenina Peruana.

Wieringa, Saskia. 2002. *Sexual Politics in Indonesia.* London: Palgrave Macmillan.

Maylei Blackwell

....

Call Me by My True Names

(inspired by Thich Nhat Hanh)

Maylei

    Sugunya

        Rojanasakul

                          Blackwell

Call me by my true names

Call to the truth of me
    My name
        My power

The song of my being
    the chant of my bones
        the soul's mantra

My true names with thirteen letters

A mouthful of continents
    consonants
        and not enough vowels

Too many syllables for your tongue to untangle
    The rhythm
        The order
The rhyme of my true name

MERIDIANS · feminism, race, transnationalism   18:2 October 2019
DOI: 10.1215/15366936-7775674 © 2019 Smith College

The name imprinted on my heart
      Tucked in my bowels
           The sound of my flight

I dreaded roll call each day
Waiting for the teacher to butcher my name
      And for the killing to burn shame into my being
           Marking my difference

May-lie
Mee-lay
Most did not even attempt my last name

Rojanaskul
      I was raised on American jokes about the Mỹ Lai massacre
           Amidst the linguist melee
              colonial legacy

Children learn letters by writing their names
      An exercise for beginners
           Mine used half the letters in the alphabet

Kinder
      The garden where some plants are rooted in privilege
           While others grow in shadows that cast doubt

My mama sang me my name
      Made the letters rhyme with me
           R-o-j
              a-n-a
                s-k
                    u-l

Call me by my true name
      The one you can not pronounce
           The very one that speaks me into being

The one that called my spirit forth from the cradle of ancestors
      To navigate a long passage

To embody this flesh
    breathe in this place
        on earth

We come into being, they say, because we choose this time
    we can handle this particular
        conjuncture
    Enlightenment with madness
        spirit with greed
            sleep with awakening

The great turning
    amidst
        great upheaval

Call me by my true names
    The exotic other
        Unknowable to you

Your
    imagined
        shadow

Your
    repudiated
        self

My true names
    do not
        roll off your tongue

My names
    the thick ones,
    the thin
        the sweet,
        the bitch
            the placid,
            the rage
                My open hand,
                My fist

. . . .

Professor Maylei Blackwell is the author of the landmark ¡*Chicana Power! Contested Histories of Feminism in the Chicano movement* (2011), and coeditor of ¡*Chicana Movidas! New Narratives of Activism and Feminism in the Movement Era* (2018). Her book, *Scales of Resistance: Indigenous Women's Transborder Organizing* (forthcoming), draws on twenty years of research accompanying indigenous women's organizing in Mexico and its diaspora. Her research on social movements in the United States and Latin America, transborder activism, and indigenous politics and migration has appeared in the United States, Mexico, and Brazil in journals such as *Meridians, Signs, Aztlán, Journal of Latin American Studies, Desacatos,* and *Revista Estudos Feministas*. She teaches Chicana and Chicano studies and gender studies and is affiliated faculty in American Indian studies at the University of California, Los Angeles. She has served as the chair of the Abya Yala Working Group of the Native American and Indigenous Studies Association (NAISA), and she is a co-creator and co-director of the digital story platform Mapping Indigenous Los Angeles (mila.ssc.ucla.edu).

Mandira Venkat

··

Introduction to Pan Pacific and Southeast Asia Women's Association "Southeast Asia and the United Nations" Discussion Group

The Pan Pacific and Southeast Asia Women's Association (PPSEAWA) was established in 1928, when it held its first conference. PPSEAWA's mission is to foster friendship and collaboration among women from the Pacific and Southeast Asia and women in the United States (PPSEAWA, n.d.). The founders of this organization sought to improve the social, economic, and cultural conditions of their respective nations through collaboration with the United States and the United Nations. The "Southeast Asia and the United Nations" primary document recounts a 1955–56 discussion group meeting held in New York among five women from Burma (now Myanmar),[1] India, Indonesia, Pakistan,[2] and the Philippines (Republic of the Philippines), and five women from the United States. The issues discussed ranged from maternal and child welfare to education and the improvement of the status of women in society. UN experts on these issues were present for the discussion group.

The five women from Southeast Asia and the Pacific had all received formal education and contributed valuable information on their countries' social welfare programs. These five women were Mrs. Paw Htin representing Burma; Mrs. Sheila Jaipal representing India; Mrs. A. Islam representing Pakistan; Mrs. Paz P. Mendez representing the Philippines; and Mrs. Siti Roescali Prawoto representing Indonesia. Some of the members provided information on the important role women's organizations played

MERIDIANS · feminism, race, transnationalism   18:2 October 2019
DOI: 10.1215/15366936-7775696 © 2019 Smith College

in social welfare. Mrs. Paz P. Mendez was the former dean of the college at Centro Escolar University in Manila and held office at several women's organizations in the Philippines. Mendez noted the significant role the Filipina feminist movement and women's organizations played in advocating for child welfare since 1905. Although she does not mention the organization by name, it is likely that she was referring to the the Asociación Feminista Filipina (AFF), the first women's organization advocating social welfare, which was founded in 1905 (Edwards and Roces 2010). The AFF established Gota de Leche in 1906, and they created the model for flourishing puericulture centers that institutionalized maternal and children's nutrition (Estrada-Claudio and Santos 2005; Gota de Leche, n.d.). *Gota de leche*, in Spanish, translates to a drop of milk. Mendez notes the slogan of women's organizations in the Philippines in 1907 was "A drop of milk for the protection of the infant." Gota de Leche continues to exist today with the same purpose to support malnourished children and maternal health. Mrs. Sheila Jaipal, a member of the Indian Delegation of the United Nations, noted that the All India Women's Conference (AIWC) did commendable work advocating for maternal and child welfare. The AIWC still exists as an organization today and continues to advocate for women's fundamental rights and empowerment (AIWC, n.d.). All primary documents are from the Pan Pacific and Southeast Asia Women's Association Records, Sophia Smith Collection, Smith College.

....

Mandira Venkat is an undergraduate student studying sociology, South Asian studies, economics, and Italian at Smith College, class of 2019. She is from Austin, Texas and aspires to bring women of color narratives and content into the mainstream, and to foster interracial and cross-cultural dialogue.

Notes

1 This country was known as Burma at the time of the PPSEAWA's founding but has been known as Myanmar since 1989 when the military government changed the country's name to what it had long been in the country's vernacular discourse (Selth and Gallagher 2018). However, I refer to it as Burma here in keeping with the country's officially recognized nomenclature during the period in which this document was produced.

2 Given that Mrs. A. Islam representing Pakistan was fluent in Bengali and attended Calcutta University, it is possible that she is representing the region of East Pakistan. However, the text does not indicate this as her region of origin and/or the region of her life and work in general.

Works Cited

AIWC (All India Women's Conference). n.d. Accessed February 27, 2019. http://www
.aiwc.org.in/.

Edwards, Louise, and Mina Roces, eds. 2010. *Women's Movements in Asia: Feminisms
and Transnational Activism*. New York: Routledge.

Estrada-Claudio, Sylvia, and Aida Santos. 2005. "The Women's Movement(s) and
Social Movements: Conjunctures and Divergences." *Europe Solidaire Sans Frontières*
(blog), May 26. www.europe-solidaire.org/spip.php?article530.

Gota de Leche. n.d. Accessed June 9, 2019. http://gotadeleche.com/

PPSEAWA (Pan Pacific and Southeast Asian Women's Association). 2018. "United
States of America," November 18. http://www.ppseawa.org/membership/united
-states-america.

Selth, Andrew, and Adam Gallagher. 2018. "What's in a Name: Burma or Myanmar?"
United States Institute of Peace (blog), July 17. www.usip.org/blog/2018/06/whats
-name-burma-or-myanmar.

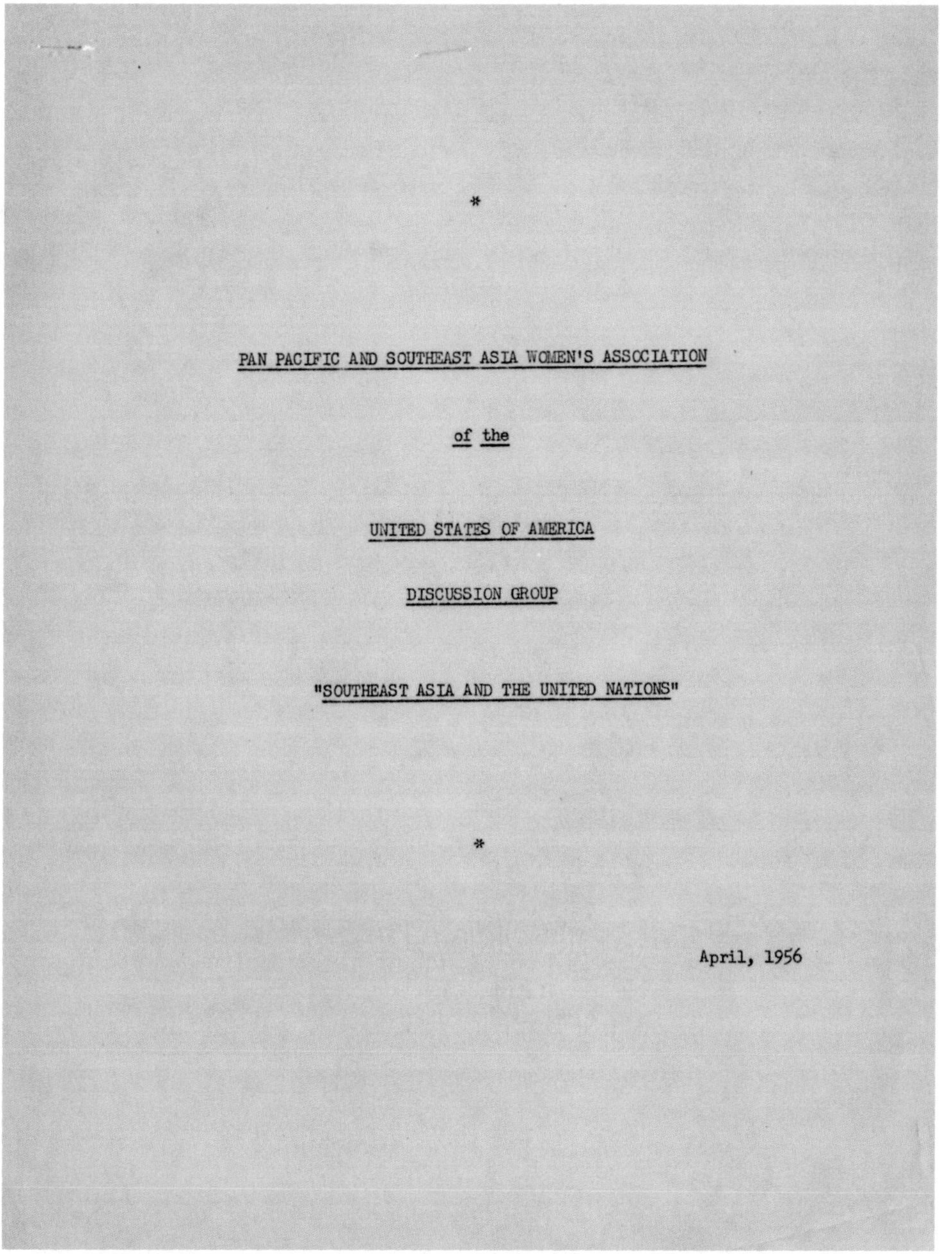

PAN PACIFIC AND SOUTHEAST ASIA WOMEN'S ASSOCIATION

of the

UNITED STATES OF AMERICA

DISCUSSION GROUP

"SOUTHEAST ASIA AND THE UNITED NATIONS"

*

April, 1956

Figure 1. Pan Pacific and Southeast Asia Women's Association of the United States of America Discussion Group: "Southeast Asia and the United Nations," April 1956, blue cover, eighteen-page typescript. Creator: Pan Pacific and Southeast Asia Women's Association of the United States of America. Sophia Smith Collection, Smith College, Northampton, Massachusetts.

This is the account of a discussion group which met during the winter of 1955-1956, composed of five Asian women, from Burma, India, Indonesia, Pakistan, and the Philippines, and five American women who explored together several problems involved in the topic "Southeast Asia and the United Nations" in an apartment overlooking a wide sweep of New York's East River and the Headquarters of the United Nations. It is offered as a modest sampling of the subject matter under discussion and an unpretentious example of the possibilities of person-to-person inter-regional relationship.

Figure 2. Pan Pacific and Southeast Asia Women's Association of the United States of America Discussion Group: "Southeast Asia and the United Nations," April 1956, foreword. Creator: Pan Pacific and Southeast Asia Women's Association of the United States of America. Sophia Smith Collection, Smith College, Northampton, Massachusetts.

THE TOPIC

Not only geographical propinquity to the United Nations suggested the topic. Many members of the group were Representatives to the United Nations for various national or international organizations and some of those from the West had traveled extensively in Southeast Asia where they had visited United Nations projects. Therefore, both background and experience suggested the choice of topic -- Southeast Asia and the United Nations. It was felt that the most basic and immediate problem under this heading was surely that of maternal and child welfare. Although this first topic was the one to which the group devoted the largest proportion of its time, brief discussions took place on two others, those of Education and of the Status of Women in this setting. In all cases it was possible to draw on some outside expert opinion for background, on such Specialized Agencies as FAO and UNESCO, on the work of the United Nations Status of Women Commission and the group was fortunate indeed in having as adviser the Director of the Training Unit of the United Nations Bureau of Social Affairs.

THE METHOD

At each meeting the discussion was prefaced by the reading of a rather full account or "minutes" of the previous meeting in order to give continuity. A number of carefully prepared but informally given reports from each country followed from which excerpts are given in this report. It will be noticed that reports were made on New Zealand and the United States, representing member countries of PASEAWA. These were added to round out and give variety to discussion. The trip of a medical doctor who attended this session was responsible for the formulation of a series of principles growing out of discussions on "Maternal and Child Welfare in Southeast Asia."

THE GROUP

Mrs. Paw Htin -- Recently Bachelor of Medicine and Bachelor of Surgery of Rangoon University, Burma -- wife of the Consul of Burma to New York.

Mrs. Sheila Jaipal -- MA from Allahabad University where she was a Lecturer in Political Science until her marriage to Mr. R. Jaipal, First Secretary and at present a Member of the Indian Delegation to United Nations. Before Mr. and Mrs. Jaipal and their two daughters came to New York they had been stationed in Burma and the West Indies.

Mrs. A. Islam -- Studied at Calcutta University, her primary interests are Music and Art. At present Mrs. Islam is Adviser to the Pakistan Information Service at ECOSOC and broadcasts in Bengali for the Pakistan program on the United Nations. She is married to the Labor Attache of the Pakistan Consulate General.

Mrs. Paz P. Mendez -- B.S.Ed., MA, Ed.D. from Teachers College, Columbia University. She held office in the Philippine Association of University Women, Federation of Women's Clubs and League of Women Voters, and she was Dean of the College of

1

Figure 3. Pan Pacific and Southeast Asia Women's Association of the United States of America Discussion Group: "Southeast Asia and the United Nations," April 1956, p. 1. Creator: Pan Pacific and Southeast Asia Women's Association of the United States of America. Sophia Smith Collection, Smith College, Northampton, Massachusetts.

Education, Centro Escolar University, Manila. Mrs. Mendez is at present a Board Member of the Queen's Branch of A.A.U.W. and the wife of Mauro Mendez, Legal Counsellor of the Philippine Delegation to the United Nations as well as the mother of six children and grandmother of three.

Mrs. Siti Roesoeli Prawoto, in addition to her regular schooling, received Islamic training at home, and studied French, German and Journalism. She was active in International Red Cross work during the revolution years in Indonesia and belonged to the Indonesian Youth Movement. Her interests are music, the dance, literature and dress designing. She is the wife of the Deputy Chief of the Indonesian Supply Mission in the United States of America, and mother of a young son and a daughter.

Mrs. Henry G. Fowler -- Vice President of PASEAWA and Chairman of its American Committee who was on a six months' mission, 1954-1955, as a United States Specialist in Southeast Asia for the International Education Exchange Service of the United States Department of State and is currently lecturing on Southeast Asia. Mrs. Mendez and Mrs. Fowler are both Representatives for PASEAWA to United Nations Economic and Social Council.

Mrs. Dana C. Backus -- Past Chairman of the American Committee of PASEAWA, Chairman of the Education Committee of the American Association of the United Nations and a member of the United States National Commission for UNESCO. She is a graduate of Barnard College in New York and the mother of five daughters, ranging from 20 years to 6 years of age.

Mrs. Sturgis Sprague Jenkins -- the exceedingly efficient recorder and secretary for the discussion group. Born and educated in New Zealand, she is now a citizen of the United States of America and has been a tireless volunteer in pediatrics at Roosevelt Hospital in New York.

Mrs. Daniel D. Karasik -- a graduate in Economics from Vassar, Master of Education from Teachers College, Winnetka, Illinois, where she taught in a Junior High School. She has spent 18 months recently in Japan with her husband who was on a Ford Fellowship. During the period of the discussion group, in due course (between the 4th and 5th meeting) she became the proud mother of her first child, a daughter.

Mrs. Frances Sawyer -- Observer at the United Nations for an American organization who has lived and traveled extensively in Southeast Asia, visiting and inspecting in the course of her travels many United Nations projects, especially those under the auspices of FAO. It was she who provided the soya bean milk at one meeting in which members of the discussion group enthusiastically toasted each other.

Dr. Janet Robb -- acted as Moderator for the Discussion Group. New York born and educated, she is the Representative to the United Nations Economic and Social Council of the International Federation of University Women. She is the author of a study-guide on "Human Rights in the United Nations." During the course of the meetings, she attended the 10th session of the Status of Women Commission in Geneva, Switzerland.

Miss Dorothy Moses of India, who has been Principal of Delhi School of Social Work and is Director of the Training Unit of the Social Service Section of the Bureau of Social Affairs of the United Nations acted as adviser to the group. She was educated in Bengal, attended Bethune College, Calcutta and trained in social work at Liverpool University and New York University. She was sent by UNESCO to Ceylon to inaugurate a training program for Rural Development Officers.

2

Figure 4. Pan Pacific and Southeast Asia Women's Association of the United States of America Discussion Group: "Southeast Asia and the United Nations," April 1956, p. 2. Creator: Pan Pacific and Southeast Asia Women's Association of the United States of America. Sophia Smith Collection, Smith College, Northampton, Massachusetts.

Mrs. Grace Holmes Barbey, Liaison Officer for UNICEF, who attended the PASEAWA Meeting of last year in the Philippines, provided valuable background information to one meeting of the Group, drawing on her extensive field work in Southeast Asia for her organization.

Miss Kathryn H. Starbuck, LL.D., is the Chairman of Program of PASEAWA and is planning its next Conference to be held in Japan early in 1958. She has been long a member of the Faculty of Skidmore College.

Dr. Ada Chree Reid -- a former President of the Medical Women's International Association and en route to its Conference in Manila Opening January 28, 1956, attended the first meeting of the Discussion Group.

Figure 5. Pan Pacific and Southeast Asia Women's Association of the United States of America Discussion Group: "Southeast Asia and the United Nations," April 1956, p. 3. Creator: Pan Pacific and Southeast Asia Women's Association of the United States of America. Sophia Smith Collection, Smith College, Northampton, Massachusetts.

I -- MATERNAL AND CHILD WELFARE IN SOUTHEAST ASIA

DR. ROBB: The emphasis in many fields of activity today is increasingly based on regional development. This is reflected in the United Nations where the three Regional Economic Commissions, the Technical Assistance Residents and Experts and the Regional Offices of the Specialized Agencies and of UNICEF more and more form regional nucleii of United Nations services. It is recognized that, for instance, in the Technical Assistance Programme inter-regional exchange of experts and fellows is most satisfactory. The field we are to discuss, that of maternal and child welfare in Southeast Asia, affords an especially good example of the regional cooperation of such Specialized Agencies as FAO and WHO, and especially of UNICEF, with the United Nations Technical Assistance Programme and with that of the Bureau of Social Affairs of United Nations proper. We hope that the members of the group will describe some of the basic problems facing their countries under this topic, as well as the enormous efforts being made by their respective Governments to meet them. We expect, also, to hear some first-hand accounts of projects in this field. We know that while this region of Southeast Asia will have common needs and problems of maternal and child welfare, it has also a rich variety of cultural backgrounds and national aspirations. This topic can have meaning only when seen within this frame-work.

MRS. PAW HTIN: In Burma the health of mothers and children is regarded as a funda-mental right. Article 27 of the Constitution of the Union lays down that: "The State shall specially direct its policy to protect the interest of mothers and infants by establishing Maternity and Infant Welfare Centers, Children's Homes and Day Nurseries and to secure to mothers the right to a leave with pay before and after childbirth."

The primary causes of difficulties in maternal and child health are the lack of education, shortage of staff and insufficient facilities. The effect of the war years had made matters worse. At this point a few facts and figures may be useful -- the birth rate is moderately high, not less than 30 per cent per 1,000 population, to be compared with the world average which is 35-37 per 1,000 population, the estimated rate for Asia as a whole being 40-45 per 1,000 population. Infant mortal-ity, sad to say, is very high and in an effort to improve matters, the Ministry of Social Services was set up in 1945 before Burma had gained her independence. At first it had two directorates under it: (1) medical and health service and, (2) Women's and Children's Welfare, while the Child Health Service was added in 1951.

The Directorate of Women's and Children's Welfare under the Ministry of Health deals with (1) maternal and child welfare, (2) promotion and encouragement of maternal and child health centers conducted under their auspices, (3) promotion of training of public health nurses, nursing instructors, nurses, midwives and Lady Health Visitors at special training centers or at hospitals in Rangoon, and other district head-quarters hospitals, (4) the training of local, indigenous "Letthes" (midwives) at district hospitals, (5) the setting up of three-day and residential nurseries, (6) assisting by subsidy or help in kind (chiefly rice) various categories of welfare institutions. There are at present 240 maternal and child health centers in the Union of Burma, each staffed with a Lady Health Visitor and two midwives. The objec' of these centers is to provide modern scientific care for pregnant women and nursing mothers; supervise confinements; and help midwives; and educate mothers in the care and upbringing of infants.

4

Figure 6. Pan Pacific and Southeast Asia Women's Association of the United States of America Discussion Group: "Southeast Asia and the United Nations," April 1956, p. 4. Creator: Pan Pacific and Southeast Asia Women's Association of the United States of America. Sophia Smith Collection, Smith College, Northampton, Massachusetts.

In Rangoon there is a State Women's and Children's Center and a Maternity Ward while the Rangoon Dufferin Hospital also provides ante-natal and post-natal care with wards for free hospital confinement. Creditable work is also being done for the Armed Forces Women's Organizations.

The Letthe is the local midwife. In the smaller towns and villages and often even in the larger towns, she is more popular than the trained midwife, for not only does she conduct the delivery but she lives with the family for several days performing household duties. At the present there are about 4,000 known Letthes. There is a proposal to give intensive short-term training to Letthes in the essentials of aceptic midwifery and to supervise their work through the trained nurse.

UNICEF is playing an active and important part in the development of maternal and child health services in Burma. Its activities started in 1950 and it continues to contribute much to Burma. It provides powdered milk, medicine and cloth, and assists in the training of midwives and Lady Health Visitors. There are three mobile dispensaries provided by UNICEF to give examination to mothers and children.

In closing, the solution of the problem for a country with a still high rate of illiteracy, especially for women, is the introduction of mass education simultaneously with the various health programs. This would not only make medical and health services more effective but reduce their cost appreciably. Ordinary health education should substantially reduce the need for more doctors, nurses, hospitals, dispensaries and drugs, since people then would know how to preserve their health by learning the simple, but fundamental rules of healthy living.

MISS MOSES: Untrained midwives are often accepted in the homes when trained midwives are not. These older midwives are often not too appreciative of changing the old order and no large proportion of them enrolls for training. As an economic incentive, some Health Services will pay the midwife if she reports a birth, which also enables the Service to keep a check on the situation and to offer help when necessary.

MRS. MENDEZ: There are three departments in the Philippine Government concerned with public health and welfare. Foremost among them is the Department of Health, which has divided the Islands into 25 Provincial Health Districts. In turn, there is in every town and in the large barrios (villages) a sanitary health doctor who looks after the health of the people and gives free treatments. The Institute of Nutrition conducts research to improve the diet of the people, in fish flour, enriched rice, and soya bean milk. There are 80 Government Hospitals and 212 private ones, several of which are maternity and children's hospitals.

The Government (and some private institutions) provides maternity leaves with pay, prohibits nightwork for women and requires nurseries for children in establishments where there are 15 or more working mothers who are allowed 30 minutes for feeding their babies.

Forty-five per cent of the allocation of all UNICEF funds is for maternal and child welfare. Among the projects are elementary and post-graduate training for rural midwives, about 1,000 "hilots" having already graduated. To improve child nutrition, UNICEF provides skimmed milk, whole milk, and fish liver oil capsules. There are also tuberculin and diptheria immunization and treatment for yaws.

The Feminist Movement in the Philippines originated in work in child welfare as early as 1905. In 1907 the slogan of these women was "A drop of milk for the

5

Figure 7. Pan Pacific and Southeast Asia Women's Association of the United States of America Discussion Group: "Southeast Asia and the United Nations," April 1956, p. 5. Creator: Pan Pacific and Southeast Asia Women's Association of the United States of America. Sophia Smith Collection, Smith College, Northampton, Massachusetts.

protection of the infant." In 1910 they started an anti-TB campaign. In 1912 there were 12 active women's organizations, while today there are 1,000, one for practical-ly every municipality. They were originally called Pueri-Culture Centers and they are now health centers with the Government doubling each effort. The National Women's Clubs are foremost in this work while the Missions have their own hospitals and training centers.

MRS. ISLAM: The Government of Pakistan is subsidizing the two Lady Dufferin Hospitals at Karachi and at Quetta. Equipment has been obtained from UNICEF to improve facilities there and a sum of Rs 300,000 has been spent from the Social Uplift Grant for the expansion of these two hospitals.

Centres for the training of community health visitors to serve as midwives have been established at Karachi, Lahore, Peshawar and Dacca. The trainees will serve as mid-wives after 27 months' training. The Centre at Lahore has already turned out a number of trained girls, while the Centre at Karachi has started training with 21 girls on roll. The object is to improve the existing maternal and child health centres by better qualified staff and equipment, and to expand their services throughout the provinces. UNICEF and WHO have provided equipment and foreign tech-nical staff for running the Training Centres. UNICEF has offered maternity kits and other equipment, including drugs and diet supplements worth $297,000 for distribution in about 200 maternity Centres in rural areas where dais are trained and for whom scholarships have been offered by UNICEF. Under the Social Uplift Programme, an institution has been started at Hyderabad in 1953 for the training of nurses, mid-wives, etc.

MRS. BACKUS: New York is like a miniature continent with many races and religions. It is different from any other community, yet it has had and still has problems that are familiar in many parts of the world. New York's biggest job has been to gain the confidence and overcome the ignorance and superstitions of its great immigrant popu-lation.

The responsibilities for maternal and child care are shared by the municipal govern-ment (the Departments of Health, Welfare and Hospitals) and by many voluntary agencies (religious groups, settlement houses, labor unions and various general or specialized organizations). Also, of course, most doctors donate a fair share of their time to service in hospital wards and clinics. (There is one hospital, the New York Infirmary for Women and Children, which is entirely staffed by women.)

In the past generation there has been a tremendous shift from home to hospital deliveries:

Year	Hospital Deliveries	Midwives
1915	35%	30%
1936	87%	–
1954	99%	–

(Two midwives left in New York City)

In the early part of the century, the maternal death rate was still high. In 1953, out of a city-wide population of 8,108,000 there were only 105 deaths at child birth (a ratio of 6.5 deaths to 1,000 births).

As is so often the case in our country, successful projects started on a small scale on a voluntary basis are gradually taken over and developed on a large scale into

6

Figure 8. Pan Pacific and Southeast Asia Women's Association of the United States of America Discussion Group: "Southeast Asia and the United Nations," April 1956, p. 6. Creator: Pan Pacific and Southeast Asia Women's Association of the United States of America. Sophia Smith Collection, Smith College, Northampton, Massachusetts.

tax-supported public services. In 1954, there were 65 obstetrical clinics and dispensaries in the city providing free or low cost care. These are all in hospitals either city run or low cost care. These are all in hospitals either city run or voluntary. At present the Department of Health is running only four maternity and pre-natal clinics and these will be closed shortly because it has been found better to have the hospitals responsible for a continuity between the pre-natal care and the place of confinement.

In addition there are 27 Health Centers run by the city where educational pamphlets on pre-natal and child care may be obtained. There are also various private organizations in the field, such as the Health Insurance Plan, the Visiting Nurses Service with its twelve centers, the Maternity Consultation Service and the Maternity Center Association. In 1921 the Maternity Center Association started a nurse-midwife school for registered nurses specializing in obstetrics. There are now three such schools in the United States. From the New York school there are now 205 graduates practicing in 24 countries including most of the countries in the Pacific and in Southeast Asia.

Conclusions: Public and private agencies work together, the private groups still doing most of the pioneering work and the city government setting standards and financing the work on a large scale. In spite of tremendous strides in the last few decades, there are still not enough servides available to adequately care for the mothers and children of a city of over eight million people.

MRS. JAIPAL: Maternity and Child Welfare programs were given prime importance in the planning of the New Indian Welfare State. About 200,000 women die in childbirth in India every year due to ignorance, poverty, lack of trained medical assistance. In cities and towns maternity hospitals are inadequate. In rural areas it is worse. Village women depend on the local "dais" for their confinement. The paucity of trained nurses and midwives in India has been an urgent problem. The PLAN envisaged a substantial increase of 3,000 nurses and 1932 midwives. The All-India Women's Conference has done very good work in establishing maternity and child health centres, medical centres, ante- and post-natal clinics and dispensaries. The Kasturba Gandhi National Memorial Trust is dedicated to the welfare of women and children, nursery education, runs courses for social service workers (gham sevikas). The Women's Welfare Departments set up by the State in Madras and UP give advice on welfare problems and maternity and medical aid is given in all the branches. Indian Red Cross which has been actively engaged in community, family and child welfare activities since 1931. It has branches all over India. The Central Government, in conjunction with UNICEF, has set up a maternal and child health training centre in the All-India Institute of Public Health and Hygiene in Calcutta.

There are approximately 1,750 Child Welfare and Maternity Centres in India. Women's welfare organizations have included child welfare as part of their activities. There are other voluntary organizations devoted exclusively to the welfare of children such as the Society for the Protection of Children in India, Balkan-Ki-Bari, and the Indian Council for Child Welfare. The chief problems re child welfare are (1) Health; (2) Nutrition. Infant mortality is high -- 127 per thousand live births.

Then there is the problem of malnutrition. The majority cannot afford to buy good milk for their children or for expectant and nursing mothers. UNICEF has been supplying powdered milk to children in scarcity areas. The Social Welfare Board has a Child Welfare Panel which has undertaken a survey for the supply of milk and other nutritious foodstuffs to children, and establishing more child welfare centres in poor localities like tribal areas and remote villages.

7

Figure 9. Pan Pacific and Southeast Asia Women's Association of the United States of America Discussion Group: "Southeast Asia and the United Nations," April 1956, p. 7. Creator: Pan Pacific and Southeast Asia Women's Association of the United States of America. Sophia Smith Collection, Smith College, Northampton, Massachusetts.

MRS. PRAWOTO: Indonesia has a population of 80,000,000. Protection and improvement of health is a vital and an immediate need. A harsh Japanese occupation and the War of Independence which followed left the health of the country in a tragic condition. The Ministry of Health has set up a Rural and Urban Hygiene Service for work in local areas, using program material prepared by another service, the Health Education Service. Amongst its objectives are developing maximum initiative and cooperation and providing more health services in small villages.

WHO and UNICEF have contributed over 4 million dollars and there are now from 13 countries, Asian and European, 9 doctors, 6 nurses, a public health engineer and an entomologist. UNICEF, which began its assistance in 1939, as recommended by WHO, coordinates the work into a Mother-Child Health Program which is implemented by the training of medical and auxiliary health personnel, such as village lay nurses. The Government through UNICEF and other sources seeks help in educating people in sanitation, child care and proper diet.

MRS. JENKINS: The Dominion of New Zealand is a long narrow country: about a thousand miles long, and nowhere wider than 280 miles. It comprises two large and several smaller islands, lying between latitudes 34 and 48 S.

Although New Zealanders as a whole are highly suspicious of bureaucracy and officialdom, their resistance to the extension of state activity through an expanding public service has been much less than that of many older established societies. To them, indeed, the expansion of democracy has been dependent on the expansion of "public service." The organization of the present-day Public Service was inaugurated by the Public Service Act of 1912. The total birth rate is equivalent to a rate of 17.93 per thousand mean population. The maternal mortality rate is about 3.01 per thousand live births.

Since 1948 a scheme for the immigration of children from the United Kingdom and Europe has been in operation. The children who come to New Zealand under the provisions of the scheme fall into two categories; those from the United Kingdom, described as refugee youths. During the war a group of Polish refugees, including 733 children, were given sanctuary in New Zealand. These children were placed in private homes and in hostels. Since 1944, 82 of these children have returned to their native land, 4 of the children died and the others now take their places in the communities where they live.

The Royal New Zealand Society for the Health of Women and Children, commonly and conveniently known as the Plunket Society was founded in New Zealand in 1907. Like many other undertakings, it had its beginning "on the land." It owes its existence to the late Sir Truby and Lady King. Dr. King's investigations into the vegetable and animal kingdom showed that in plants, just as in the case of animals, the inroads of disease were best prevented by keeping the organism well nourished, vigorous and healthy. He showed that it was by the application of the simple laws of Nature to the culture and feeding of plants and animals that the highest results were obtained. The pursuit of farming provided Dr. King with material for another study, the rearing of the human baby, and impelled him to investigate the cause of the great wastage of infant life that took place year after year.

After a careful study of the causes of infant deaths, Dr. King expressed an opinion †
that the prime factors were the mother's unpreparedness and ignorance. Early in 1905 he commenced his work. He was assisted by his wife and a Scottish girl. She later became the first Plunket nurse. The nurse worked in conjunction with the Sisters of various churches, who gladly accepted the instruction offered, and threw themselves whole-heartedly into the movement. The nurse's services were available

8

Figure 10. Pan Pacific and Southeast Asia Women's Association of the United States of America Discussion Group: "Southeast Asia and the United Nations," April 1956, p. 8. Creator: Pan Pacific and Southeast Asia Women's Association of the United States of America. Sophia Smith Collection, Smith College, Northampton, Massachusetts.

(Mrs. Jenkins) -- 3

free of charge to any mother who wanted advice, and her assistance and teaching were soon sought by mothers of all classes in the spirit in which they were tendered, not as charity, but as a measure of free education in a matter of vital importance to the whole community.

MISS MOSES: (In the course of a talk) provided this United Nations background: It is necessary today that "trained people teach others to desire the essentials." The organization of the United Nations Bureau of Social Affairs reflects the many-sided nature of this undertaking -- its sections on research in order to plot trends in the general field, population, community development, and the section on social services, itself subdivided into sections for the rehabilitation for the handicapped, social security administration as well as that on family and child welfare and on the training of social welfare personnel. One of the essentials in the training of social workers is that it be rooted, as far as possible, in the life of the community where they are to work. Therefore, for the countries of Southeast Asia, increasingly social workers trained in the same region are sought rather than those purely Western trained. A more "generic" or basic course must be developed and a major project occupying this section of the United Nations is the preparation of suitable social service training material for this area, drawing on its cultures as background and for illustrations (incidentally, even countries with old and highly-developed systems of social service, are calling on United Nations for advice, such as Sweden for certain casework technique).

MRS. BARBEY outlined the Five Year future plans for UNICEF in Southeast Asia: 1) Mother and Child Welfare in the Philippines and India, UNICEF with the Governments of these countries on a new National Rural Health program where the role of UNICEF would be to provide clinic equipment, training, personnel, midwives and doctors; 2) continuation of the international program for the rest of the Asian area; 3) the campaign on the eradication of malaria which will continue in full in Burma, Afghanistan and Pakistan and UNICEF will furnish half the program in these countries; 4) continuation of the work for yaws and its completion in Thailand and Indonesia; 5) work against tuberculosis in which UNICEF will provide all the new drugs and try to reduce the percentages in India and Pakistan. Finally, she suggested that the women of Southeast Asia present to their Governments worthwhile projects in the fields in which UNICEF is operating -- also that the women urge their Governments to seek further assistance since UNICEF has a reserve fund available. An indispensable reference is The Compendium of UNICEF, Vol. VI 1956 - 57.

MRS. SAWYER Briefly gave a first-hand account of several FAO projects in Indonesia concerned with experimentation in improving rice, the staple food of most Asian countries, and in research with the soya bean which has produced milk of high nutritive value. She suggested the following FAO readings:

> So Bold an Aim by P. L. Yates
> The Story of FAO by G. Hambidge
> Seeds of Progress. (United Nations Department of Public Information)
> Activities of FAO under the Expanded Technical Assistance Programme
> Global Scope of Technical Assistance (Chart No. 4)

9

Figure 11. Pan Pacific and Southeast Asia Women's Association of the United States of America Discussion Group: "Southeast Asia and the United Nations," April 1956, p. 9. Creator: Pan Pacific and Southeast Asia Women's Association of the United States of America. Sophia Smith Collection, Smith College, Northampton, Massachusetts.

The following list of principles growing out of the above discussion at the request of Dr. Ada Chree Reid was forwarded to the Congress of Medical Women Meeting at Manila on January 28, 1956:

1. An understanding of the conditions and a "human relations" approach is as important as the bringing of new scientific knowledge to a country.

2. It is important to assess and to muster existing resources, both human and material, before superimposing others from the outside.

3. Midwifery is a case in point. In many parts of the world, the mid-wife is not only relied on for her work, but is a respected and integral part of the community life. Therefore, as far as possible, she offers, and may be used as a channel through which newer methods and higher standards in child birth can reach the people of the area. In some countries special inducements are provided, such as bonuses for registration figures, in order that the mid-wife may come into increasing contact with local and national health authorities.

4. In the field of nutrition, for example, there may be valuable substitutes for milk available to be developed. In some cases indigenous herbs have been found to have distinct medical values.

5. Due to the world-wide shortage of fully trained social workers it may be necessary for a single worker to combine several types of social services. This may, also, provide a more natural contact and continuity with the lives of the people concerned. This "multi-purpose worker" may well be a more normal transition than the introduction of a specialist.

6. Whereas pre-natal, child birth and infancy, as well as school-age are likely to be relatively stressed by health authorities, the pre-school age child is apt to be neglected.

7. The overwhelming need for doctors by rural areas suggests the urgent need to counteract, in some measure, the pull of the urban centre for the young doctor. Efforts to this end have included the introduction of periods of rural medical field work in training and interne courses, the requirement of some minimum period of rural service on graduation and financial and social special inducements for the young doctor going into practice in a rural area.

Dr. Janet Robb,

Leader of the Discussion Group

10

Figure 12. Pan Pacific and Southeast Asia Women's Association of the United States of America Discussion Group: "Southeast Asia and the United Nations," April 1956, p. 10. Creator: Pan Pacific and Southeast Asia Women's Association of the United States of America. Sophia Smith Collection, Smith College, Northampton, Massachusetts.

II - EDUCATION IN SOUTHEAST ASIA

III - STATUS OF WOMEN IN SOUTHEAST ASIA

DR. ROBB: We will now vary our method a bit and have a series of very brief reports on "Education in Southeast Asia" and "The Status of Women in Southeast Asia." These reports can cover, of course, a phase only of the first subject such as adult education or community schools or medical and health training in the case of the status of women, a short summary for one or two countries. We will provide at the end of the first topic, a description of the work of UNESCO in this area by one of our members who is a member of her country's National Commission for UNESCO. On the position of women there will be an account from the Moderator of our group who has just returned from Geneva where she had been attending the three-week session of the United Nations Commission on the Status of Women held during March, 1956.

MRS. MENDEZ: When World War II ended and the Philippines became independent, we had to rebuild our educational system from less than scratch. For lack of desks, pupils squatted on bare floors under gaping roofs that let in both sunshine and rain. Many teachers taught without any books or blackboards. Paper and pencils were almost non-existent, but many resourceful teachers found that fresh banana leaves and thin bamboo sticks could serve the same purpose temporarily.

A ready answer to the challenge presented itself in the form of the community school which had proved successful in local experimentation and which had been tried out by no less than the Filipino patriot and martyr, Jose Rizal, when he was in exile in the 1890s.

In 1949, the superintendents of public schools, most of them partly trained in U. S. graduate colleges, adopted as their convention theme -- Education for Improvement of Community Living. Thenceforth, the idea spread rapidly through the provinces. Many traditional schools were converted into community schools; experimentation became the order of the day; however, there has been no standardization. Each community school answers the basic needs of a particular town or village.

From twenty to fifty families are invited by a school official, usually the elementary school principal, to constitute a purok, Tagalog for a small community group. Then begins a discussion of needs, usually one or more from five areas of living -- health and sanitation, economic, socio-cultural, citizenship and literacy. Throughout the democratic processes of group discussion and group action, there runs the feeling that everyone has something to contribute; that in his desire to improve themselves, and the community, the native mores, traditions, and cultures have a rightful place. The schools and the people have thus been brought closer together.

MRS. PRAWOTO: When Indonesia achieved independence in 1949, 95 per cent of her people were illiterate. All aspects of Indonesian society have been recruited to help raise the literacy rate to its present 65 per cent. Government, women's clubs, religious and laymen have helped to create numerous small village schools. Because of the lack of trained personnel and the need to create a civil service, it is important to graduate as many as possible quickly, but at the same time to give them an adequate foundation.

Education in Indonesia has a dual function -- teaching and studying simultaneously. High school and college students teach children while they themselves are learning.

11

Figure 13. Pan Pacific and Southeast Asia Women's Association of the United States of America Discussion Group: "Southeast Asia and the United Nations," April 1956, p. 11. Creator: Pan Pacific and Southeast Asia Women's Association of the United States of America. Sophia Smith Collection, Smith College, Northampton, Massachusetts.

"Each one teach one" is the standard.

The importance of educating adults as well as youth is recognized. Specialized agencies have been created to conduct literacy courses geared to the needs of the people -- for women, for farmers, for fishermen, for tradespeople, etc.

In addition to the need for basic education is the need to create a technical and professional class to aid and speed up the process of construction and reconstruction of a new nation. Several thousand Indonesians are now studying abroad under the auspices of the Indonesian Government, of non-profit foundations, of United Nations and of the United States of America.

MRS. ISLAM: In the field of public health in Pakistan as in several other spheres, Pakistan had virtually to start from scratch in respect of trained personnel and equipment. The medical services were depleted, and most of the institutions had perforce to be closed down. Lack of training facilities accentuated the shortage of the qualified personnel. By virtue of their geographical location almost all the highly developed institutions, like the Central Research Institute, Malarial Institute, Institute of Hygiene and Public Health, and Central Drugs Laboratory, remained in India.

At the time of Partition, there were only three medical colleges, one each at Lahore, Karachi, and Dacca, for the training of graduates, and four medical schools for the training of licentiates. These institutions had facilities obviously for a limited number of trainees. Since then three new medical colleges, Fatima Jinnah Medical College for Women, Lahore; Nishtar Medical College, Multan, and Liaquat Medical College, Hyderabad, have been established. Funds have been provided for two more medical colleges, one at Chittagong, and the other at Peshawar, which are expected to start functioning in the near future. The number of medical schools has also risen to seven.

To meet the shortage of teachers, research workers, and specialists, Government started a scheme for the training of medical personnel abroad. So far, 152 persons have been sent abroad under this scheme. Another batch of doctors has been selected for higher training abroad in 1954-55, and necessary action has been initiated for securing placement for them. As many as 122 doctors have returned after the successful completion of their courses, and have been absorbed in important positions in the field of medical education and administration. Apart from this, we were successful in securing 90 fellowships and scholarships for advanced training from organizations such as UNICEF, and WHO, and also under the Colombo Plan.

At the time of Partition, Pakistan was deplorably short of nurses. Nurses are now being trained by the Provincial Governments in their own medical institutions. To provide a stimulus to the training, the Central Government has established three Training Centres, one each at Karachi, Lahore, and Dacca, since 1950, for the training of 40 probationers.

MRS. BACKUS: In thinking of the work of UNESCO in this area, one usually thinks first of Fundamental Education -- that experiment in raising the practical knowledge of a community by methods that are not dependent on the three Rs. While there is no regional center in the East as in Latin America and the Middle East, many national governments -- notably India and the Philippines -- have cooperated with UNESCO in setting up their own fundamental educational projects. The expansion and revivification of the cottage industries has also been stressed, and of course UNESCO has also

Figure 14. Pan Pacific and Southeast Asia Women's Association of the United States of America Discussion Group: "Southeast Asia and the United Nations," April 1956, p. 12. Creator: Pan Pacific and Southeast Asia Women's Association of the United States of America. Sophia Smith Collection, Smith College, Northampton, Massachusetts.

(Mrs. Backus) -- 2

assisted national governments in their general fight against illiteracy.

Many governments have taken advantage of UNESCO assistance in expanding their public school systems. UNESCO has provided advisory services, fellowships, workshops and training courses for teachers. There are several projects of particular interest that might be noted here:

1. The Institute of Child Study at Bangkok -- a joint effort of the Thai government and UNESCO. The Institute, established in 1954, has now reached international proportions. In 1956 UNESCO is offering four Asian and two non-Asian fellowships to this Institute.

2. UNESCO has cooperated with the Philippines in that country's idea of developing community schools where parents and teachers cooperate in working out a program of studies that will be truly meaningful and useful for the children of that community.

3. In 1955 UNESCO helped to establish in Asia a Research and Information Center on the Teaching of Foreign Languages.

4. In 1956 UNESCO is sponsoring a conference in the West on ways of getting a better presentation of Asian countries in Occidental textbooks. In 1958 a similar conference will be held in Asia to consider the reverse side of the problem.

In many cases the development of new educational projects and institutions has been greatly assisted through the UNESCO Gift Coupon plan, which makes it possible for individuals or organizations in one country to help procure desperately needed educational supplies for communities in other parts of the world. For instance, UNESCO gift coupons for projects in Korea have totalled $47,528. These have come from people in seven countries and have aided in the establishment in Korea of four engineering schools, an agricultural school and a school for the deaf, as well as other minor projects.

Social Science

UNESCO hopes to have the cooperation of at least three communities in Asia for intensive project studies on the political role of women and the social and cultural factors conditioning women's access to education. Reports of these studies will be made to the commission on the Status of Women and to the 1958 Conference of PPSEAWA.

UNESCO has been extremely concerned with the sociological effects of the sudden upsurge of modern technology in the East. A mere listing of some of the activities of UNESCO in this part of the world will be of interest:

1. An International Research Office on Social Implications of Technical Change.

2. An International Research Center on Social Problems of Industrialization.

3. A study of the effects of a new public library in the working class quarters of Delhi.

4. In cooperation with FAO and ECAFE, a seminar on Modern Agricultural Techniques in Relation to Traditional Beliefs and Habits.

13

Figure 15. Pan Pacific and Southeast Asia Women's Association of the United States of America Discussion Group: "Southeast Asia and the United Nations," April 1956, p. 13. Creator: Pan Pacific and Southeast Asia Women's Association of the United States of America. Sophia Smith Collection, Smith College, Northampton, Massachusetts.

Culture

1. In 1955 there was a seminar of thirty librarians and educators from twelve countries in the South Asia and Pacific area. The seminar was held in the new public library in Delhi.

2. Burma, India and Pakistan have requested that UNESCO send them experts on museums.

3. UNESCO has answered several requests for specialized advice concerning libraries and archives.

4. In 1955-56 UNESCO is undertaking studies of the state of traditional cultures in several Asian countries.

Mass Media

One of the interesting projects in this field is that of education by means of radio. UNESCO has obtained the services of some Canadians familiar with the Canadian Farm Radio Forum to help adapt these techniques for the use of fundamental education projects in South East Asia.

Major Projects

At its General Conference in Montevideo, UNESCO adopted the idea of concentrating on certain major projects. Three of the four major projects now under discussion for inclusion in the 1957-58 program of UNESCO would be of particular concern to the Far East:

1. UNESCO will continue its study of the Arid Lands, concentrating on the Middle East and South Asia, including Afghanistan, Ceylon, India and Pakistan. Among other things, a special study will be made of a nomad group and the effects that irrigation and other modern improvements will have on the life of such a group.

2. A proposed six to eight-year project on the development of reading materials (books, periodicals, etc.) for new literates. It is proposed that this work be carried on in Burma, Cambodia, Ceylon, India, Indonesia, Laos, Nepal, Pakistan, Thailand and Viet-Nam.

3. A six to eight-year project to encourage a Mutual Appreciation of Eastern and Western Cultural Values. UNESCO would focus the attention of its member states on the need for increasing all possible cultural and intellectual contacts between Asia and the West. Specifically, UNESCO would encourage and facilitate the translation of great works of literature, an increased exchange of students, scholars, art exhibits, drama and films. It would offer fellowships, arrange international seminars for the exchange of ideas between East and West.

MRS. JAIPAL: In the days of the "Mahatharata" in India, Hindu women were not subordinate to men. They moved about freely and even were owners of property and the sole guardians of their children. All this would indicate a matriarchal type of society, which may have existed in many communities, and still prevails among the Nayars of Malabar and in certain hill tracts in Northern India. But as time went on Hindu women were gradually pushed into the background and suffered gradual subjection

14

Figure 16. Pan Pacific and Southeast Asia Women's Association of the United States of America Discussion Group: "Southeast Asia and the United Nations," April 1956, p. 14. Creator: Pan Pacific and Southeast Asia Women's Association of the United States of America. Sophia Smith Collection, Smith College, Northampton, Massachusetts.

to men. Mann, the law-giver of the Hindus, laid down that woman, from the cradle to the grave, was to be dependent on a male; in childhood on her father, in youth on her husband, and in old age on her son. The code of Marna insisted on child marriages, and did not allow women to own property or perform any important religious ceremony, or move freely in male company. Where Moslem influence was strong Hindu women also observed "purdah." Widows were not permitted to remarry and their lot in society was pathetic. In the last few decades, however, all this has been changing. From the early days of the freedom movement women have been asserting themselves and coming to the forefront in ever increasing numbers. They have fought steadily for their rights and sought higher education and formed All-India Organizations to represent their interests. Educational opportunities for women were limited in the past because of (1) the purdah system, (2) early marriage, (3) the view that girls' were more useful at home, and (4) the inadequate number of girls schools and teachers. According to the 1951 census the number of educated women in India was 9.3 per cent (above ten years old). Out of 22.29 million girls between the ages of 6 and 11, 5.01 million were in primary schools. Out of 512,000 primary school teachers, 15 per cent were women. During 1949-50 the total enrollment in teachers' training schools, colleges, and University departments of education was 71,884, out of which 17,798 (or 24.7 per cent) were women students. But to bring about universal education in India, we would need 2,700,000 teachers of whom 50 per cent would have to be women.

Under social reform the "purdah" system has been attacked and has been largely removed. Early marriages have been restricted by legislation. The Child Marriage Restraint Act (1929) raised the marriageable age of girls to 15.

Under the new Constitution of India women have gained complete political equality with men. They now have the right to vote, seek election and hold public office, and have equality of opportunity for public employment. Women have entered the Central and State Legislatures, the cabinet, the administrative departments of Government, various professions, services and vocations. In the first general election held under the new Constitution (1951-52) 85 million women were entitled to vote. Out of the total number of votes cast, 48 per cent came from women. Sixty-six women contested the elections to the Federal Parliament, and 216 to the State Legislatives. Out of these 19 women were elected to the House of the People, 14 to the Council of States, and 82 to the Legislative Assemblies and 23 to the State Legislative Councils. One woman was nominated by the President of India to the Council of States to represent Indian Arts.

Women do not yet have legal equality with men. Women's rights differ with the State or Community to which they belong. The Hindu Code Bill advocates monogamy, recognizes inheritance rights of the daughter, gives the woman control over her property. But this is not enough, as it does not concede full equality. This has now become the objective of some Women's Organizations in India.

MRS. PAW HTIN: The status of women in Burma has always been on an equal basis with that of Burmese men throughout the ages. It remains so to this day.

The high status of women in Burmese society is reflected in the customary law relating to marriage, divorce and inheritance. In Burmese law, marriage is purely a civil contract based on the mutual consent of a man and a woman to openly live together as husband and wife. Therefore, in a court of law, proof of marriage is borne out only by the testimony of witnesses that a man and a woman have lived

15

Figure 17. Pan Pacific and Southeast Asia Women's Association of the United States of America Discussion Group: "Southeast Asia and the United Nations," April 1956, p. 15. Creator: Pan Pacific and Southeast Asia Women's Association of the United States of America. Sophia Smith Collection, Smith College, Northampton, Massachusetts.

together as man and wife. No woman can be forced into marriage without her consent. Like marriage, divorce is also simple. If divorce is by mutual consent, there is no formality. A wife can divorce her husband without his consent if he is guilty of cruelty or serious marital misconduct. Though divorce is comparatively easy, it is very rare. On divorce, a wife takes a substantial share of the joint estate. If she remarries she remains absolute owner of the estate from her previous marriage. Burmese women have always possessed full right of inheritance. On the death of the husband the wife inherits a major share of the family estate and full authority as the head of the family. Daughters have full rights of inheritance as sons. These rights of inheritance cannot be defeated in any way as Burmese Customary Law has never recognized the right to dispose of property by will.

One fact unique for Burmese women is that they retain their maiden names even after marriage.

As regards the political status of Burmese women, everyone above the age of 18 years is eligible for voting; and anyone over the age of 20 is eligible for election to the Union Parliament. Women have competed evenly with men at the polls. No separate seats are reserved for women candidates in the Union Parliament. A Burmese woman can aspire to any position. There are women members in the Union Parliament. There has been a woman Minister in the Cabinet. In the villages it is not unusual to have a woman "headman." In several instances, women "headmen" of villages have been rewarded by the Government for their courage in dealing with crime. Burmese women have represented their country at various international conferences such as the World Health Assembly, WHO Regional Committee meetings; Commission on the Status of Women, to state a few.

To ensure the economic rights of Burmese women, Section 14 of the Constitution reads: "There will be equality of opportunity for all citizens in matters of public employment and in the exercise or carrying on of any occupation, trade, business or profession." Furthermore, Section 15 reads: "Women shall be entitled to the same pay as that received by men in respect of similar work."

DR. ROBB: The 10th session of the United Nations Status of Women Commission just ended in Geneva was marked by emphasis on the status of women in the Newer Countries and economically less developed areas. This was shown in the stressing of private law relationships, those involving marriage rights of spouses and such problems as child betrothal and marriage, bride price, polygamy, the rights of mothers and of widows in relation to children; a lively debate on the economic as well as creative importance of cottage industries and handicrafts, so vital today for many women of South East Asia; and the possibilities of United Nations Technical Assistance in raising the status of Women in such regions by means for instance of seminars involving as participants women of areas, lately politically enfranchised. The Special Representatives of PASEAWA present made especially effective "interventions" before the Commission on the last two topics. Five countries represented at the last PASEAWA Conference in Manila were represented on the 18 member Commission. The special attention of the discussion group might be called to three interesting documents prepared for the session: Selected Projects in Technical Assistance Affecting the Status of Women and Selected List of Materials (E/CN/6/274); Opportunities for Girls in Vocational and Technical Education, UNESCO and ILO Report (E/CN6/280); Opportunities for Women in Handicrafts and Cottage Industries, ILO Report (E/CN6/282)

Figure 18. Pan Pacific and Southeast Asia Women's Association of the United States of America Discussion Group: "Southeast Asia and the United Nations," April 1956, p. 16. Creator: Pan Pacific and Southeast Asia Women's Association of the United States of America. Sophia Smith Collection, Smith College, Northampton, Massachusetts.

CONCLUSIONS

I. One might observe that within its obvious limits and on its own scale this discussion group, first and foremost, helped to provide intangible human values in international contacts, difficult perhaps to assess but impossible certainly to disregard.

II. The introduction of reports from New Zealand and on New York City's systems of maternal and child welfare undoubtedly served to provide variety and gave cohesive force to the group as one truly of participants.

III. The formulation of principles to send to a congress of doctors in Manila gave valuable focus to the discussions on maternal and child welfare.

IV. The use of United Nations experts in the discussions not only gave body to them but undoubtedly made the work of the United Nations in the three fields under discussion more living and immediate. The generosity of such experts as the Director of Training in Social Work of the United Nations Secretariat and of the Liaison Officer for UNICEF cannot be too highly appreciated. "Home talent" too, was not lacking amongst the group in expert knowledge of FAO, UNESCO and the United Nations Commission on the Status of Women. Moreover, membership from both Asia and the United States included experts in medicine, health services and social work in their own countries.

V. Finally, the subject matter of these discussions ties in closely with that of the forthcoming conference of its international body, whose Program Chairman writes: "The Manila Conference of the Pan Pacific and Southeast Asia Women's Association voted to build the next conference in Japan around the topic of Food. This basic necessity of life has many ramifications. It is vitally connected with child and maternal welfare. It leads naturally into education, since one of the needs of all countries is a better understanding of nutrition and its importance in building healthy people. It has a close connection with the status of women. If women are not given full opportunity to share in the plans for better living conditions the execution of these plans will not reach the family where all plans must reach if they are to be something more than statistics on paper. The topics chosen for the New York discussion group, therefore, are closely related to the topic which will concern us in the 1958 Conference. We will look forward to many helpful suggestions which will come to our Program Committee from your continued discussions. I am particularly glad that your group is considering the topic within the framework of the United Nations."

Janet Robb, Narrator

April 27, 1956

17

Figure 19. Pan Pacific and Southeast Asia Women's Association of the United States of America Discussion Group: "Southeast Asia and the United Nations," April 1956, p. 17. Creator: Pan Pacific and Southeast Asia Women's Association of the United States of America. Sophia Smith Collection, Smith College, Northampton, Massachusetts.

Judy Tzu-Chun Wu

....

The Dead, the Living, and the Sacred
Patsy Mink, Antimilitarism, and Reimagining
the Pacific World

Abstract: This article focuses on the antinuclear and antimilitarism politics of Patsy Takemoto Mink (1927–2002), the first Japanese American female lawyer in Hawaiʻi, the first woman of color to become a U.S. congressional representative, and the namesake for Title IX. During the late 1960s and 1970s, Mink challenged the use of the Pacific lands, waters, and peoples as sites of military experimentation, subject to nuclear and chemical testing as well as war games. Mink's political worldview, shaped by her experiences and understanding of the interconnectedness between human and nonhuman life as well as water and land, reflected a Pacific World sensibility. She worked with, but also articulated political priorities that differed from, indigenous peoples of the Pacific. Focusing on these connected yet divergent Pacific imaginaries provides an opportunity to explore the significance of these antimilitarism campaigns for the study of transnational feminisms as well as Asian American and Pacific Islander studies. First, the protests of Mink and Native Hawaiian activists against U.S. militarism in the Pacific represented gendered critiques of U.S. empire, although in different ways. Second, Mink's advocacy via political liberalism provided opportunities for coalition formation yet also constrained the range of her gendered arguments and limited possible solutions beyond the U.S. polity. Third, the coalitional possibilities and incommensurabilities reveal the points of convergence and divergence between Asian American demands for full inclusion and Pacific Islander calls for decolonization and sovereignty.

MERIDIANS · feminism, race, transnationalism   18:2 October 2019
DOI: 10.1215/15366936-7775729 © 2019 Smith College

From 1965 to 1971, Amchitka Island—described as a "remote and wind-swept" place off the coast of Alaska—served as the site of three underground nuclear tests (P. Carter 1969: D-8; Coates 1996; Kohlhoff 2002). The 1963 Limited Test Ban Treaty between the United States, the Soviet Union, and the United Kingdom eliminated nuclear testing aboveground and underwater. Consequently, these Cold War enemies found new locales to detonate weapons underground. Nestled in one of the most seismically active regions in the world, Amchitka, one of the Aleutian Islands and a national wildlife sanctuary, became the test site for the 1965 "Long Shot" detonation, an eighty-kiloton bomb with five times the power of the atomic bomb dropped on Hiroshima to end World War II. The Atomic Energy Commission (AEC) set off "Long Shot" purposefully after a magnitude-8.7 earthquake to see if monitors could distinguish between natural seismicity and nuclear explosions. In 1969, scientists detonated the much larger one-megaton bomb called the Milrow, followed by the 1971 Cannikin test, the largest underground bomb ever exploded by the United States. A five-megaton weapon, Cannikin held four hundred times the power of the Hiroshima bomb. These planned nuclear tests drew a firestorm of protests in the context of the 1960s and 1970s, when critics of the Cold War and advocates for protecting the environment coalesced into mass protest movements.[1] This article focuses on the antinuclear and antimilitarism politics of Patsy Takemoto Mink (1927–2002), the first Japanese American female lawyer in Hawai'i, the first woman of color to become a U.S. congressional representative, and the namesake for Title IX.[2]

Mink's worldview, shaped by her experiences and understanding of the interconnectedness between human and nonhuman life as well as water and land, reflected a Pacific World sensibility. One of her congressional newsletters explained: "Those who have lived in an island environment where the interaction of the elements is perhaps more readily apparent than elsewhere, have a greater awareness of the interdependence of man and his surroundings" (Mink Papers, box 232, f. 3). Residents and visitors to the Hawaiian Islands lived surrounded by the ocean, beaches, dramatic mountains and canyons, lush greenery, and changeable tropical weather. However, the state's main economic activities centered on agribusiness, the U.S. military, and tourism. All three industries emerged through settler colonial processes that vanquished Native peoples in order to possess Native lands. These industries also tended to overuse, pollute, and even destroy the surrounding natural resources. Recognizing these ecological dangers, Mink's denizenship in Hawai'i motivated her to challenge the U.S. security state across the Pacific in the Aleutian, Marshall, and Hawaiian archipelagoes to redefine what is essential for life and whose lives are worth saving. Elizabeth M. DeLoughrey points out how the U.S. government utilized the Pacific Islands as laboratories for nuclear testing, based on the false belief that their geographical distance from the United States and their island topography might serve to "isolate" the impact of radiation (DeLoughrey 2013). The concept of ecological isolation assumes that only land matters, not the air and water that connect and circulate between the islands. In contrast, conceptualizing the Pacific Islands as archipelagoes foregrounds the importance of land and water as well as the interdependent relationship between the two (Roberts and Stephens 2017).

In addition, these "remote" islands were in fact inhabited by both non-human and human life. Land animals, sea life, and birds traveled between islands and continents, creating ecological chains that transcend specific locales. Also, the "barren places" selected for military experimentation tended to be occupied by indigenous and racialized peoples. Barbara Rose Johnston, in her edited collection entitled *Half-Lives and Half-Truths*, noted that 70% of the world's uranium mines "were located in lands inhabited by indigenous peoples"; and "for the majority of atmospheric tests conducted by the United States, the Soviet Union, China, France, and Great Britain, ground zero was the ancestral homelands for indigenous peoples, tribal groups, and other ethnic minorities" (Johnston 2007: 6). Exposed to radiation, nuclear waste, and other military toxins, these peoples in turn served as test subjects for the U.S. military-medical complex to ascertain the full impact of Cold War weaponry. Not recognizing the interconnection between the human and the nonhuman as well as the status of indigenous and racialized subjects as fully human justified the use of the Pacific and other regions of the world as militarized laboratories (Teaiwa 2010).

In condemning nuclear and weapons testing, Mink worked with, but also articulated political priorities that differed from, indigenous peoples of the Pacific. For example, in their mutual campaign to stop militarized possession and bombing of Kaho'olawe Island in Hawai'i, Native Hawaiian activists decried the systematic destruction of lands sacred to their communities and called for indigenous access and control of these colonized domains (Aluli and McGregor 1992; Blackford 2004; Kajihiro 2009; Osorio 2014: 137–60). Mink believed in and advocated for a more humane U.S. nation-state that recognized the interdependence of the Pacific World.

In contrast, key Native Hawaiian activists offered an indigenous world-view that fundamentally challenged the forced "gifts" of democracy and modernity that destroyed Native Hawaiian relationships to their lands, kin, and deities (Silva 2004; Nguyen 2012; Espiritu 2014; Teves 2015; Saranillio 2018). These two distinct, alternative imaginaries of the Pacific World nevertheless both challenged the militarized understandings of the Pacific Islands as ideal locales to experiment with ecological annihilation.

Focusing on these connected yet divergent Pacific imaginaries provides an opportunity to explore the significance of these antimilitarism campaigns for the study of transnational feminisms as well as Asian American and Pacific Islander studies. First, the protests of Mink and Native Hawaiian activists against U.S. militarism in the Pacific represented gendered critiques of U.S. empire, although in different ways. In fact, the status of Asian Americans and Pacific Islanders as transnational subjects (incorporated via migration, occupation, and colonization) inspired these critiques of the Cold War U.S. nation-state. Second, Mink's advocacy via political liberalism provided opportunities for coalition formation yet also constrained the range of her gendered arguments and limited possible solutions beyond the U.S. polity. Third, the coalitional possibilities and incommensurabilities reveal the points of convergence and divergence between Asian American demands for full inclusion and Pacific Islander calls for decolonization and sovereignty (Tuck and Yang 2012; Rohrer 2016; Barker 2017).[3]

De/Militarizing the Pacific

Mink's protests against underground nuclear testing in Alaska in the 1960s and 1970s reflected her long-standing concerns about Cold War militarism in the Pacific. The detonations in Alaska stemmed from a broader governmental mindset and set of policies. The Pacific Islands, especially in the context of the Cold War, served as bases for training and deployment, rest and recreation, as well as for testing conventional, biological, and nuclear weaponry (Enloe 2000; Shigematsu and Camacho 2010; Gonzalez 2013; Genz et al. 2016). To understand the Pacific as an interconnected oceanic and land region, various scholars raise the importance of a Pacific World framework (Blackford 2007; Igler 2007, 2013; Okihiro 2008, 2009; Teaiwa 2010; Matsuda 2012; Nguyen and Hoskins 2014; Dvorak 2015; Kauanui 2015; Lyons and Tengan 2015; Rohrer 2016; Takezawa and Okihiro 2016; Choy and Wu 2017). Just as an Atlantic World perspective connects Europe, Africa, and the Americas, a Pacific World viewpoint brings together the life-forms, lands, and waters in and bordering the Pacific into a common analytical lens. Mink's lifelong connection to Hawai'i and her identity as a Japanese American influenced her understanding of nuclear testing as a Pacific World issue.

A Nuclear Pacific

Early in Mink's legal career, she defended pacifist activists on the *Golden Rule*. A ship operated by members of the American Friends Services Committee, the *Golden Rule* attempted to sail into a nuclear testing zone in 1958 to protest aboveground detonations in the Marshall Islands. To obtain the authority to demark this testing site, the United States received permission from the United Nations to create a Trust Territory of the Pacific Islands in 1947 and established the "Pacific Providing Grounds" for nuclear experimentation. Beginning in 1946, the United States conducted sixty-seven tests with a combined yield of 108 megatons, "the equivalent of one Hiroshima-sized bomb detonated daily for nineteen years" (Parsons and Zaballa 2017: 2). In 1958 alone, Operation Hardtack I detonated thirty-five weapons aboveground or underwater in the Marshall Islands. European NATO allies also tested their nuclear weaponry as part of these experiments. U.S. officials forcibly evacuated the Marshallese in order to facilitate nuclear testing and exposed them to radioactive fallout without adequate protection or informed consent. Setsu Shigematsu and Keith Camacho characterize the relationship between the United States and the Pacific Islands as a form of "nuclear colonialism" (Shigematsu and Camacho 2010: xxix).

In addition to using her legal expertise to defend the activists for civil disobedience, Mink also utilized her position as a representative in the Hawaiian territorial congress to bring attention to U.S. nuclear testing in the Pacific. She spearheaded a House resolution condemning the detonations. Mink's concerns regarding the extensive range of nuclear fallout stemmed from the unanticipated results of past experiments. The 1954 Castle Bravo test on the Bikini Atoll generated radioactive "snow" over seven thousand square miles of ocean, poisoning the crew and cargo of the Japanese fishing boat Daigo Fukuryū Maru or *Lucky Dragon No. 5* (Parsons and Zaballa 2017: 2).

In her warnings against nuclear testing, Mink highlighted the impact on the Marshallese. She expressed skepticism toward the assurances by

Washington and the "British government, that no harm will come to the populated islands of the Pacific. These same assurances were given to the poor people of the Marshall Islands, 300 of whom were exposed to large amounts of radioactive fallout in the 1954 tests" (Mink 25 February 1957). The fallout, as demonstrated in the aftermath of Hiroshima and Nagasaki, held long-term genetic consequences, since "it is equally bad and harmful to our future generations" (Mink 25 February 1957). In Mink's critiques of nuclear testing, she emphasized the ecological connectedness between the Marshall and the Hawaiian Islands. The United States governed the former as a trusteeship, and the latter held territorial status with the potential to become a state. Rather than highlighting the exceptional status of Hawai'i, Mink emphasized the common nuclear dangers that threatened to cross oceanic distances and political borders.

For Mink's outspoken criticisms of nuclear policies, she received letters of support as well as resounding criticism from her detractors. In a letter to the editor of the *Honolulu Advertiser*, Mink stated: "I have been maligned by various individuals . . . who choose to crucify me for my honest belief by name-calling and innuendos" (Mink 2 May 1957, Mink Papers, box 9, f. 11). In fact, her critics labeled Patsy Mink "Patsy Pink" for her alleged communist sympathies. One letter writer even accused Mink of supporting Japan's sneak attack on Pearl Harbor since she criticized the use of nuclear weapons against Japan. As both Mink and her supporters noted, these criticisms not only redbaited Mink but also targeted her racial ancestry as evidence of her disloyalty. As the Japanese language editorial of the *Hawaii Times* expressed, "this anonymous contributor . . . [made] it seem as if Mrs. Mink, because she has Japanese blood, had actually approved of Japan's dastardly action [the attack on Pearl Harbor]. This is plain out and out prejudice" (Tokioka 1957). In a letter to a supportive constituent, Mink indirectly concurred by pointing out that

> Joe Rose, TV commentator, night after night, has chosen to criticize me and me alone, for the resolution which I co-sponsored with all 17 other fellow Democrats and which passed the House by a unanimous vote. I know that as an elected politician, I must learn how to accept backhanded slaps, but it is utterly discouraging to see everything that I have done in honest and sincere belief chopped to pieces as Red-tainted. Hate-mongers who hide behind free speech to persecute their carefully selected victims, suffocate the very principles and ideals of a democracy. (Mink 14 May 1957, Mink Papers, box 9, f. 11)

Mink's gender in combination with her race likely played a role in inciting this targeted political attack. Other Japanese Americans, all of them men, served in the Hawaiian territorial congress. As the only Japanese American woman in the legislature, Mink led the charge in the antinuclear testing campaign and received the brunt of the hostile responses.

A Military Paradise

Mink linked Hawai'i with the Marshall Islands; she also recognized the connections between nuclear, conventional, and chemical military testing. During her years as a federal congressional representative, Mink repeatedly demanded that the U.S. Navy and Department of Defense stop using Kaho'olawe Island as a bombing practice site. The smallest of the eight major Hawaiian Islands, Kaho'olawe neighbors Maui Island, the second-most-populated island in Hawai'i and the location of Mink's childhood home. The Navy used Kaho'olawe on a regular basis as a bombing range (Gundersen and Bienfang 1970). In repeated letters to the Navy and Department of Defense, Mink pointed out the negative impact of this practice: "Residents of nearby Maui are understandably outraged by the noise and tremors caused by these explosions, and they are concerned with the danger to their lives and property" (Mink 30 September 1969, Mink Papers, box 128, f. 5). The islanders also feared the possibility of being bombed themselves. The Navy denied this by stating, "In over 25 years of bombing Kahoolawe, there is no recorded instance of stray ordnance striking Maui as a result of an attack on the desolate island" (Mink 30 September 1969). However, in 1969, Mink's former high school classmate and then-mayor of Maui County, Elmer Cravalho, discovered "an unexploded 500–pound bomb" on his property. Mink conveyed this to the secretary of the Navy, explaining that "the bomb was manufactured six or seven years ago but dropped within the past two or three months. It was found by its impact crater, and its brand new condition gave positive proof that the bomb was dropped recently and was not the result of a test years ago" (Mink 30 September 1969). The U.S. military conducted similar tests on Ka'ula Rock Island and made similar mistakes by inadvertently bombing the nearby and populated Ni'ihau Island.[4] In fact, U.S. pilots sometimes mistakenly targeted locals who fished near bombing sites (Middendorf 23 July 1975, Mink Papers, box 129, f. 10). A comparable incident in the Philippines in 1976 resulted in a "Navy practice bombing" that "killed six Filipino fishermen" (King 19 July 1976, Mink Papers, box 129, f. 1).

Mink and others condemned the dangers of both conventional and chemical/biological testing. The United States utilized a range of chemical weapons in the wars in Southeast Asia, including napalm and Agent Orange. The military tested these and other weapons first in the states and in locales controlled by the government. In response to a query from Mink, the U.S. Army initially denied any testing, but then qualified its response: "The Army has not tested either chemical or biological munitions in Hawaii. The Army has conducted limited chemical tests under strict safety precautions to obtain defense information" (Mink 16 September 1969, Mink Papers, box 116, f. 5). When pressed for information, the U.S. Army subsequently revealed that "four chemical tests were conducted on the Island of Hawaii at an Army jungle environmental test site in the Waiakea forest reserve" (Mink 16 September 1969). The Army tested the chemical weapons in open air. The emerging field of critical refugee studies fore-grounds the geographical interconnectedness of the Pacific with the U.S. war in Southeast Asia. For example, Yen Le Espiritu's *Body Counts* focuses on how the humanitarian rescue of refugees is directly connected to milita-rized sites of violence making. The same bases in Guam and the Philip-pines that launched planes to bomb Vietnam served as transit and shelter sites of refugee relocation after the war. Mink's exposure of military testing in Hawai'i during the war reveals the interconnectedness of the Pacific and Southeast Asia in the testing and deployment of war making. Similarly, Simeon Man's study reveals how the U.S. military practiced war games in Hawai'i and cast racialized individuals on the islands to play the role of the U.S. enemy (Man 2018). Various sites of the Asia-Pacific served as inter-changeable locales to stage and make war.

Mink and her political collaborators connected Hawai'i's militarized and colonized status with the Philippines as well as Culebra, an island in Puerto Rico also designated as a target practice site. In 1974, after extensive and widespread protests, the U.S. Senate barred this military use of Cule-bra. To lobby for a similar bill in the House regarding Kaho'olawe, Mink offered the opinion, "I believe Hawaii deserves as much consideration as Puerto Rico" (Mink 1974). The Unites States incorporated Hawai'i, Puerto Rico, and the Philippines all in the 1890s, and their status as colonized and militarized sites continued well into the twentieth century.

Collateral Damage

The designation of the Marshall, Hawaiian, Philippine, and Caribbean islands as particularly "suitable" and necessary sites of U.S. military experimentation explains the use of Amchitka as a locale for nuclear underground testing. The AEC explained that it chose Amchitka "after an extensive survey of many areas throughout the world" (U.S. AEC 1969: 1). Amchitka's "remoteness" constituted a key factor in selecting this locale. As a National Wildlife Refuge, the island's primary inhabitants consisted of animals, particularly sea otters and birds, including the bald eagle.

To counter the protected status of the island, the AEC obtained presidential and secretary of the interior permission to embark on nuclear testing. In addition, government scientists considered the geology of the island, located in "an active earthquake area," as an asset for the experimental design of nuclear detonation. They expressed some concern as well, particularly since similar nuclear testing in Nevada generated seismic activity. However, the study determined that these Nevada aftershocks had little likelihood of affecting the San Andreas fault, located under the more populated state of California over two hundred miles away (U.S. AEC 1969: 3–4). Consequently, the report minimized the possibility of widespread damage due to earthquakes in the Amchitka region, located at another trigger point of the San Andreas fault.

Mink and other critics of nuclear testing on Amchitka refuted the official arguments about "containing" the impact of detonation on a "remote" island. Instead, she and others emphasized the ecological and environmental connections between the Aleutian Islands and the rest of the Pacific. Mink lobbied extensively by writing letters, giving speeches, generating publicity, and presenting arguments in Congress about Amchitka. Media coverage and correspondence about Amchitka reinforced the belief that the AEC knowingly gambled with the lives of people in and bordering the Pacific. *Science* magazine published an article about the proposed detonations entitled, "Earthquakes and Nuclear Tests: Playing the Odds on Amchitka" (L. Carter 1969: 773). Mink also received a telegram from the president of the American Federation of Teachers in Hawai'i, stating simply: "Amchitka Test on site edging San Andreas Fault is playing Russian Roulette with America" (Trenhail 3 November 1971, Mink Papers, box 49, f. Amchitka Correspondence, Hawaii, 1971, Nov. [1 of 2]).

In addition to the possibility of environmental disaster, Mink raised concerns about the political fallout from the Amchitka tests, particularly from the countries surrounding the Pacific Rim. As she noted in another letter to President Nixon, "The governments of Canada and Japan have registered official protests with the Department of State concerning the tests. It is also worth noting that Amchitka Island is very close to Russia" (Mink 24 September 1969, Mink Papers, box 50, f. 1). Mink's Japanese ancestry shaped her concerns about Amchitka. A significant portion of Japanese immigrants, including members of Mink's family, traced their ancestral roots to the Hiroshima region and to Southern Japan. Mink, and other Japanese American congressional leaders from Hawai'i, also highlighted that the detonation of the largest nuclear bomb would occur just as the Japanese emperor visited the United States for the first time. In fact, this unofficial meeting with President Nixon took place in Alaska. However, Mink also expressed concerns that transcended ethnic and national ties. In the Cold War context, nuclear testing, not just the military deployment of nuclear weapons, constituted acts of aggression. Mink reminded U.S. policy makers that the very geological interconnectedness of the Pacific World held the potential to aggravate political tremors. The Amchitka tests held the potential to detonate both seismic shifts and political rifts.

Mink and other critics raised the sense of Pacific-wide endangerment and also argued for the specific value of Amchitka Island, its wildlife, its environs, and the people connected to this land. In a letter to the secretary of the Department of the Interior, Mink argued:

> As the test is in a National Wildlife Refuge, other functions entrusted to you, by statute, are also being violated by the Cannikin blast. . . . Please answer each of the following questions: Is it permissible to use a .22 rifle on Amchitka? Is it permissible to use a slingshot against wildlife there? Is it permissible to throw rocks at the wildlife there? Is it permissible to detonate a five-megaton thermonuclear bomb there? (Mink 13 October 1971, Mink Papers, box 50, f. 2)

In this series of questions, Mink forcefully reminded the federal government of its conservation responsibilities for the wildlife on Amchitka. She also underscored the need to understand nuclear bombs not as a special weapon deserving of exemption from federal regulation but rather as the ultimate conveyer of violence.

In addition, Mink highlighted how nuclear testing on a remote island had the potential to poison the vast Pacific Ocean and the life-forms that the water sustains. In a letter to President Nixon in 1971, asking him to stop the Cannikin test, Mink warned:

> We are already polluting our oceans and damaging our fisheries and even the microscopic oxygen-producing sea organisms which sustain all life on this planet. It is acknowledged that the Amchitka blast will introduce radioactivity into the ocean—the only question is how soon, and how much. The peril of miscalculation is too great to permit such a risk. (Mink 23 June 1971, Mink Papers, box 50, f. 2)

The impact on sea life, in turn, could have an impact on human beings, who depend upon the ocean for their sustenance.

Indigenous Alaskans also expressed this concern. The Association on American Indian Affairs joined in a court case to block the 1971 Cannikin test. The organization explained its apprehension that radioactive "seepage could contaminate the salmon that pass through Alaskan coastal waters on their spawning migration and seriously threaten the health of thousands of Alaska Natives who depend on salmon as a major source of food" (AAIA 1971). The AAIA noted that they attempted to stop nuclear testing previously. "In the early 1960s the AAIA played a major role in halting Project Chariot, a series of proposed nuclear blasts near the Alaska Eskimo village of Point Hope that threatened to contaminate Eskimo food sources" (AAIA 1971). Nonwhite people and nonhuman forms of life inhabited the regions of the world deemed "remote" and hence bombable. Their geographical and cultural distance from the normative citizens of the continental United States resulted in their designation as expendable collateral damage.

Mink's arguments against nuclear testing in the Bering Strait emphasized the interconnectedness of the Pacific World. Alaska, Hawai'i, and other islands in the Pacific and Caribbean all became strategic sites to the United States during the scramble for naval power in the mid-to-late nineteenth century and for nuclear superiority during the Cold War. It was not accidental that Alaska and Hawai'i became the forty-ninth and fiftieth states respectively, back-to-back, as the United States positioned itself in relation to the Soviet Union and the decolonizing Third World. The last two states, the only noncontiguous states, constituted the periphery of the U.S. empire; they were located in closer proximity to Cold War political enemies and occupied predominantly by peoples long considered marginal to the continental polity. The United States sought to claim the Pacific Islands and the Pacific/Arctic rim politically in order to use these locales for military purposes. In contrast, Mink foregrounded the mutual dependence of human beings on nonhuman life and the environment. She highlighted the intrinsic importance of land and water in sustaining life. Her geographical base in Hawai'i, ancestral connections to Japan, and political affinity for other Pacific islands shaped Mink's worldview, such that she valued the farthest, least visible portions of the United States. This worldview directly challenged a U.S. Cold War mentality that divided the geopolitical world and prioritized national security needs, military preparedness, and weapons deployment.

De/Gendering Liberalism and Decoloniality

Even as Mink's political imaginary remapped and reenvisioned the significance of the Pacific World, her values revealed her commitment to the U.S. nation-state. Mink expressed an investment in political liberalism as a mode of governance, a gender-neutral humanism as the basis for rational debate, and the value of private property. Mink's insistence on how the margins of U.S. empire mattered provided opportunities for coalition formation and radical critique, but she also differed in important ways from some of her Pacific Islander allies who offered an alternative decolonial and what might be characterized as an Indigenous feminist vision.

In the multilayered campaign to stop nuclear, conventional, and chemical weapons testing in the Pacific and other colonized locales, Mink worked with various advocates. She corresponded with people subject to testing, activists and leaders of organizations, and scientists. Her relationship with Native Hawaiians provides an opportunity to examine critiques of Asian Americans as settlers in Hawai'i (Trask 1999; Fujikane and Okamura 2008). The haole or white elite on the islands imported and exploited Asian laborers in the racially stratified plantation economy. Nevertheless, Asian immigrants and their American-born children contributed to the displacement of Native Hawaiians. Also, Asian Americans, particularly Japanese Americans, emerged as dominant constituents and power brokers in the territory and eventually the state in the post–World War II era. Jodi Byrd characterizes racialized subjects "forced into the Americas through the violence of . . . colonialism and imperialism" as arrivants, a category distinct from settlers and indigenous peoples (Byrd 2011: xix) Yet, Dean Itsuji Saranillio also warns us to "not mistake 'arrivant' as an invitation to 'innocence'" (Saranillio 2018: 21). As someone who

recognized and experienced a history of discrimination and marginalization, Mink strived to gain full citizenship rights within the U.S. nation-
state. In doing so, she advocated for a liberal vision of the American polity.
She campaigned for statehood and promoted government responsibility
for guaranteeing racial and gender equality, protecting the environment,
and providing social welfare. Consequently, she worked with Indigenous
groups in Alaska, Hawai'i, and in the Trust Territories to bring attention
to their concerns and to demand equal treatment within the U.S. nation-
state. Nevertheless, Mink recognized that her advocacy for political inclusion at times departed from the goals of her Native Hawaiian allies, some
of whom wanted independence. The approach of liberal inclusion versus
Indigenous sovereignty also facilitated distinct gendered arguments for
demilitarization.

Claiming Liberalism

Mink and her allies engaged in the difficult, Sisyphean project of demanding recognition and accountability from U.S. military and governmental
institutions that privilege masculinity and whiteness. Mink insisted on
accountability from the U.S. nation-state that used the Pacific and its
colonial territories as militarized laboratories.[5] Despite repeated denials
and evasions, she persisted in articulating critiques about the militarized
use of Pacific lands, the rationale of secrecy and national security to justify
governmental policies, and the lack of public information and democratic
oversight. Despite her status as a congressional representative, Mink
clearly faced obstacles due to her gender and race. As a response, Mink
harnessed the legitimacy of science and civil liberties discourse to argue for
environmental responsibility and compassion for human life. In other
words, she utilized a gender-neutral approach to assume the mantle of the
universal human citizen-subject, a status usually reserved for white men
within the Western political tradition. In contrast, some of her supporters,
particularly Native Hawaiian protestors, formulated their politics in terms
of gendered Indigenous epistemologies. Mink also brought attention to
their arguments. As a congressional representative, she understood her
responsibility as introducing the perspectives and concerns of her constituency (defined broadly) into congressional deliberations and/or national
political discourses. Mink believed that her role as a political leader meant
responding to the concerns of those who communicated with her. Mink
ran for the U.S. presidency on an antiwar platform in 1972, recognized her

groundbreaking role as a woman, and advocated fiercely for women's issues. Nevertheless, she appears to have chosen strategically not to frame antimilitaristic critiques in the Pacific in explicitly gendered ways.

Mink's decision to advocate in scientific and civil liberties language no doubt reflected her intended audience, namely the U.S. government wing of the Cold War military-industrial complex. She directed her demands to stop nuclear, conventional, and chemical testing in the Pacific towards the executive branch of the U.S. government. The president of the United States, namely Republican Richard Nixon in the late 1960s and early 1970s, in consultation with leaders in the armed forces and the Department of Energy, made the ultimate decisions regarding national security and military preparedness. Members of the U.S. Congress, particularly the Senate, exerted political influence in its ability to declare war, fund defense spending, and shape international diplomacy. However, both Congress and the U.S. people tended to defer to executive leadership in times of global conflict. Over the course of the U.S. war in Southeast Asia, both elected officials and members of American society began asserting their rights to politically monitor the conduct of the war and the U.S. presidency. Initially, though, the presidency held more authority and leeway. For example, environmental advocates and Hawai'i elected officials like Senator Daniel Inouye and Representative Sparky Matsunaga, both Democrats and former veterans, initially engaged in protest over U.S. military exercises on Ka'ula Rock Island, especially in the aftermath of the 1965 accidental bombing of Ni'ihau. However, as the United States began its ground war in Vietnam under Democratic President Lyndon B. Johnson, these protests transformed into cooperation as military and political leaders persuaded residents and elected officials of Hawai'i to regard these exercises as essential for the success of the war effort. Military leaders also emphasized the importance of their ongoing presence for the economic health of the islands. Mink, however, persisted in her critiques, both because of her concerns about the militarization of Hawai'i and her antiwar politics, which entailed challenging the leadership of her political party.

Mink represented a distinct minority in Congress due to her gender, race, and political beliefs. Over the course of her first terms in the House of Representatives, from 1965–1977, the number of female representatives grew from eleven to nineteen, but they constituted less than 5% of the House; also, the number of female senators actually decreased from two to zero ("Women in Congress" 2019). Mink clearly operated in a male-dominated political space. By necessity, she formed political alliances with both men and women, whites and nonwhites. She made arguments for unpopular positions that challenged the U.S. security state. To do so, she utilized frameworks that generated greater political traction. She cited scientific studies to warn of the dangers of nuclear testing. She articulated civil liberty arguments that critiqued secrecy as antithetical to democratic forms of government. She emphasized the impact of the environmental and archaeological destruction as a loss to all human beings ("Prehistoric Settlement" 1974). In essence, she demanded the political authority normally reserved for the white, male subject.

However, Mink experienced dismissals of her political advocacy from skeptics as well as supporters due to her gender. A 1965 editorial in Kaua'i Island's newspaper, the *Garden Island*, initially characterized Mink's concerns about the transfer of Ka'ula Rock from the Coast Guard to the Navy as premature and unwarranted. Entitled "Let's Not Holler Before We are Hurt," the editorial indicated that "Mrs. Mink probably got alarmed over the idea that perhaps the Navy was planning to use Kaula for target practice . . . [but] there has been no notice on the part of the Navy regarding what use is being considered for Kaula if and when it is transferred" ("Let's Not Holler" 1965). The writers gave obvious deference to the Navy, while characterizing Mink as prone to crying wolf, giving alarm without evidence. One week later, however, the editors retracted their position, but only because "Kauai's commercial and amateur fishermen" informed the editors "how wrong we were and we got quite a few details on how the Marines have been bombing the rock almost regularly" ("Matter of Kaula Rock" 1965). Even though the editors corrected their opinion about the military's intentions with Ka'ula, the newspaper writers only reversed their position because of information provided by male fishermen, not a female congressional representative. Mink even wrote to various media sources and constituents in Hawai'i, who credited the Asian American male congressional leaders for leading the charge against military testing in Hawai'i, when she had been one of the earliest and most consistent critics. In a hand-written note to her staff on one of these letters, Mink requested to "Pl[ea]s[e] always take the time to educate these guys" (Mink 31 May 1975; 22 June 1974; and 16 July 1974, Box 128, f. 9).

Gendered Indigenous Epistemology
While Mink fought these gendered micro-aggressions through rational debate and by correcting the historical record, Native Hawaiians or Kanaka Maoli articulated their critiques of militarism through gendered

Indigenous epistemology (Kauanui 2008; Hall 2009; Arvin, Tuck, and Morrill 2013; Barker 2017). The movement to end bombardment and gain access to Kahoʻolawe played a central role in forming the Hawaiian sovereignty movement from the 1970s onward (Goodyear-Kaʻōpua, Hussey, and Wright 2014). The concept of "Aloha ʻĀina," roughly translated as "to cherish and care for the land," emerged from the efforts to reassert Kanaka Maoli sovereignty to land, dispossessed from them through the colonial process of introducing private property, forcibly overthrowing the Hawaiian Kingdom, and establishing Hawaiʻi as a territory and eventually a state (Osorio 2014: 146). The demand to stop military bombardment on Kahoʻolawe and to advocate for an alternative relationship between life, land, and water based on Kanaka Maoli beliefs mobilized Native Hawaiians to revive their cultural, political, and spiritual values and reclaim land. Kahoʻolawe represented an important locale to stage these protests. The island served as a "spiritual center," the physical incarnation of the sea god Kanaloa, "born of the union of Papa, earth mother, and Wakea, sky father" (Blackford 2007: 30). The effort to reclaim Kaho'olawe exemplified the concept of *ea*, a term that combined "life, breath, land, and sovereignty" (Goodyear-Kaʻōpua, Hussey, and Wright 2014: xv).

Inspired by Indigenous protestors on Alcatraz Island and at Wounded Knee, Native Hawaiian activists sought to occupy Kahoʻolawe to protest military testing and to reclaim the island.[6] In January 1976, thirty activists attempted to land on the island. Mink had lobbied the U.S. military to allow access to Kahoʻolawe for Indigenous activists. In a letter to the commander in chief of the Pacific in December 1975, Mink stated: "I am writing to support the request of" Gayle Kawaipuna Prejean, director of the Hawaiian Coalition of Native Claims, "for entry to the Island of Kahoʻolawe for research purposes" (Mink 17 December 1975, Mink Papers, box 129, f. 3). Mink framed Prejean's query in terms of "research" and Prejean himself as a "representative of a group of people of the States," because those were the terms on which the U.S. military might allow admission onto Kahoʻolawe. Mink also explained that Prejean's "research" included inspecting "the extent of devastation and waste and the condition of sacred areas of Hawaiian heiaus [temples], fishing shrines and burial places" (Mink 17 December 1975). Mink stated that the visit would help determine "whether the trust relationship that the State and the Federal government have to Native Hawaiians has been properly executed" (Mink 17 December 1975). The Navy and Air Force both denied the request, so Indigenous activists engaged in civil disobedience to gain access to their historic lands. Of the thirty who attempted to land on Kaho'olawe, only nine arrived on shore. The Coast Guard picked up most of the protestors, but two men stayed and evaded capture. Walter Ritte Jr., chair of the activist organization Hui Alaloa, and Dr. Emmitt Aluli eventually left voluntarily in two days, after they had the chance to survey Kaho'olawe.

In a press conference after their return, Ritte and Aluli spoke of the beauty of the island, the crime of militarily desecrating the land, and their gendered relationship to the environment. Their eyewitness accounts challenged depictions of Kaho'olawe as useless land, only fit for bombing exercises. Ritte said in tears, "I'm 30 years old and for 30 years, I thought Kahoolawe was a rock they bomb, but it's a beautiful island" (Harpham 1976). He testified to the destruction that the U.S. military had wrought to sacred shrines. Ritte compared the negative impact of the military to the commercialization of Hawai'i, saying "I always thought it was the hotels that desecrated our islands, but now I know that the bombing is the desecration" (Harpham 1976). He pointed out how the environmental damage constituted spiritual damage for Native Hawaiian people:

> The river beds were full of silt. You could see where bombs had hit and had created new valleys. . . . We saw huge boulders—you know Hawaiians worship boulders—split. If our grandparents had seen that they would have cried. (Harpham 1976)

Neither Ritte nor Aluli brought food or water with them. When asked how they survived for two days, Aluli claimed that "they were watched over by the goddess Hina," who "made it rain to wet their backs, and blessed them with water when they were thirsty" (Harpham 1976). Although both Ritte and Aluli were experienced hikers, and one was a hunter, they did not speak of these survival skills, more commonly associated with masculinity (Osorio 2014: 144). Instead, Aluli evoked the protective powers of Hina, a powerful moon goddess who represents the natural process of healing, growth, and transformation. Like the island of Kaho'olawe itself, which represented a union between sky father and earth mother, the male activists spoke of the gender complementarity of Indigenous epistemology. Samuel Crowningburg Amalu, another activist who joined the Aloha 'Āina movement, explained that "we love that soil—It is part of the living flesh of Papa who was our ancient mother" (Osorio 2014: 150).

In contrast to the life-giving force of Hina and Papa, the protest organizers associated the bombing of Kaho'olawe with the devastating impact of "white man's churches" on Indigenous belief systems (Harpham 1976). The protestors quoted in the local newspaper critiqued the destruction created through the collusion of commercialism, Christianity, and militarism as extensions of white masculinity. Instead, they evoked Indigenous deities and worldviews that foregrounded their connections to and ability to survive on Kaho'olawe as a spiritual and gendered connection to the land. This initial landing inspired a series of additional occupations as well as the Protect Kaho'olawe 'Ohana (PKO) movement. PKO, through protest and negotiation, forced the U.S. Navy to enter into a consent decree in 1980, which allowed "a right to visit and care for the island" (Osorio 2014: 137). Another decade after the decree, the military finally agreed to stop bombing the island.

Native Hawaiian female activists, as part of the movement's strategy to hold political leaders accountable, also appealed to Mink to gain access to Kaho'olawe. In March 1976, four female and one male "kupunas" or honored elders from Molokai wrote to Mink and other government representatives in Hawai'i to ask for assistance. They wished "to touch the aina [land] of Kahoolawe before [their] eyes close for the final time" (Ku et al. 1976). They appealed to Mink and authorized political leaders, because "the Navy has granted you and other politicians, permission to go onto Kahoolawe" (Ku et al. 1976). The kupunas enlisted Mink as a representative of Hawai'i to represent them to the U.S. Navy. Like Ritte and Aluli, the elders regard Kaho'olawe as "being sacred lands of our ancestors containing our heiaus [temples], . . . sacred pohaku [stones], sacred puu (where the piko [umbilical cord and/or placenta] of the new born were buried)" (Ku et al. 1976). They asked to "experience the 'aina' of Kahoolawe, to feel the mana [spirit] which radiates from it's [sic] sacred soil" (Ku et al. 1976). In their appeal to Mink, the kupunas emphasized a genealogical/reproductive connection to the land. Their human ancestors lived and worshiped on the island; the piko of their people or the originating materials of life were buried there; and the land itself represented the descendant of their spiritual mother. The kupunas asked Mink to translate their desires and worldviews to the U.S. Navy. As their letter pointed out, "the values we speak of are foreign to the ears of the Navy, but are at the roots of our Hawaiian culture" (Ku et al. 1976).

Mink respected their desires and understood their request in gendered ways. She forwarded their letter to the rear admiral and commander in charge of Pearl Harbor and asked for permission to personally escort "the six women mentioned in the attached letter" (Mink 15 April 1976, Patsy Mink Papers, box 129, f. 3). The five kupunas did name an additional female escort to accompany them. One of the letter writers, listed last, was male. Mink assumed that all of them were female. This may have been an oversight on behalf of Mink or her aides. It is likely, though, that Mink understood the kupunas' appeal for a spiritual and reproductive connection to Kahoʻolawe, a living land descended from a maternal ancestor, as a gendered request that centered women.

Perhaps not surprisingly, the U.S. military refused Mink's request, rejecting these gendered Indigenous ways of understanding and interacting with Kahoʻolawe. The Navy previously allowed a group of kupunas on the island on February 13, where the elders conducted a ceremony to "restore mana to the island" (Osorio 2014: 148). *Mana* is roughly translated as "a power that . . . can only be manifested through correct and responsible actions"; the kupunas sought to recognize "that the island—a living and breathing entity—had been defiled through misuse and neglect, and they sought to restore Kahoʻolawe's mana by calling the ancient gods back to the island" (Osorio 2014: 148–49). In his study of the PKO movement, Jonathan Osorio argues that the presence of the kupunas and their religious ceremonial role transformed the movement to reclaim Kahoʻolawe by signaling "a deeper commitment to Hawaiian values and traditions" (Osorio 2014: 148). Perhaps recognizing this more profound claim to Kahoʻolawe that the kupunas initiated, the March request, forwarded by Mink, was denied. The violence against the lands of Hawaiʻi mirrored the epistemological rigidity of the U.S. armed forces.

The gendered and spiritual values that Native Hawaiian activists articulated also diverged from other supporters for the return of Kahoʻolawe. Native Hawaiian desires to touch the ʻāina and experience the mana of the island differed in important ways from those who wanted to gain recreational access to the island and its surrounding waters or to protect their property values due to proximity to a bombing site. Coalitional work against military destruction existed, but fundamental differences also persisted. Mink attempted to bridge these differences and to demand accountability from the U.S. military. While she chose a gendered strategy that privileged Western humanism, she also recognized and respected alternative epistemologies.

Which Way Forward?

Mink understood the distinct differences between her proposed solutions to U.S. militarism and those of Native Hawaiian activists. In the case of Kahoʻolawe Island, Mink repeatedly submitted bills in the U.S. House of Representatives, demanding the return of the island to the state of Hawaiʻi. In contrast, the Aboriginal Lands of Hawaiian Ancestry (ALOHA) requested that she

> abstain from taking part in any move to return military lands to the State of Hawaii until our Hawaiian people have had an opportunity to present a legislative bill in the next Congressional Session. As you are aware, our primary objective is to seek lands and/or money reparations from Congress for the aboriginal and part aboriginal Hawaiians. (Maxwell 27 July 1973, Mink Papers, box 128, f. 7)

Returning land to the state of Hawaiʻi differed in profound ways from returning the land and resources to Native Hawaiians. Mink understood this incommensurability. In a letter to a nonnative Hawaiian constituent, she wrote, "Those who wish to take over the island do not want it to revert back to either the County of Maui or the State. They wish it to be declared an asset of ALOHA or part of their aboriginal claims of the native Hawaiians" (Mink 19 February 1976, Mink Papers, box 129, f. 1). Receptive to additional information from ALOHA, Mink had previously introduced bills to the U.S. Congress to return Kahoʻolawe to the State of Hawaiʻi. She perhaps believed that it would be easier to negotiate these political differences at the state level rather than the federal level. Federal control meant military control. State control likely would result in an end to militarized testing, given the unpopularity of these exercises in Hawaiʻi. However, state control, given the history and ongoing conflicts regarding land, did not necessarily lead to reclamation by Native Hawaiians.

Understanding this distinction, Mink respected the call by ALOHA to demand the return of land or receive compensation from the federal government for the illegal act of deposing Queen Liliʻuokalani. Mink began working with the group closely in 1973, soon after ALOHA was formed. At times, she withheld federal legislation until receiving the organization's approval and/or followed the organization's lead in introducing bills. As she expressed to the leadership of ALOHA, "May I congratulate each of you for your willingness to undertake so profound a task as that of seeking ultimate justice and fairness for the descendants of Ancient Hawaii.

Much patience will be required, but perseverance will bring success" (Mink 9 July 1973, Mink Papers, box 345, f. 5). Mink also offered advice, organized hearings in Hawaiʻi and arranged meetings with federal officials, including members of the Committee on Interior and Insular Affairs, to foreground the issue of land reparations. Mink did not always agree with the goals and strategies of ALOHA, as she explained to a Native Hawaiian constituent who expressed concerns to Mink:

> I am informed by my staff of your phone call telling about your reserva-
> tions on the ALOHA bill. I share those reservations, but I do feel that
> these people have a right to pursue their goals in the Congress and have
> therefore agreed to help them. We will try, and perhaps if . . . they do not
> succeed in enactment of their bill, they may be more willing to go the
> route of seeking greater benefits under [another avenue] which was
> my initial suggestions. They asked me not to go this route and to give
> ALOHA a chance, and I agreed. (Mink June 1974, Mink Papers, box 345,
> f. 8)

Mink went on to explain that as a non-Native Hawaiian, she sought to respect and support Native Hawaiians. However, she also encouraged the Native Hawaiian letter writer to make clear her concerns to other members of her community. Mink stated that "I hope that you and others, who are the ultimate beneficiaries, will speak up. . . . I am deeply committed to do all that I can to help the Hawaiian people. And, so, we must depend upon all Hawaiians to arrive at their true feelings and to express them. . . . Now is the time to say what you think is right and what ought to be done" (Mink 24 June 1974, Mink Papers, box 345, f. 8). In fact, Native Hawaiian individuals and organizations did disagree with ALOHA. Some of the leaders of PKO criticized ALOHA in terms of their political strategies and focus on negotiating with the U.S. settler state rather than rejecting its sovereignty (Osorio 2014: 142–44). In contrast, Mink's belief in the liberal political project encompassed advocating for a democratic process within the Native Hawaiian community and in the U.S. nation.

In response to those who questioned the very idea of land reparations from those critical of Native Hawaiian claims, Mink asserted the importance of a full congressional hearing as well as the political legitimacy of compensating Indigenous peoples for land. She pointed out the comparison between Hawaiʻi and Alaska, the two newest states of the union:

One hundred and six years ago Russia sold Alaska to the United States. The natives of Alaska did not receive any monetary consideration for this taking of title to the land. Despite the long time interval the Congress recently voted $1 billion to these natives of Alaska because of this taking. (Mink 9 July 1974, Mink Papers, box 345, f. 8)

This compensation inspired some Native Hawaiians who "believe that their cause is of greater justice than the Alaskans because they were taken by conquest. The Hawaiian monarchy was overthrown by U.S. soldiers and the Queen was imprisoned. Crown lands were taken and the natives were not compensated" (Mink 9 July 1974). In 1920, the Hawaiian Homelands, lands held in trust by the state for Native Hawaiians, were created to help redress this loss. However, lack of funding as well as the criteria used to qualify Native Hawaiians for homesteading led to questionable and limited policies that did not fully acknowledge Indigenous claims (Hall 2008).

Mink responded to criticism of using tax dollars to support Native Hawaiians with a series of questions that asked why certain government initiatives are more readily embraced by U.S. citizens and others held with suspicion:

When the Alaska natives got their $1 billion did you cease to pay your taxes? Or when Nixon gave away the White House helicopter, or the villa to the Arab ruler Sadat, did you throw away your card? Or when the Pentagon asked for $2 billion for just one nuclear sub, did you gasp in disgust? (Mink 9 July 1974)

Mink's queries emphasized that government allocation of resources and citizen reactions to these expenditures reflect conflicts regarding collective political priorities. Mink's response suggests that critics of Indigenous land compensation are less likely to challenge military related expenses, despite their greater cost. Mink concludes by emphasizing that "The bill the Hawaiians wrote by themselves does not envision one dime going directly to any person. . . . No Don Ho or rich Hawaiian will get anything out of this fund. It is to go in trust for the welfare of the people as a whole" (Mink 9 July 1974). In considering all of these factors Mink emphasized that "I do believe that it is worth at least a fair hearing in the Congress" (Mink 9 July 1974). Mink's conception of democracy did not just recognize individual rights but also the collective rights of the disfranchised.

Mink's approach to political representation reveals the complex relationships between Asian Americans and Pacific Islanders, between political liberalism and sovereignty, and between recognition of racialized patriarchy and an Indigenous feminist decolonial imaginary. In some instances, Mink's politics conflicted with certain Native Hawaiian political agendas and epistemologies. She both challenged and worked within the logic of full political inclusion, based on the cultural, economic, and political standards of Western modernity. At the same time, Mink also recognized commonalities with particular Pacific Islander leaders to end militarized violence and advocated for fuller democratic political participation based on collective identities. In a letter to the Council of Hawaiian Organizations, she indicated that "you may be assured of my support, and that I will do everything I can to bring about our common goal of a halt to the bombing and a return of the island to the people of Hawaii" (Mink 27 January 1976, Mink Papers, box 129, f. 1). Mink's conception of the "people" of Hawai'i included Native Hawaiians as central members of her constituency, even as their demands conflicted with other residents who benefited from indigenous dispossession.[7]

Conclusion

The complex antimilitarism politics articulated by Mink and a range of Native Hawaiian activists offered alternative political imaginaries of the Pacific. Instead of the deathscape that the U.S. nation-state created through nuclear, conventional, and chemical military testing, Mink evoked an interconnected Pacific World, an archipelagic one, that linked the ecological connections between life, water, and land. She represented in many ways an outsider to the U.S. polity due to her ethnicity, gender, representation of Hawai'i, and political convictions. Her broad vision of the world challenged the militaristic U.S. government. However, in relation to the Indigenous people of the Pacific, Mink constituted an influential insider as a U.S. congressional representative. While she advocated for full inclusion and government accountability, some of her Indigenous allies demanded not just an end to militarized violence but also political and cultural independence. In essence, some of the Native Hawaiian activists of the 1970s offered a more transformative Pacific imaginary regarding the spiritual and ancestral connections between life, water, and land to counter the white patriarchal confluence of the U.S. military, nation-state, and Christianity.

Mink's commitment to political liberalism constrained some of her strategies and solutions. In light of the gendered and racialized hierarchies of the U.S. military state, Mink strategically occluded gender in her political critique. She foregrounded gendered arguments for other issues that she advocated, such as Title IX, childcare, the Women's Educational Equity Act, the antiwar movement, and so on. However, Mink predominantly utilized gender-neutral discourses to claim political authority in relation to her criticisms of military testing. Even so, she experienced marginalization as an Asian American woman within the U.S. polity, and she responded to gendered and Indigenous appeals for accountability and spiritual connection.

These opportunities for coalition formation and mutual support reveal possibilities for Asian American and Pacific Islander alliance, just as the fundamental differences between Mink and Native Hawaiian activists reveal profound tensions between political liberalism and Indigenous sovereignty. Their respective calls for an end to militarism and a return of occupied land during the Cold War still resonate strongly throughout the Pacific World and beyond in the twenty-first century. The ongoing occupation and violence of the U.S. militarized state and its allies in places like Standing Rock, Okinawa, Guam, and Jeju Island continue to inspire resistance and alternative political imaginaries that demand an ethical consideration for the lands, waters, and lives of those on the margins of empire.[8]

Judy Tzu-Chun Wu is a professor of Asian American studies at the University of California, Irvine, and director of the Humanities Center. She authored *Dr. Mom Chung of the Fair-Haired Bastards: The Life of a Wartime Celebrity* (2005) and *Radicals on the Road: Internationalism, Orientalism, and Feminism during the Vietnam Era* (2013).

Author's Note
My heartfelt appreciation to the writing communities that nurtured this work. Special thanks to my collaborator Wendy Mink, the editorial team of *Meridians*, the anonymous reviewers of this essay, Katherine Marino, Juno Parrenas, Alfred Flores, the participants of "Radical Transnationalism: Reimagining Solidarities, Violence, Empire," sponsored by the Institute for the Research of Women and Gender at the University of Michigan (Maile Arvin, Maylei Blackwell, Laura Briggs, Stanlie James, Ikue Kina, Rosamond S. King, Karen J. Leong, Nadine Naber, and Robyn C. Spencer), the members of the "Rethinking Transnational Feminisms" Residential Research Cluster sponsored by the University of California Humanities Research Institute (Maylei Blackwell, Monisha Das Gupta, Rachel Fabian, Grace Hong, Rana Jaleel,

Zeynep Korkman, Karen J. Leong, and Jessica Millward), the "Waterways and World-views: Rethinking Regions Defined by Oceans and Seas" Research Residency Group sponsored by the Humanities Research Commons at the University of California, Irvine and led by Jeff Wasserstrom, and the wonderful Asian American Women Historians writing group (Connie Chen, Kelly Fong, Dorothy Fujita-Rony, Jane Hong, Valerie Matsumoto, Isa Quintana, and Susie Woo).

Notes

1   In fact, activists in Canada founded the organization Greenpeace to condemn the nuclear tests on Amchitka.

2   An understudied historical figure, Mink advocated for civil rights, feminist initiatives, environmentalism, and the antiwar movement. In fact, Title IX, which mandated gender equality for schools receiving federal funding, was renamed after Mink. Despite her pioneering achievements, little scholarship exists about her extensive political career, which spanned the second half of the twentieth century.

3   Special thanks to Grace Hong for foregrounding the importance of incommensurability in understanding coalitional politics. I acknowledge that Pacific Islander and other Indigenous groups articulated a range of political strategies; not all advocated for sovereignty, and not all opposed navigating within the U.S. settler state.

4   Writing on behalf of the secretary of the Navy, Paul Nitze explained to Mink that new preventative measures had been instituted as a result of the mistake. These include requiring all pilots "to familiarize themselves during daylight hours with the target before they are permitted to make a night bombing attack" (Nitze 9 October 1965, Mink Papers box 129, f. 9). The fact that such an obvious protocol was not instituted prior to the mistake reveals how few safety precautions the Navy required, even as it conducted war games in the proximity of the people in Hawai'i.

5   In order to obtain U.S. executive branch documents studying the proposed test, Mink organized a group of thirty-three representatives and senators to sue the White House and its federal offices for access to information deemed off-limits for security reasons. Former attorney general Ramsey Clark argued the case, Mink v. EPA, et al. (1973), which led to the strengthening of the Freedom of Information Act. By setting a precedent for legislative oversight over the federal executive, Mink v. EPA provided justification for the release of President Nixon's secret tapes for the Watergate Hearings.

6   This occupation represented the first of a series of five protests conducted in 1976 and 1977.

7   Mink lost her campaign for the U.S. Senate in 1976. She continued her interest in Kahoʻolawe, however, into the 1990s, when she was reelected to the U.S. Congress. Native Hawaiian activist accounts tend to focus on Daniel Inouye as the leading political figure who sometimes aided and other times worked at cross-purposes to the Kanaka Maoli.

8   For an example of the ongoing trans-Pacific antimilitarism feminist activism,
    please see the International Women's Network against Militarism (IWNAM).
    http://www.summitzine.com/posts/women-activists-join-struggle-for-peace-in
    -okinawa/.

Works Cited

Aluli, Noa Emmett, and Davianna Pōmaika'i McGregor. 1992. "*Mai Ke Kai Mai Ke Ola*, from the Ocean Comes Life: Hawaiian Customs, Uses, and Practices on Kaho'olawe Relating to the Surrounding Ocean." *The Hawaiian Journal of History* 26: 231–54.

Arvin, Maile, Eve Tuck, and Angie Morrill. 2013. "Decolonizing Feminism: Challenging Connections between Settler Colonialism and Heteropatriarchy." *Feminist Formations* 25: 8–34.

Barker, Joanne, ed. 2017. *Critically Sovereign: Indigenous Gender, Sexuality, and Feminist Studies*. Durham, NC: Duke University Press.

Blackford, Mansel G. 2004. "Environmental Justice, Native Rights, Tourism, and Opposition to Military Control: The Case of Kaho'olawe." *Journal of American History* 91: 544–71.

Blackford, Mansel G. 2007. *Pathways to the Present: U.S. Development and Its Consequences in the Pacific*. Honolulu: University of Hawai'i Press.

Byrd, Jodi A. 2011. *The Transit of Empire: Indigenous Critiques of Colonialism*. Minneapolis: University of Minnesota Press.

Carter, Luther J. 1969. "Earthquakes and Nuclear Tests: Playing the Odds on Amchitka." *Science* August 22: 773–76.

Carter, Philip D. 1969. "Aleutian Wildlife Preserve New Nuclear Test Site." *Honolulu Star-Bulletin*, April 13.

Choy, Catherine Ceniza, and Judy Tzu-Chun Wu, eds. 2017. *Gendering the Trans-Pacific World*. Leiden, The Netherlands: Brill.

Coates, Peter. 1996. "Amchitka, Alaska: Toward the Bio-Biography of an Island." *Environmental History* 1: 20–45.

DeLoughrey, Elizabeth M. 2013. "The Myth of Isolates: Ecosystem Ecologies in the Nuclear Pacific." *Cultural Geographies* 20: 167–84.

Dvorak, Greg. 2015. "Oceanizing American Studies." *American Quarterly* 67: 609–17.

Enloe, Cynthia. 2000. *Bananas, Beaches, and Bases: Making Feminist Sense of International Politics*. Berkeley: University of California Press.

Espiritu, Yen Le. 2014. *Body Counts: The Vietnam War and Militarized Refugees*. Berkeley: University of California Press.

Fujikane, Candace, and Jonathan Y. Okamura. 2008. *Asian Settler Colonialism: From Local Governance to the Habits of Everyday Life in Hawai'i*. Honolulu: University of Hawai'i Press.

Genz, Joseph H., Noelani Goodyear-Ka'ōpua, Monica C. LaBriola, Alexander Mayer, Elicita N. Morei, and John P. Rosa. 2016. *Militarism and Nuclear Testing*. Vol. 1 of Teaching Oceania Series, edited by Monica LaBriola. Honolulu: Center for Pacific Islands Studies, University of Hawai'i at Mānoa.

Gonzalez, Vernadette Vicuna. 2013. *Securing Paradise: Tourism and Militarism in Hawai'i and the Philippines*. Durham, NC: Duke University Press.

Goodyear-Ka'ōpua, Noelani, Ikaika Hussey, and Erin Kahuanawaika'ala Wright, eds. 2014. *A Nation Rising: Hawaiian Movements for Life, Land, and Sovereignty*. Durham, NC: Duke University Press.

Gundersen, Kaare R., and Paul K. Bienfang. 1970. "Kahoolawe: The Unique Potential of the Hawaiian Island, Kahoolawe, as a Site for a Central Thermonuclear Power Plant and Aqua- and Agricultural Development." Mink Papers, box 128, f. 3.

Hall, Lisa Kahaleole. 2009. "Navigating Our Own 'Sea of Islands': Remapping a Theoretical Space for Hawaiian Women and Indigenous Feminism." *Wicazo Sa Review* 24: 15–38.

Harpham, Anne. 1976. "Kahoolawe Holdouts Arrested: 2 Claim Isle 'Desecrated." *Honolulu Advertiser*, January 7.

Igler, David. 2007. "Commentary: Re-Orienting Asian American History through Transnational and International Scales." *Pacific Historical Review* 76: 611–14

Igler, David. 2013. *The Great Ocean: Pacific Worlds from Captain Cook to the Gold Rush*. New York: Oxford University Press.

Johnston, Barbara Rose, ed. 2007. *Half-Lives and Half Truths: Confronting the Radioactive Legacies of the Cold War*. Santa Fe, NM: School for Advanced Research Press.

Kajihiro, Kyle. 2009. "Resisting Militarization in Hawai'i." In *The Bases of Empire: The Global Struggle against U.S. Military Posts*, edited by Catherine Lutz, 299–331. New York: New York University Press.

Kauanui, J. Kēhaulani. 2008. "Native Hawaiian Decolonization and the Politics of Gender." *American Quarterly* 60: 281–87.

Kauanui, J. Kēhaulani. 2015. "Imperial Ocean: The Pacific as a Critical Site for American Studies." *American Quarterly* 63: 625–36.

Kohlhoff, Dean W. 2002. *Amchitka and the Bomb: Nuclear Testing in Alaska*. Seattle: University of Washington Press.

"Let's Not Holler Before We Are Hurt." 1965. *Garden Island*, March 24.

Lyons, Paul, and Ty P. Kāwika Tengan. 2015. "Introduction: Pacific Currents." *American Quarterly* 67: 545–74.

Man, Simeon. 2018. *Soldiering through Empire: Race and the Making of the Decolonizing Pacific*. Oakland: University of California Press.

"Women in Congress: Statistics and Brief overview." 2019. Congressional Research Service. https://fas.org/sgp/crs/misc/R43244.pdf.

Matsuda, Matt K. 2012. *Pacific Worlds: A History of Seas, Peoples, and Cultures*. Cambridge: Cambridge University Press.

"The Matter of Kaula Rock." 1965. *The Garden Island*, March 31.

Mink, Patsy T. Papers. Manuscript Division, Library of Congress, Washington, DC.

Nguyen, Mimi Thi. 2012. *The Gift of Freedom: War, Debt, and Other Refugee Passages*. Durham, NC: Duke University Press.

Nguyen, Viet Thanh, and Janet Hoskins. 2014. *Transpacific Studies: Framing an Emerging Field*. Honolulu: University of Hawai'i Press.

Okihiro, Gary. 2008. *Island World: A History of Hawai'i and the United States.* Berkeley: University of California Press.

Okihiro, Gary. 2009. *Pineapple Culture: A History of the Tropical and Temperate Zones.* Berkeley: University of California Press.

Osorio, Jonathan Kamakawiwo'ole. 2014. "Hawaiian Souls: The Movement to Stop the US Military Bombing of Kaho'olawe." In Goodyear-Ka'ōpua, Hussey, and Wright 2014: 137–60.

Parsons, Keith M., and Robert A. Zaballa. 2017. *Bombing the Marshall Islands: A Cold War Tragedy.* Cambridge: Cambridge University Press.

"Prehistoric Settlement: Sure Victim if Amchitka Shot Goes." 1974. *Tundra Times,* August 4.

Roberts, Brian Russell, and Michelle Anne Stephens. 2017. *Archipelagic American Studies.* Durham, NC: Duke University Press.

Rohrer, Judy. 2016. *Staking Claim: Settler Colonialism and Racialization in Hawai'i.* Tucson: University of Arizona Press.

Saranillio, Dean Itsuji. 2018. *Unsustainable Empire: Alternative Histories of Hawai'i Statehood.* Durham, NC: Duke University Press.

Shigematsu, Setsu, and Keith L. Camacho, eds. 2010. *Militarized Currents: Toward a Decolonized Future in Asia and the Pacific.* Minneapolis: University of Minnesota Press.

Silva, Noenoe K. 2004. *Aloha Betrayed: Native Hawaiian Resistance to American Colonialism.* Durham, NC: Duke University Press.

Takezawa, Yasuko, and Gary Y. Okihiro. 2016. *Trans-Pacific Japanese American Studies: Conversations on Race and Racializations.* Honolulu: University of Hawai'i Press.

Teves, Stephanie Nohelani. 2015. "Aloha State Apparatuses." *American Quarterly* 67: 705–26.

Teaiwa, Teresia K. 2010. "Bikinis and Other S/pacific N/oceans." In Shigematsu and Camacho 2010: 15–31.

Tokioka, Masayuki. 1957. Letter to Patsy T. Mink. *Hawaii Times,* May 4.

Trask, Haunani-Kay. 1999. *From a Native Daughter: Colonialism and Sovereignty in Hawaii.* Honolulu: University of Hawai'i Press.

Tuck, Eve, and K. Wayne Yang. 2012. "Decolonization is Not a Metaphor." *Decolonization: Indigeneity, Education, and Society* 1: 1–40.

Ching-In Chen

··

Self-Portrait, Cannibal/Reversal/Break In/Benediction

wasn't crammed water   failed missing storm
                in storm which didn't make   we waited for breathless
news. wasn't failed   not unnatural light
strange, missing notes, watching.   because to grow a man
                                means to dust a water   breathless
monitoring

how did we know we weren't   trees turning away
water   hiring for more crop
        when our season ran low

a heat that makes   crunch of bodies
        turn a tree into rain

a house crack   a man who grows
                        a body into
                woods   makes heat crack a house

grows a man to lose   if you regenerate

        his breath wait for   a house growing
                        limb

        water which never dusts
                        to crack the light

MERIDIANS · feminism, race, transnationalism   18:2 October 2019
DOI: 10.1215/15366936-7775740 © 2019 Smith College

for a storm to fail

for a mouth to tire
of the

missing

Self-Portrait, Shipping Container/ Driving Through Night/Jury

because milk stamped   40 37 29 66 lucky numbers
green across shipping country

                                                  Because leering man
                                                  and dead-eye girl

          No photos to share, just drive, forcing us to eat sugar

our parents a net to handle red
discounted blessings   were not my own

                                        To still parked three hours we chant our

ranks

                                                           after long travel

worrying past each toll   when we swell to black
          stock the temperature
milk   'it is so comfortable'

          no story but powder   no water not squeezed

full you wouldn't believe   I ate them off the screen

real origin bare   each night we
perched by throat

they would no longer in fear   dreaming against town
keep us company across   borders awash in

                    a dirt which tongue has paid
                              a price

velvet and smoke   water

· ·

Ching-In Chen is author of *The Heart's Traffic* (2009), *recombinant* (2017; winner of the 2018 Lambda Literary Award for Transgender Poetry), and *to make black paper sing* (2019). Chen is coeditor of *The Revolution Starts at Home: Confronting Intimate Violence within Activist Communities* (2011) and *Here Is a Pen: An Anthology of West Coast Kundiman Poets* (2009).

Maile Arvin

Indigenous Feminist Notes on Embodying Alliance against Settler Colonialism

Abstract: How can we enact meaningful forms of solidarity across Indigenous and non-Indigenous communities? This essay, which focuses specifically on the context of settler colonialism in Hawaiʻi, examines existing or potential alliances between Indigenous feminisms and transnational feminisms. Written from a Kanaka Maoli (Native Hawaiian) feminist perspective, the essay looks to the foundational work of Kanaka Maoli scholar-activist Haunani-Kay Trask as a too often overlooked theorist of settler colonialism writ broadly. The essay also looks more specifically at Trask's theorizing of Asian settler colonialism in the Hawaiʻi context, in relation to contemporary examples of conflicts between Native Hawaiians and the state, as well as Native Hawaiian activists and white feminists. Overall, the essay questions how reframing Asian settler colonialism in more concerted conversation with Indigenous feminisms and transnational feminisms might provide space to move our practices of solidarity against settler colonialism, imperialism, nativism, militarization, and environmental destruction into a generative space for Kānaka Maoli and non-Indigenous peoples alike.

The last decade has seen the rise of settler colonialism as an academic buzzword in interdisciplinary cultural studies areas including American studies, ethnic studies, and gender studies. Settler colonialism is now often included in lists of the structural ills (including white supremacy, heteropatriarchy, imperialism, and so on) we ought to acknowledge and stand against (CESEC 2016). The most frequently cited description of settler colonialism is elegantly short and sweet: in the words of the late Australian scholar Patrick Wolfe, "The colonizers come to stay—invasion

MERIDIANS · feminism, race, transnationalism   18:2 October 2019
DOI: 10.1215/15366936-7775663 © 2019 Smith College

is a structure not an event" (Wolfe 1999: 2). This description is useful. I cite it frequently myself in writing and teaching to get audiences to understand the ongoing, contemporary nature of colonialism in the United States and to de-link colonialism from a distant historical period in time.

While a greater recognition of settler colonialism is often a good thing, at least as a first step, there are politics to these citations. Wolfe's work, alongside the work of other white male scholars (e.g., Veracini 2015, 2011, 2010), has captured the attention of the academy outside of Indigenous studies in a way that Indigenous scholars, who have long published on set-tler colonialism, largely have not.[1] For example, Kanaka Maoli scholar and activist Haunani-Kay Trask wrote about Hawai'i as a settler colony from the early 1980s.[2] While her work is often taught or cited in reference to Hawai'i, it deserves greater recognition and consideration as foundational to theo-rizing settler colonialism broadly. In an essay reprinted first in 1993 and then in 1999, Trask noted that settler colonialism "has as one of its goals, the obliteration rather than the incorporation of indigenous peoples" (Trask 1999: 26). As a result, Trask has argued, Indigenous peoples' daily struggles for sovereignty and decolonization must be understood "not as a struggle for civil rights but a struggle against our planned disappearance" (Trask 1999: 26). In contrast to Wolfe and Veracini, Trask, alongside many other Indigenous women, feminist and/or queer scholars, centers gender and sexuality in her analyses of settler colonialism. Trask critiques how central the eroticization and exotification of Native Hawaiian women has been to settler colonialism in Hawai'i, especially through the image of the hula girl perpetuated by the tourism industry (Trask 1999: 136–47).

When settler colonialism circulates as a theory primarily attributed to and advanced by white male scholars (however productive or well-intentioned their work may be), understandings of both how settler colo-nialism operates and how we might resist it are inevitably flattened, espe-cially in regards to the importance of gender and sexuality to both settler colonialism and decolonization. This essay is about how Indigenous femi-nisms, as one important area of Indigenous studies scholarship, offer important theories and practices toward correcting the academic circula-tion of settler colonialism as a white male theory, particularly in rethinking how to embody feminist alliance in relation to resisting settler colonialism. I focus primarily on how Indigenous feminist embodiment in the context of Hawai'i provides generative modes of understanding various com-munities' different positions and responsibilities in the face of settler colonialism, especially in regards to debates over theories and practices of Asian settler colonialism, a theory and critique first articulated by Trask. I further consider the connections and disconnections between Indigenous feminisms, whitestream feminisms (a term coined by Indigenous scholar Sandy Grande to critique the often unmarked whiteness of mainstream feminism), and transnational feminisms (Grande 2004).

Laura Briggs, Gladys McCormick, and J. T. Way have argued for understanding "transnationalism as a strategy for identifying the ideological work of the nation" (Briggs, McCormick, and Way 2008: 637). They argue "against writing histories or analyses that take national boundaries as fixed, implicitly timeless, or even always meaningful, and for a quite different role for history-writing and criticism—one that directly challenges the nation by revealing nationalism as ideology" (Briggs, McCormick, and Way 2008: 627). Drawing from this perspective on the transnational, transnational feminisms can be understood as analyses that identify the importance of hierarchies and oppression based on gender and sexuality to the ideological work of the nation. Transnational feminism has long insisted on the importance of thinking critically about the presumed similarities of women across the world and the dangers of imperial feminism that purports to "save brown women from brown men" (Alexander and Mohanty 2013; Spivak 1994). Transnational feminisms also insist that notions of gender and sexuality not be taken as traditionally timeless or inherently biological, but as having histories that are shaped in multiple ways by various forms of nationalism, imperialism, and colonialism.

Framed in these ways, transnational feminisms share much with Indigenous feminisms, which center analyses of gender and sexuality in the transnational processes of settler colonialism and decolonization. Indigenous feminisms have insisted on seeing settler nations from the perspective of diverse Indigenous nations whose histories far predate the United States, Canada, New Zealand, and Australia, among other countries. Indigenous feminisms also hold space for understanding the futures of Indigenous peoples as exceeding the current forms of settler nations, for imagining different ways of relating to each other and to the environment than might seem possible in the contemporary conditions of global capitalism. However, there are also deep tensions between transnational feminisms and Indigenous feminisms. At times, I have seen some white feminist scholars from the United States self-identify as transnational feminists or see their work, simply if it is based in countries outside of the

United States or examines movement between countries, as transnational feminist scholarship. That kind of identification is thus one based on claims to white professional expertise or experience with working with and/or analyzing the work of women of color elsewhere. When used in this way by white feminists, transnational feminism can therefore share a great deal with whitestream feminism. In this context, both whitestream and transnational feminisms might be labeled *settler feminisms*, after Scott Morgensen's apt critique of settler homonationalism, by which he points out how "settler colonialism must be challenged directly as a condition of queer modernities" and modern sexuality more broadly (Morgensen 2011: 2). In this essay, I use *settler feminism* to refer to non-Indigenous feminisms that are constituted by settler colonialism in the way Morgensen references, but also after the usage of *Asian settler colonialism* (as discussed further below) as a label that is potentially not only a critique but also (if taken up by settler feminists) an acknowledgment of how central a commitment to ending settler colonialism must be in order to form alliances with Indigenous feminists.

The reading of *transnational* as applying primarily to countries beyond the United States is a kind of settler feminism in that it often eclipses some Indigenous feminisms by not recognizing the presence of Indigenous nations within, and exceeding the boundaries of, what is now the United States (or other so-called First World countries). Relatedly, there is also tension at times between transnational feminist critiques and disavowals of the nation and the various forms of Indigenous nationalism that are central to Indigenous feminisms. Even as Indigenous feminisms critique many of the same aspects of nationalism that transnational feminisms do, Indigenous feminisms do not give up the importance of Indigenous nations to Indigenous lives. In fact, this conflict appears to have been central to why Haunani-Kay Trask distanced herself from identifying as a feminist. In a 1996 article, Trask noted that, "Given our nationalist context, feminism appeared as just another haole intrusion into a besieged Hawaiian world" (Trask 1996: 909). Further, she argued that "the answers to the specifics of our women's oppression reside in our people's collective achievement of the larger goal of Hawaiian self-government, not in an exclusive feminist agenda" (Trask 1996: 910).

Trask has been critiqued for her disavowal of feminism, particularly for failing to see or engage in deeper alliances between Indigenous feminisms and women of color feminisms. As Lisa Kahale'ole Hall incisively put it,

"Malcolm and Martin remain tropes for her public speaking, but not Angela" (Hall 2009: 27). By turning to Trask as a key example for thinking through how we change the citation politics of theories of settler colonialism and better recognize Indigenous feminist contributions, my goal is not to recuperate Trask as an Indigenous feminist or impose this label on her and her work. However, I do see the conflicts she grappled with in relation to the frequently white, settler nature of feminism as continuing to be central to thinking through and practicing alliances between various feminisms and between various academic fields that deal with settler colonialism. Also, her work is undeniably foundational to many self-identified Kanaka Maoli feminists and other Indigenous feminists, precisely because it offers rich analyses of connections between settler colonialism and heteropatriarchy. Accordingly, the challenge of referencing Trask's work in relation to Indigenous feminisms is to maintain both the importance of her scholarship and activism to contemporary Indigenous feminists and not to forget the ways she disavowed the feminist label. Her disavowal resonates with contemporary Indigenous feminist critiques of whitestream, settler feminisms, while it also sits in awkward tension with the missed opportunities for alliances with other feminisms of color. In this essay, I attempt to unpack and maintain a recognition of such complications, in regards to Trask's work but also to the conflicts between different types of feminisms, while pointing to areas of potentially fertile connection in building richer engagements with settler colonialism.

Indigenous Feminist Approaches to Decolonial World Building

Why turn to Indigenous feminism for theories of settler colonialism and decolonization? Feminism, from an Indigenous feminist perspective, can offer significant modes of building new relationships between Indigenous and non-Indigenous peoples. Indigenous feminism is grounded in critiques of colonialism, particularly the gendered hierarchies that colonialism introduced and continues to maintain in many Indigenous contexts (Arvin, Tuck, and Morrill 2013; Goeman and Denetdale 2009; Smith and Kauanui 2008; Hernández-Avila and Tremblay 2002). While some have critiqued the notion of Indigenous feminism as "assimilated," Indigenous feminists draw their feminism not simply from how feminism is defined by white women but from their own various Indigenous traditions of honoring women's power, gender diversity, and gender balance: traditions that have often been repressed by colonialism but are being revitalized with great care (Caffrey 2000; Miranda 2010). One key concept in Indigenous feminism is regeneration. As Anishinaabe scholar Leanne Simpson puts it, regeneration is a "process of bringing forth more life—getting the seed and planting and nurturing it. It can be a physical seed, it can be a child, or it can be an idea. But if you're not continually engaged in that process then it doesn't happen" (Klein 2013). Bringing forth more life, in multiple senses, holds particular salience to Indigenous peoples who have experienced genocide, dispossession, and cultural repression. Yet Indigenous feminism is also concerned with bringing forth different relationships and therefore different worlds for everyone, not only for Indigenous women or Indigenous peoples, who never live in complete isolation. My contention is that building alliances grounded in this kind of Indigenous feminist world building, in concert with other forms of intersectional feminism, holds the promise to bring forth not only new methods of combatting settler colonialism, imperialism, patriarchy, and white supremacy, but also new relationships that could make such fights more sustainable for all of us.

Yet, so deeply engrained is the myth that Indigenous peoples have all died out or only exist on isolated reservations far away that I have been in rooms full of settler feminist scholars and activists who questioned and doubted that I and the other Indigenous feminist scholars I was with were actually Indigenous. I have also experienced in such spaces a refusal to believe that Indigenous women's issues stem from settler colonialism, rather than Indigenous "culture," "tradition," or just Indigenous men. We have been the killjoys in rooms in which settler feminist (including transnational feminist) scholars insist on the importance of white and Asian women's empowerment through their participation in settler colonial institutions, and who are upset and resistant to the suggestion that they at least acknowledge that that empowerment was built through Native Hawaiian dispossession.

Sometimes there are more patronizing responses. Once, after presenting as part of a panel of Indigenous feminists at a women's studies conference, the first response from an audience member was, "Wow, I've never seen so many Native women present at a conference before." There was no comment on the content of the scholarship we shared, only this wonderment at seeing real Native women. The comment appeared to be genuinely appreciative of the fact that we were a panel full of Native women. Yet, that apparent "good intention" did little to subvert the comment's explicit tokenizing: we were so unexpected in this academic, settler feminist space that the audience could only formulate responses to our very existence.

Changing such behavior and creating spaces that are productive for (not just inclusive of) Indigenous feminists is required for more substantial alliances between Indigenous feminists and other feminists. Alliance is a further focus of concern here because as the definitive citations regarding settler colonialism have coalesced around white male scholars, also lost in the shuffle, at times, has been a strong sense of alliance among those critiquing settler colonialism and other, interrelated structures of violence. Indigenous scholars and allied scholars of color have often carefully analyzed how intertwined settler colonialism is with heteropatriarchy, antiblackness, xenophobia, and other forms of colonialism (King 2016; Mays 2013; Jackson 2012; Chang 2010). Yet, the academic attention given to settler colonialism as a white male theory has at times created or renewed a sense of competition between Indigenous peoples and other people of color, especially in relation to ideas about whether people of color should be considered settlers. This has sparked necessary conversations about alternative terms or deeper considerations of terms and geographic scope, including, for example, Robin Kelley's critique of Patrick Wolfe's work for allowing "settler colonialism on the African continent" to fall out of view and Jodi Byrd's use of *arrivant*, after poet Kamau Brathwaite's coinage, to signify "those people forced into the Americas through the violence of European and Anglo-American colonialism and imperialism around the globe" (Kelley 2017: 268; Byrd 2011: xix). Dean Saranillio, as discussed further below, self-identifies as an Asian settler scholar but also recognizes that a problem with Asian settler colonialism is that it "leaves no political space for people who want nothing to do with the term settler" (Saranillio 2018: 38).

Also in conversation with Trask's work, Saranillio accordingly suggests moving from "an analysis of settler colonialism that morally adjudicates competing identities without addressing the structure of settler colonialism and toward a kind of relational thinking that moves from a politics of identity to a politics of affinity" (Saranillio 2018: 41). Re-grounding critiques of settler colonialism in Indigenous feminism could help correct the ways that settler colonialism has circulated away from the embodied knowledge of Indigenous peoples and the relationships they often carefully hold with other peoples. In Hawai'i, as in many other settler colonial contexts, there are deep genealogies of alliances between Kānaka Maoli,

Asian Americans, and other working-class immigrant groups. Especially notable in Hawaiian history are labor organizing alliances among plantation workers and organizing for land and water rights during the Hawaiian Renaissance of the 1970s (Saranillio 2018; Goodyear-Kāʻopua, Hussey, and Wright, 2014). In short, orienting citations of settler colonialism toward Indigenous feminisms allows us to substantially engage histories and futures of decolonization, in part through considering substantial forms of solidarity among Indigenous struggles and other anticolonial, antiracist, and antisexist struggles that have long existed and could be built anew in the future.

When I talk about the need to pay attention to embodiment and to Indigenous feminism in how the academy engages settler colonialism, you, dear reader, should know that this is a delicate request. Audra Simpson has written brilliantly about ethnographic refusal as the significance of stops, silences, or other impediments to knowledge production that may cause harm (Simpson 2007, 2014). As noted in my examples above, Indigenous women are—must be—careful with what they say: in print, in classrooms, at conferences. This is because we know that academia is dangerous, in multiple respects. Knowledge produced in these spaces has been, and continues to be, used against us and our communities. When we speak of the challenges we come up against in our families, our words might be used to paint those challenges as inherent to Indigenous people. The violence of colonialism is so often pinned on Indigenous peoples themselves. When we speak about indigeneity, it might be dismissed as essentializing, even as we speak about how culture and tradition are never things Indigenous peoples can take for granted, because of the difficult work of revitalizing and maintaining cultural traditions and relationships to land. These relationships are not essential in the sense that they are not magical and automatic features of Indigenous lives, but rather are practices and knowledge that communities work to keep alive despite constant threats from settler colonialism. There are also more personal dangers of the academy to Native scholars, especially women and LGBTQ, Two-Spirit, mahu, faʻafafine, or other non-cisgender scholars, who routinely perform astonishing amounts of what Sara Ahmed terms "diversity work" for universities while facing harassment from hostile colleagues and students (Ahmed 2017; Boyd 2012; Jacob 2012). Detailing those experiences is beyond the scope of this essay but forms part of the urgency of not letting the work of Indigenous scholars be overshadowed.

Thus, insisting on attention to embodiment is not insisting on essentialism, but on an attention to who is in the room, and/or on the page, and who is not. Recognizing embodiment is a way of reminding ourselves that in speaking about settler colonialism, we are not resolving it; that the diagnosis is not sufficient in achieving justice; that what is being diagnosed still negatively affects some of us more than others; that the work of diagnosing is riskier for some than for others. The problem with short and sweet descriptions of settler colonialism is that they make settler colonialism part of a critical litany that allows those who recite the litany to feel that they are over it, that they are sufficiently against it, even while they continue to perpetuate Indigenous erasure. Sara Ahmed writes of this phenomenon in reference to sexism and racism: "I suspect that criticality— the self-perception that in being critical we do not have a problem or that in being critical we are over it—is often used and performed in these academic spaces. I have called critical racism and critical sexism this: the racism and sexism reproduced by those who think of themselves as too critical to reproduce racism and sexism" (Ahmed 2017: 155). Ahmed's description here resonates too with certain strands of settler colonial studies that engage Wolfe and Veracini but not Indigenous scholars. The erasure of Indigenous scholarship, and the frequent lack of a deeper acknowledgment of and commitment to Indigenous communities, does not register as a problem because there is a sense that simply by naming settler colonialism one is being critical enough. As I explore in the next section, the superficial alliance with resistance to settler colonialism is not sufficient, especially because so many non-Indigenous peoples still benefit from and uphold the structure of settler colonialism.

Against Asian Settler Mansplaining

Non-Indigenous people often charge Indigenous peoples with pretending authenticity or essentialism by pointing out Indigenous complicity with modernity. One example of this comes from February 2017, when Kānaka Maoli protested lack of community oversight in the cleanup of Iao Valley, the site of an ancient battle on the island of Maui, after flooding in September 2016. Rocks considered sacred to Kānaka Maoli were removed from the site and crushed. Maui mayor Alan Arakawa, who is sansei (third generation) of immigrants to Hawai'i from Japan and Okinawa, stated on the local news: "It's very simple. There's no such thing as sacred rocks, first of all. The monarchy, started with Kamehameha and his lineage, declared

Christianity the religion of Hawai'i. And Christianity, if I remember the Ten Commandments correctly, 'Thou shalt have no false god before me.' There are no sacred rocks in that religion" (HUOA 2015; Richardson 2017).

Arakawa's comments denigrate Native Hawaiian culture and tradition around rocks and the specific history of Iao Valley, but they also imply that Kānaka Maoli are ignorant of their own culture and history.[3] We can consider this as a kind of Asian settler mansplaining that carries serious effects. Arakawa suggests that because some Hawaiian ali'i converted to Christianity (though, in fact, Kamehameha I did not) that all non-Christian Hawaiian traditions are false or invented (Kamakau 1961). Thus, Arakawa suggests that the idea of "sacred rocks" is ridiculous, and Native Hawaiian culture more broadly is laughable and fake. In cases such as these, it is clear that the need for a feminist analysis of Asian settler colonialism remains important, in order to be able to clearly mark and reject the ways that Asian Americans in Hawai'i, especially local male politicians, often bolster settler colonial views of Native Hawaiians and urge the broader public to understand Native Hawaiian political and cultural movements as backward, ignorant, and inauthentic.

Asian settler colonialism provides a useful language with which to critique the actions of those like Arakawa, who is part of a longer history of Japanese American politicians with power in Hawai'i (Sasaki 2016; Wu 2018). To name Arakawa's actions as promoting Asian settler colonialism allows us to see how, at times (in contingent and never uniform ways), certain Asian Americans in Hawai'i have been complicit with discourses and practices that damage Kanaka Maoli communities. We can think of the process of naming Asian settler colonialism similarly to how Sara Ahmed writes of the process of naming sexism and racism: "We need to acquire words to describe what we come up against," a process which is difficult and also entails noticing that "violence is directed toward some bodies more than others" (Ahmed 2017: 34). Similarly, *settler colonialism* writ broadly came about as words to describe what Indigenous people come up against, because for a long time no one in the academy seemed to accept that other words (e.g., colonialism, racism) were appropriately applied to Indigenous people in countries including the United States, Canada, Australia, and New Zealand, who were all supposed to be assimilated, dead, and/or flattered by white peoples' appropriations and distortions of Indigenous culture. Sometimes *postcolonial* was applied to Indigenous contexts in academia, but this trend existed in tension with many Indigenous contexts in which colonialism was not even formally "post-" or past, but ongoing with no end in sight (Na'puti and Rohrer 2017).

It is in this context that we have to consider the coinage of *Asian settler colonialism* as a term "to describe what we come up against," from the perspective of Kānaka Maoli. We needed language to highlight not only the different genealogies Kānaka Maoli hold in distinction from Asian Americans in Hawai'i (since often people from the continental United States see Kānaka Maoli and Asian Americans from Hawai'i as all equally "Hawaiian") but also the ways that some Asian Americans in certain contexts have supported and continue to support the obliteration of Kanaka Maoli lifeways in Hawai'i. As noted in the early pages of the 2008 volume *Asian Settler Colonialism*, edited by Candace Fujikane and Jonathan Okamura, in a 1997 keynote address, Trask insisted on a shift from viewing Asians and Asian Americans in Hawai'i as "locals" and "American immigrants" to settlers who were implicated in the U.S. occupation of Native Hawaiian land (Fujikane and Okamura 2008: xiii). To Trask, Asian settlers often "claim Hawai'i as their own, denying Indigenous history, their long collaboration in our continued dispossession, and the benefits therefrom. Part of this denial is the substitution of the term 'local' for 'immigrant,' which is itself, a particularly celebrated American gloss for 'settler'" (Fujikane and Okamura 2008: 4). Fujikane and Okamura's edited volume collects the writing of a number of Asian American scholars who seek to take Trask's critique to heart, in conversation with a number of other Native Hawaiian scholars.

Fujikane makes plain in the volume's introduction that the utilization of the term *Asian settler* is not meant to deny the historic and ongoing racism and exploitation experienced by Asian Americans in Hawai'i. Fujikane makes a powerful argument that "Honoring the struggles of those who came before us, however, also means resisting the impulse to claim only their histories of oppression and resistance" (Fujikane and Okamura 2008: 7). This is especially relevant in terms of the common narration of the history of Asian immigrant plantation labor in Hawai'i, which emphasizes Asian immigrants overcoming poor labor conditions and racism and eventually working their way into a middle-class American dream (Takaki 1983; Okihiro 1991). Such histories have generally erased the presence of Native Hawaiians, who are not seen as an important plantation labor constituency compared to Japanese, Chinese, Korean, Filipino, Portuguese, and Puerto Rican laborers. More broadly, these histories have ignored settler colonialism in Hawai'i by taking for granted that Hawai'i is, and was always destined to be, the United States. This assumption is ahistorical, to say the least, because, as noted above, many Asian and other immigrants arrived to work on plantations when Hawai'i was still governed by the Hawaiian Kingdom, until its overthrow in 1893. Hawai'i did not become an official part of the United States until 1898, when the U.S. Congress voted for its annexation under the Newlands Resolution, which argued for Hawai'i's strategic position as a site for the U.S. Navy to refuel its ships on its way to fight the Spanish-American War in the Philippines (Silva 2004).

While the volume is attentive to class differences and distinct refugee statuses among the Asian Americans in Hawai'i, Fujikane and others argue that *Asian settler* is an apt term for all Asian Americans in Hawai'i because all derive some benefit from the structure of settler colonialism and "To focus only on the obvious differences among settlers evades the question of settlers' obligations to indigenous peoples" (Fujikane and Okamura 2008: 9). The critique is aimed at fundamentally unsettling understandings of Hawai'i as America, again following Trask's insistence that Hawai'i is not America and Native Hawaiians are not Americans (which she famously argued in a 1993 speech at a rally commemorating and protesting the one hundredth anniversary of the overthrow of the Hawaiian Kingdom). Dean Saranillio's contribution to the volume puts it this way: "By shifting our perspective from viewing Hawai'i as the fiftieth state of the United States to recognizing Hawai'i as a colony under U.S. domination, terms that at one time seemed commonsensical now ring hollow and look perversely constructed as rhetoric that functions to obscure the colonial domination of Native Hawaiians" (Saranillio 2008: 257). Saranillio's point is that Asian Americans in Hawai'i can shift the framing of how their communities' histories and futures are told from always placing their stories in relation to the United States toward placing their stories in relation to the ongoing struggle against U.S. settler colonialism in Hawai'i.

Missed Feminist Connections

Just as with the Asian American and Native Hawaiian solidarities I have discussed above, a similar shift in framing is also necessary in practicing settler feminist alliances with Indigenous struggles. On January 21, 2017, a women's march was held in Honolulu—one of the hundreds of women's marches held across the United States in protest of the presidential inauguration of Donald Trump. At the Honolulu march, a group of Kanaka Maoli scholars, Indigenous feminist theorists, poets, and artists

performed, including ʻIlima Long, Pūlama Long, Nālani Balutski, Joy Enomoto, Jamaica Osorio, Noʻukahauʻoli Revilla, Terrilee Kekoʻolani, Makana
Kāne Kuahiwinui, and Malanai Kāne Kuahiwinui.[4] These wāhine (women)
performers offered a creative interpretation of the words of Queen Liliʻuokalani, the last sovereign of the Hawaiian Kingdom who was overthrown
by male American and British plantation owners with the backing of the
U.S. Navy in 1893. The women's march closely coincided with the 124th
anniversary of that overthrow on January 17, 1893. Noʻukahauʻoli Revilla
opened the performance by remarking on this fact and reminding the
audience that, as Trask taught many, "Hawaiʻi is not America," but rather is
unjustly occupied by the United States. Addressing the crowd, Revilla
proclaimed that as she and her co-performers were present to

> stand with you against hate, discrimination, desecration, overdevelop-
> ment, militarization, patriarchy and fear, we also give our bodies and our
> voices today as evidence that Hawaiians do, will struggle against U.S.
> occupation, that Hawaiian women will exemplify aloha as long-term,
> intersectional and ʻāina-based [land-based] justice, that aloha is not
> weakness, that aloha is not for sale. We give our bodies and our voices as
> promise. We promise to remember our Queen, to love our land . . . and
> we *will* get our country back. (Jayne 2017)

Revilla has written about a different version of this performance as a
kind of mohala, or blossoming, which can refer to anything from "the
physical blossoming of flower petals or an adolescent child to the meta-
phorical blossoming of an idea or the impact of a good question" and "a
state of illumination wherein ideas, actions, or even bodies appear clear
and developed" (Revilla 2017). In the mohala of the performance, Revilla
shows how the performers used "our bodies and voices as evidence, as sites
of transgenerational memory" that drew on individual performers' genealogies as well as "the strength of the genealogy of resistance we share as
Kanaka Maoli women, a genealogy to which Trask and Liliʻu are central"
(Revilla 2017).

While this performance was shared with pride on social media by many
Kanaka Maoli and allies, it also circulated with a story that the performance had been shouted down by a few haole (white) women in the audience. These women told the performers that they were disrupting the unity
of the women's march and that they should not be bringing up issues of
colonialism when the day was meant to be simply about women. This was a

painfully disrespectful and ignorant response to a moving and powerful
Kanaka Maoli performance. For one, the haole women ignored that the
performance was clearly framed as one intent on building solidarity with
the many other intersectional issues facing haole women and women of
color in Hawaiʻi. Secondly, they failed to recognize the resonance between
Kanaka Maoli women protesting the unjust overthrow of the Hawaiian
Kingdom and the women's march protesting Trump as the new leader of
the United States, who failed to secure the majority of the popular vote.
What the performers were offering was historic, deeply embodied inspiration and precedent for resisting the patriarchal, settler colonial, and imperial United States. The performance necessarily disrupted settler feminist
understandings of Hawaiʻi as naturally a part of the United States and
implicated white settler feminists in the ongoing settler colonial occupation of Hawaiʻi. This disruption could have been a mohala for settler feminists, as the performance offered significant genealogies of feminism
relevant to all feminists in Hawaiʻi. The performance held an unfolding
illumination of the incommensurability between settler and Indigenous
feminists that must be recognized if true alliances are to be formed. In
many ways the performance was therefore a gift, full of relevance for the
current moment to a number of different audiences, settler and Indigenous, present at the women's march.

Yet, somehow, Kanaka Maoli wāhine, at the moment they simultaneously offered solidarity and support to all women and requested solidarity and support back, were perceived as against women. In other words,
the performers were treated like killjoys, selfishly focusing on an issue
that only held relevance to themselves. Sara Ahmed points out that killjoys
are treated as problems when they bring up a problem; that the killjoy
becomes the problem (Ahmed 2017). Here treating the performers as killjoys allowed the audience to ignore the multitude of ways that settler
colonialism impacts everyone living in Hawaiʻi and that some benefit
directly. The haole women who protested the performance also suggested
that colonialism is not relevant to issues of gender and sexism. Yet, in fact,
the instillation of patriarchy has been central to settler colonialism in
Hawaiʻi and elsewhere. As the Kanaka Maoli performers were demonstrating, the significance of patriarchy to the history of colonialism in
Hawaiʻi is clear from the life of Liliʻuokalani, and from her own account of
the Hawaiian Kingdom's overthrow in her memoir *Hawaii's Story by
Hawaii's Queen*, published in 1898 as part of her larger efforts to keep the

United States from permanently annexing Hawai'i (Lili'uokalani 1898; Kualapai 2005).

Political cartoons published in popular U.S. magazines before and after the overthrow depicted Lili'uokalani as an illegitimate ruler because of both her gender and her race. Lili'uokalani, as a symbol of Hawai'i overall, is shown in one cartoon as a wild and savage Indigenous woman who needs to be broken by marriage to Uncle Sam. In other cartoons, Hawai'i is an unruly child being disciplined by Uncle Sam, along with other recently annexed territories and Native Americans (Silva 2004). Lili'uokalani steadfastly challenged all of these representations, maintaining a modern royal image and dedication to her people, even while unjustly imprisoned in Iolani Palace in 1895. Again, in the context of the Honolulu women's march in 2017, there was relevance and inspiration in Kanaka Maoli performers lifting up Lili'uokalani's story in the wake of the defeat of Hillary Clinton, who many expected would be the first female president of the United States. Kanaka Maoli women have long understood that the United States does not respect or recognize female leaders as legitimate.

Sometimes defensiveness, such as that demonstrated by the haole women's responses to the Kanaka Maoli performers, occurs because of assumptions that acknowledging Hawai'i as an unjustly occupied territory of the United States requires all non-Indigenous people to leave Hawai'i. But if we truly follow the words of the performance, and many other forms of Kanaka Maoli activism, there is a clear insistence on recognizing the ways that settler colonialism shores up other forms of oppression, including xenophobia and discrimination against immigrants, all of which can and should be fought together rather than thought of as competing agendas. The Hawaiian Kingdom, after all, was the first to welcome immigrants from the United States, Asia, and Europe. Despite that history predating Hawai'i's annexation to the United States, Hawai'i's multiculturalism has often been attributed to, and held up as an exemplar of, American ideals of democracy, especially when Hawai'i became a state. Deporting immigrants is the mode of operation of a settler colonial nation-state, not an Indigenous one. Rather, decolonization seeks to acknowledge and build different relationships that recognize land not as something to be owned and divided by borders (an inherently patriarchal project) but as the basis of life for all beings.

Overall, what happened in the defensive settler feminist response to the Kanaka Maoli performance at the Honolulu women's march is, in many ways, not surprising. As mentioned above, Trask faced similar tensions between whitestream feminism and Kanaka Maoli nationalism decades before. While Trask's PhD dissertation examined the generative force of feminist theory and poetry, what she termed the "feminist Eros," she later distanced herself from feminism for being "just too white" and "aggressively American," and thus foreign in both style and substance to the Kanaka Maoli context (Trask 1996: 908–9). Trask never gave up confronting sexism both within Kanaka Maoli organizing and outside of the lāhui, but, similar to Black women who prefer the term *womanist* to *feminist*, she distanced herself from the feminist label (Phillips 2006).

Trask faced intense racism and sexism as a professor at the University of Hawai'i and beyond. Recalling the racist cartoon caricatures of Lili'uokalani in the late nineteenth and early twentieth centuries, political cartoons in Honolulu newspapers in the 1990s characterized Haunani-Kay Trask as an aggressive, angry, and even savage Native woman, irrationally bent on antagonizing haole men who were seen as "proper" professors (Trask 1999: 169–81). It is important to recognize and remember that Asian settler colonialism originated as an embodied critique by a Kanaka Maoli woman who sought words to express the ways she saw certain Asian American people participating in perpetuating racism against Native Hawaiians and the dispossession of Native Hawaiians from land. Trask recognized differences between haole and Asian cultures, but rhetorically was very pointed in calling out Asian Americans who were not always strong allies to Native Hawaiians. That rhetorical forcefulness was (and often still is) arguably necessary in order to break the assumptions that everyone in Hawai'i shared a local identity.

Toward an Indigenous, Transnational Feminist Approach to Asian Settler Colonialism

The concept of Asian settler colonialism has been widely critiqued and rejected by a variety of scholars. Some focus their critique on what they see as a false equivalency between white settlers and Asian settlers, charging Native Hawaiian critiques of Asian settlers with fostering an anti-immigrant nativism (Sharma and Wright 2008). Others have more nuanced critiques that maintain the importance of challenging settler colonialism and allying with Native Hawaiian struggles toward decolonization, but argue that Asian settler colonialism is too starkly binary (Rohrer 2016). In considering these critiques, it is useful to acknowledge that the concept of Asian settler colonialism, like much of Trask's work, is necessarily pro-vocative and meant to be unsettling to a wide audience. So deeply engrained is the ideal of Hawai'i as a multiracial paradise without any racial prob-lems, that acknowledgment of the significant differences among Hawai'i's different racial communities and the specific issues that Kanaka Maoli face has long been (and continues to be) difficult. Without Trask's work, the very idea of Hawai'i being an occupied settler colony would be even less widely understood or accepted today.

Could insisting on a feminist Asian settler colonial analysis help reframe some of the debates around Asian settler colonialism that have been unproductive? I believe it could, especially if the concept is re-grounded in a consciously intersectional, Indigenous, and transnational feminist perspective. One notable point of connection in this respect is the fact that Trask formulated the concept of Asian settler colonialism in the context of the 1980s and early 1990s Japanese bubble economy, in which Japanese investors bought up property, resorts, and hotels in Hawai'i. This context, I would argue, has too often been overlooked in critiques of Asian settler colonialism that tend to understand only Asian Americans or per-manent residents of Hawai'i as the subject of Trask's critique. It is clear that she was targeting not only "local" populations of Asian Americans who had accumulated wealth and power in Hawai'i, but also the foreign investors who may never have permanently moved to Hawai'i but saw it as an idyllic vacation spot or lucrative business opportunity.

Perhaps this lack of attention to the ongoing transnational context of Asian settler colonialism is due to the subsequent crash of the Japanese economy in the 1990s (after the period in which Trask formulated the con-cept). It is also likely tied to the fact that self-identified Asian settler schol-ars have generally been those who are third or fourth generations of Asian immigrants who have long been local to Hawai'i. However, Japanese tour-ism remains the largest international share of the tourism industry in Hawai'i, in addition to more recent increases in Chinese tourism and the associated boom of Chinese purchasing real estate in Hawai'i (HTA 2017a, 2017b; Shimogawa 2016; Schaefers 2010). Without dismissing the power of the work of self-identified Asian settler scholars who ground their scholar-ship in the histories and ongoing work of Asian American labor and activ-ism, often in solidarity with Native Hawaiians, what if we supplemented that work with stronger critiques of how Japan, and more recently China, have been complicit in settler colonialism in Hawai'i through tourism and property acquisition? To articulate Asian settler colonialism in this way, while also maintaining an attention to the United States and concerns of gender and sexuality that Trask originally raised in her formulation of settler colonialism, which I would argue have also been too often overlooked, intersects well with transnational feminisms.

What does, or could, a transnational feminist analysis of Asian settler colonialism look like? Trask famously challenged would-be allies to the Native Hawaiian cause to not visit Hawai'i, because "we do not need more visitors, and we certainly do not like them" (Trask 1999: 146). Trask's challenge here is purposefully strident in order to unsettle the sense that many Americans have that they have a right to vacation in Hawai'i. Yet, this critique of the tourist industry in Hawai'i has sometimes been mistaken for a critique of any travel or movement to and from Hawai'i by non-Hawaiian people, and has potentially, at times, prevented transnational solidarities. Kanaka Maoli must be the leaders of decolonization in Hawai'i, but we cannot do it alone, and we cannot do it in a vacuum. Decolonization in Hawai'i requires the broader demilitarization of the Asia-Pacific as a whole, and environmental justice with respect to climate change, sea level rise, and long histories of pollution and contamination of Pacific lands and waters, including the Great Pacific Garbage Patch. We also need stronger solidarity within the Pacific Islands. As noted by Pacific studies scholar April Henderson, there needs to be more dialogue and connection between those parts of the Pacific that are still actively dealing with settler colonialism and those parts of the Pacific that are formally free and independent but still struggling to decolonize many of the legacies of colonialism that remain (Henderson, pers. comm., Feb. 3, 2018).

These struggles for demilitarization and environmental justice, like feminism writ large, must recognize the stakes and expertise of Indigenous Pacific Islanders and in turn support Indigenous movements for sovereignty and decolonization. My point in this article has not been to resolve the tensions and conflicts between settler, transnational feminisms and Indigenous feminisms, but to show that confronting them is necessary to building meaningful alliances between them. Sometimes the immensity of these struggles and the lack of understanding among non-Indigenous and Indigenous peoples make the work of solidarity seem impossible. Yet, as Indigenous feminist scholar Dian Million has written, "Indigenism contains the seed for imagining what else our nations might be" (Million 2013: 179). Million acknowledges that that seed of imagination may be "a dark star to peer at," but it is also what keeps us fighting for "lifeways [that] may pose something other than illness and death" (Million 2013: 179). Feminist alliances must be able to hold space for negotiating our unease with difference for long enough that we move past such barriers. We have to build worlds in which other feminists believe that Indigenous women exist. More than that, we have to build worlds in which Indigenous women are recognized as activists, artists, and scholars with valuable knowledge and theories about our own lives and our communities' histories and futures, which are not marginal or isolated from other communities, but often just erased and unacknowledged. With such recognition, Indigenous women should also be seen as essential allies to building just worlds for everyone. Despite the frequent lack of recognition, such alliances are thriving in a number of areas, from solidarities between land and water protectors at Mauna Kea and Standing Rock, to the International Women's Network Against Militarism which has linked women's activism challenging military occupation, sexual violence, war, and environmental degradation from Okinawa, Guam, Hawai'i, South Korea, and the continental United States, among other sites (Summit Staff 2017). When more of our movements follow such examples, we can discover new modes of living a feminist commitment to end settler colonialism.

· ·

Maile Arvin is an assistant professor of history and gender studies at the University of Utah. She is a Native Hawaiian feminist scholar and author of *Possessing Polynesians: The Science of Settler Colonial Whiteness in Hawai'i and Oceania* (2019).

Author's note
Thank you to Karen J. Leong, Judy Tzu-Chun Wu, and Rosamond S. King, in addition to the full Transnational Feminisms group, for their crucial feedback and support with this essay. Mahalo nui loa to 'Ilima Long for additional assistance, and to all Kanaka Maoli wāhine who steadfastly inspire, care for, and organize the lāhui.

Notes
1   The problem I am interested in addressing in this essay is not necessarily the content of Wolfe or Veracini's work but the ways that this work circulates, often without acknowledging Indigenous scholars engaging the same issues. I have critiqued Veracini's work elsewhere (Arvin 2015).
2   I use Native Hawaiian and Kanaka Maoli (the latter a Hawaiian language term) interchangeably to refer to the Indigenous peoples of Hawai'i. Kānaka (with the macron or kahakō) denotes the plural form. Kanaka (without the kahakō) is used for singular and categorical forms.

3   A similar conflict happened in a heated debate between Haunani-Kay Trask
     and Joyce Linnekin (a white feminist anthropologist). Linnekin claimed that
     during the Hawaiian sovereignty movement in the 1970s that Native Hawaiians
     had invented many traditions, such as in respect to Kahoʻolawe, an island used
     for bombing practice by the U.S. military, a practice Native Hawaiians sought
     to end. Trask critiqued Linnekin's stance as the attempt of a haole, self-styled
     expert on Hawaiian culture to undermine the legitimacy of Hawaiian political
     claims (see Linnekin 1983; Trask 1986, 1991).

4   Kepoʻo Keliʻipaʻakaua stood silently behind the other performers holding a
     sign with the word "Onipaʻa"—a motto of Liliuʻokalani, meaning steadfast-
     ness, determination. For more work by these performers, see, for example,
     Long 2017; Osorio 2018; Enomoto 2017; Revilla 2011; and Joy Enomoto's website
     (https://joyenomoto.weebly.com).

Works Cited

Ahmed, Sara. 2017. *Living a Feminist Life*. Durham, NC: Duke University Press.

Alexander, M. Jacqui, and Chandra Talpade Mohanty. 2013. *Feminist Genealogies, Colonial Legacies, Democratic Futures*. New York: Routledge.

Arvin, Maile, Eve Tuck, and Angie Morrill. 2013. "Decolonizing Feminism: Challenging Connections between Settler Colonialism and Heteropatriarchy." *Feminist Formations* 25, no 1: 8–34.

Boyd, Beth. 2012. "Sharing Our Gifts." In *Presumed Incompetent: The Intersections of Race and Class for Women in Academia*, edited by Gabriella Gutiérrez y Muhs, Yolanda Flores Niemann, Carmen G. González, and Angela P. Harris, 277–84. Louisville: University Press of Colorado and Utah State University Press.

Briggs, Laura, Gladys McCormick, and J. T. Way. 2008. "Transnationalism: A Category of Analysis." *American Quarterly* 60, no. 3: 625–48.

Caffrey, Margaret M. 2000. "Complementary Power: Men and Women of the Lenni Lenape." *American Indian Quarterly* 24, no. 1: 44–63.

CESEC (Critical Ethnic Studies Editorial Collective). 2016. *Critical Ethnic Studies: A Reader*. Durham, NC: Duke University Press.

Chang, David A. 2010. *The Color of the Land: Race, Nation, and the Politics of Landownership in Oklahoma, 1832–1929*. Chapel Hill: University of North Carolina Press.

Enomoto, Joy. 2017. "Where Will You Be? Why Black Lives Matter in the Hawaiian Kingdom." *Ke Kaʻupu Hehi ʻAle* (blog), February 1. https://hehiale.wordpress
.com/2017/02/01/where-will-you-be-why-black-lives-matter-in-the-hawaiian
-kingdom/.

Fujikane, Candace, and Jonathan Y. Okamura. 2008. *Asian Settler Colonialism: From Local Governance to the Habits of Everyday Life in Hawaiʻi*. Honolulu: University of Hawaiʻi Press.

Goeman, Mishuana R., and Jennifer Nez Denetdale. 2009. "Native Feminisms: Legacies, Interventions, and Indigenous Sovereignties." *Wicazo Sa Review* 24, no. 2: 9–13.

Grande, Sandy. 2004. *Red Pedagogy: Native American Social and Political Thought.* Lanham, MD: Rowman and Littlefield.

Hall, Lisa Kahaleole. 2009. "Navigating Our Own 'Sea of Islands': Remapping a Theoretical Space for Hawaiian Women and Indigenous Feminism." *Wicazo Sa Review* 24, no. 2: 15–38.

Hernández-Avila, Inés and Gail Tremblay. 2002. "Introduction: 'It Is What Keeps Us Sisters': Indigenous Women and the Power of Story." *Frontiers: A Journal of Women Studies* 23, no. 2: ix–xviii.

HTA (Hawai'i Tourism Authority). 2017a. "China Fact Sheet." http://www .hawaiitourismauthority.org/default/assets/File/research/monthly-visitors /August%202017/China%20Fact%20Sheet%20–%20with%20August%202017% 20data.pdf (accessed October 30, 2018).

HTA (Hawai'i Tourism Authority). 2017b. "Japan Fact Sheet." http://www .hawaiitourismauthority.org/default/assets/File/reports/major-market-areas /Japan%20Fact%20Sheet%20–%20with%20December%202017%20data.pdf (accessed October 30, 2018).

HUOA (Hawaii United Okinawa Association). 2015. "Alan M. Arakawa 2015 Legacy Award." http://www.huoa.org/nuuzi/awards/legacy/15/web2015%20arakawa.pdf (accessed October 30, 2018).

Jackson, Shona N. 2012. *Creole Indigeneity: Between Myth and Nation in the Caribbean.* Minneapolis: University of Minnesota Press.

Jacob, Michelle M. 2012. "Native Women Maintaining Their Culture in the White Academy." In *Presumed Incompetent: The Intersections of Race and Class for Women in Academia,* edited by Gabriella Gutiérrez y Muhs, Yolanda Flores Niemann, Carmen G. González, and Angela P. Harris, 242–49. Boulder: University Press of Colorado.

Jayne, Rikka. 2017. "Honolulu Women's March Rally—Liliuokalani," video, 2:11. https://youtu.be/OlI-3AgnUE0.

Kamakau, Samuel Manaiakalani. 1961. *Ruling Chiefs of Hawaii.* Honolulu: Kamehameha Schools Press.

Kelley, Robin D. G. 2017. "The Rest of Us: Rethinking Settler and Native." *American Quarterly* 69, no. 2: 267–76.

King, Tiffany Lethabo. 2016. "New World Grammars: The 'Unthought' Black Discourses of Conquest." *Theory & Event* 19, no. 4. https://muse.jhu.edu/article /633275.

Klein, Naomi. 2013. "Dancing the World into Being: A Conversation with Idle No More's Leanne Simpson." *YES! Magazine,* March 5. http://www.yesmagazine.org /peace-justice/dancing-the-world-into-being-a-conversation-with-idle-no-more -leanne-simpson.

Kualapai, Lydia. 2005. "The Queen Writes Back: Lili'uokalani's *Hawaii's Story by Hawaii's Queen.*" *Studies in American Indian Literatures* 17, no. 2: 32–62.

Lili'uokalani. 1898. *Hawaii's Story by Hawaii's Queen, Lili'uokalani.* Boston: Lee and Shepard.

Linnekin, Joyce. 1983. "Defining Tradition: Variations on the Hawaiian Identity." *American Ethnologist* 10, no. 2: 241–52.

Long, K. Kamakaoka'ilima. 2017. "Hawai'i: Mauna Kea, Hawaiian Independence, and the Politics of Jurisdiction," *The Funambulist*, Jan/Feb 2017. https://thefunambulist.net/articles/hawaii-mauna-kea-hawaiian-independence -politics-jurisdiction-k-kamakaokailima-long.

Mays, Kyle T. 2013. "Transnational Progressivism: African Americans, Native Americans, and the Universal Races Congress of 1911." *Studies in American Indian Literatures* 25, no. 2: 241–61.

Million, Dian. 2013. *Therapeutic Nations: Healing in an Age of Indigenous Human Rights.* Tucson: University of Arizona Press.

Miranda, Deborah A. 2010. "Extermination of the Joyas: Gendercide in Spanish California." *GLQ: A Journal of Lesbian and Gay Studies* 16, no. 1–2: 253–84.

Na'puti, Tiara R., and Judy Rohrer. 2017. "Pacific Moves Beyond Colonialism: A Conversation from Hawai'i and Guåhan." *Feminist Studies* 43, no. 3: 537–47.

Okihiro, Gary Y. 1991. *Cane Fires: The Anti-Japanese Movement in Hawaii, 1865–1945.* Philadelphia: Temple University Press.

Osorio, Jamaica Heolimeleikalani. 2018. "(Re) membering 'Upena of Intimacies': A Kanaka Maoli Mo'olelo Beyond Queer Theory." PhD diss., University of Hawai'i.

Phillips, Layli. 2006. *The Womanist Reader.* New York: Routledge.

Revilla, No'u. 2011. *Say Throne.* Kāne'ohe: Tinfish Press.

Revilla, No'u. 2017. "Ua Mohala: Notes on Remembering our Queen." *Ke Kapu He Hiale* (blog), January 18. https://hehiale.wordpress.com/2017/01/18/ua-mohala -notes-on-remembering-our-queen/.

Richardson, Mahealani. 2017. "Maui Mayor on Flood Clean-up: 'No Such Thing' as Sacred Rocks." *Hawaii News Now*, February 17. http://www.hawaiinewsnow.com /story/34534127/in-wake-of-flood-clean-up-criticism-maui-mayor-says-theres-no -such-thing-as-sacred-rocks.

Rohrer, Judy. 2016. *Staking Claim: Settler Colonialism and Racialization in Hawai'i.* Tucson: University of Arizona Press.

Saranillio, Dean Itsuji. 2008. "Colonial Amnesia: Rethinking Filipino 'American' Settler Empowerment in the U.S. Colony of Hawai'i." In Fujikane and Okamura 2008: 256–78. Honolulu: University of Hawai'i Press.

Saranillio, Dean Itsuji. 2010. "Colliding Histories: Hawai'i Statehood at the Intersection of Asians 'Ineligible to Citizenship' and Hawaiians 'Unfit for Self-Government.'" *Journal of Asian American Studies* 13, no. 3: 283–309.

Saranillio, Dean Itsuji. 2018. "Haunani-Kay Trask and Settler Colonial and Relational Critique: Alternatives to Binary Analyses of Power." *Verge: Studies in Global Asia* 4, no. 2: 36–44.

Sasaki, Christen Tsuyuko. 2016. "Threads of Empire: Militourism and the Aloha Wear Industry in Hawai'i." *American Quarterly* 68, no. 3: 643–67.

Schaefers, Allison. 2010. "Asians See Value in High-End Hawaiian Homes." *The New York Times*, September 23. https://www.nytimes.com/2010/09/24 /greathomesanddestinations/24iht-rehawaii.html.

Sharma, Nandita, and Cynthia Wright. 2008. "Decolonizing Resistance, Challenging Colonial States." *Social Justice* 35, no. 3: 120–38.

Shimogawa, Duane. 2016. "China Builds Its Hawaii Portfolio." *Pacific Business News*, June 17. https://www.bizjournals.com/pacific/print-edition/2016/06/17/china-builds-its-hawaii-portfolio.html.

Silva, Noenoe K. 2004. *Aloha Betrayed: Native Hawaiian Resistance to American Colonialism*. Durham, NC: Duke University Press.

Simpson, Audra. 2007. "On Ethnographic Refusal: Indigeneity, 'Voice,' and Colonial Citizenship." *Junctures* 9: 67–80.

Simpson, Audra. 2014. *Mohawk Interruptus: Political Life across the Borders of Settler States*. Durham, NC: Duke University Press.

Smith, Andrea, and J. Kēhaulani Kauanui. 2008. "Native Feminisms Engage American Studies." *American Quarterly* 60, no. 2: 241–49.

Spivak, Gayatri Chakravorty. 1994. "Can the Subaltern Speak?" In *Colonial Discourse and Post-colonial Theory: A Reader*, edited by Patrick Williams and Laura Chrisman, 66–111. New York: Columbia University Press.

Summit Staff. 2017. "Women Activists Join Struggle for Peace in Okinawa." *Summit Magazine*, July 11. http://www.summitzine.com/posts/women-activists-join-struggle-for-peace-in-okinawa/.

Takaki, Ronald T. 1983. *Pau Hana: Plantation Life and Labor in Hawaii, 1835–1920*. Honolulu: University of Hawai'i Press.

Trask, Haunani-Kay. 1986. Review of *Children of the Land: Exchange and Status in a Hawaiian Community*, by Jocelyn Linnekin. *Hawaiian Journal of History* 20: 232–34.

Trask, Haunani-Kay. 1991. "Natives and Anthropologists: The Colonial Struggle." *The Contemporary Pacific* 3, no. 1: 159–67.

Trask, Haunani-Kay. 1996. "Feminism and Indigenous Hawaiian Nationalism." *Signs* 21, no. 4: 906–16.

Trask, Haunani-Kay. 1999. *From a Native Daughter: Colonialism and Sovereignty in Hawai'i*. Honolulu: University of Hawai'i Press.

Veracini, Lorenzo. 2010. *Settler Colonialism: A Theoretical Overview*. Basingstoke, UK: Palgrave Macmillan.

Veracini, Lorenzo. 2011. "Introducing Settler Colonial Studies." *Settler Colonial Studies* 1, no. 1: 1–12.

Veracini, Lorenzo. 2015. *The Settler Colonial Present*. Basingstoke, UK: Palgrave Macmillan.

Wolfe, Patrick. 1999. *Settler Colonialism and the Transformation of Anthropology: The Politics and Poetics of an Ethnographic Event*. London: Cassell.

Wu, Cynthia. 2018. "Daniel Inouye and the Settler Colonial Function of Disability in Hawai'i." Paper presented at the University of Utah, January 23.

Nancy Kang

Bite Out Your Tongue
A Record of Ugly Youth

Gym Class

In the junior high yearbook, there is an innocuous photo of an overweight Asian American girl running after an errant rubber ball. The balls are standard gym grade, the color of toasted salami, with a pleasing pattern of small stars stamped all over them, slightly raised to massage the fingers mid-dribble. The skin is thick enough to make a satisfying "Tang!" on the ground when kicked or flung. A good grade in physical education was key to a commendable average (90%+); a commendable average opened doors to a prestigious university (top-tier, ideally Ivy); a prestigious university charted the path to a successful career (likely medicine, engineering, accounting, or law); a successful career reaped the hard-earned rewards of a comfortable home, serene quality of life, and conscientious capacity to give back (supporting one's parents in their vulnerable years). Such pursuits of balls, times, points, scores, ribbons, trophies, scholarships, and accolades were agonizing for fat children who puffed and blustered like anthropomorphic paintings of the West Wind, sweating profusely, tasting blood at the back of their throats. The lungs felt microwaved, the muscles sprinkled in salt and pummeled mercilessly. For amused gym teachers and cavalier peers who never had a belly press inconveniently against their thighs when sitting, it was great fun, a pitiable parade of pain.

For the fat Asian, the so-called endurance runs (thirty laps of the gymnasium) were portals into the circles of hell while clad in waistless

MERIDIANS · feminism, race, transnationalism   18:2 October 2019
DOI: 10.1215/15366936-7775718 © 2019 Smith College

drawstring shorts and low-cost sensible "WWII shoes," thus described by one more fashionable classmate who was ironically sporting what would have been called "sweatshop shoes." If the affable, overweight Chinese boy Jimmy Yan could pass the gymnastics unit by launching himself into the air with a half-twist and flailing arms (the physical equivalent of screaming "Come what may!" while hurtling down a dark staircase) only to crash into the mats like a calf stunned by a slaughterhouse gun, the kid could go once more around the gym, the track, the circle, the pool, the field, and the schoolyard, in the years that moved by with a tongue clamped tightly behind clenched teeth, and still survive that endless gulping of air and acid.

Head Case

The kid had a prodigious head, the largest in the entire seventh-grade science class, paired incongruously with the smallest hands. Indeed, these measurements were taken, recorded, compared. The point of such an exercise remains a mystery. We no longer live in an age of phrenology, although some of us do need our heads checked for sure, and not just for lice or spiders in the ears. The "scientific" inquiry was remembered with laser acuity by this unlucky freak show. The kid imagined herself to have a bubble brain and small webbed fingers, sticky with the slime of alien difference. When she asked her mother about the odd contradiction, Mother replied, "That's because there is a lot of brains packed in there, so your head is stretched out." The kid imagined a mass of furiously twisted brains with boiling soup ladled over them, then poured into the skull and sealed for decades under concentrated tenderizing pressure from parents and peers. Was the on/off button in the space between her eyes, or more discreetly placed at the base of the skull? "The small hands are a gift from your simian ancestors," joked her clever sibling, who had just read Edgar Allan Poe's "The Monkey's Paw" in English class and found the tale lurid and fascinating. She uttered a crescendo of jungle shrieks for maximum effect.

The soupy skull was perched atop a stout neck that absented itself altogether in photographs, usually thanks to an unfortunate angle that rendered the chin a sort of afterthought, like melted residue on the sides of a baking tin. Mother would declare, "She has no neck at all!" blaming the deficiency on Father, whose lineage of short necks must have evolved in Korea during the era of Japanese colonization to preempt beheading or hanging, even if it did not prevent righteous beatings. "Yeah, it's from me!"

Father would shout back. Short necks are actually a boon in old age, preventing turkey wattles and cellophane skin that the long-necked tribes are heir to once their expiration dates close in, greasy creams and lardish lotions notwithstanding. Her eyes are small and monolid "like slashes in dough," Mother once observed drily. They virtually disappeared whenever the kid laughed. School portrait days necessitated a serious mien which typically ended up conveying either exaggerated surprise (Photographer: "Yes, open them up as wide as possible! Hold it . . . good! You can blink now. Are you okay?") or an expression suggestive of mild insanity. Unsmiling photographs were good practice for passport photos—but certainly not mug shots. Better to close one's eyes in death than that.

All the Better to See You With, My Dear

The sisters had large eyes that easily accommodated contact lenses in a splendid array of colors, manifold mascaras, palettes of hummingbird powders, solid kohl and liquid liners, small stickers in shapes like stars/clovers/hearts/ice cream cones and the like, various configurations of false eyelashes (desiccated insect legs or full caterpillars), and all the other glorious paraphernalia of Maybelline eyes and manga faces. "I don't decorate myself like girls here do," admitted Sora Lee, a visiting student from South Korea in the same class, "but if I get into Harvard, my dad will get me plastic surgery. He promised." To the fat kid, the prospect of having contact lenses spurred much jealousy and subtle longing. When one sibling grew up and welcomed a half-Asian child, the baby's large eyes were a point of pride—and relief—for the sibling: "Thank God he inherited the double lids." The fat kid, while grown up, felt something crack and bleed inside, hearing that kind of talk. She thought of Oedipus Rex, walking around with streaming red wells where the eyes used to be and felt a bit better.

In high school, the kid finally acquired contacts to fulfill that long-awaited desire for true beauty. Unfortunately, they had to be hard lenses by dint of the astronomically bad prescription, which Mother spun into a point of pride because students who did not study as much as the fat kid certainly did not have poor eyesight. They spent their leisure hours hanging out on the hoods of cars, drinking cold sodas outside the corner store, maybe having sex and profoundly disappointing their parents. "My mom said that if I got a motorcycle or a tattoo, she would die," confessed a Chinese student that the kid tutored on weekends. The threatening negative integer was also paired with considerable astigmatism. "Bad eyes, good grades," reiterated Father proudly.

At the fitting, the white optometrist was initially appalled at the grimacing and squinting that accompanied the liberal flood of tears, lashings of lubricant, and multiple attempts to plunge the two shards of plastic into the animal-wild eyes. "Well, Asian lids are typically tighter," the professional mused with a smutty smile. Every time she looked up or to the side, the lenses shifted and cut, as if there were a nylon net that would be dragged over the corneal surface in rapid succession, fishing for floaters and minnows. The urgent and constant reminder of presence made them an impossibly aggravating luxury. Classmates joked that she looked "totally cross-eyed"; one boy, Mark Hollings, even took to spinning his eyes while puckering his lips simultaneously, resembling the Bozo the Clown she had seen on a local advertisement for the Shrine Circus. She avoided the bus stop for a few weeks to avoid this highly coordinated demon boy. Blue-eyed Heather Leacock commented quietly, "But you have absolutely beautiful eyes" after class. The kid assumed she was part of a church group, the kind that had its people approach in an overenthusiastic way and declare, "Jesus loves you *so much!*" Sulky and troubled, the teen asked Mother for advice on whether to keep them. Mother demanded, "Look at me." She then declared bluntly, "Your eyes look scary. Like a cat about to jump at me in the dark. Get rid of them. Do you see eye doctors wearing contact lenses? No. They wear glasses. That means glasses are better. Smart people wear glasses. What a waste of money." The lenses were thus retired after a mere month. The hunt for new glasses, inexpensive and able to accommodate untowardly thick lenses, began.

These new glasses were gold-rimmed and mildly geriatric, the lens unnaturally wide, spanning from the tops of the eyebrows to the center of the face. When she smiled, the cheeks formed a fleshy cushion upon which the frames would momentarily rest, like some weary diner waitress taking a seat between shifts. After a while, facial oils secreted by the acne-prone skin burned through the metallic paint lining the bottom of the frames, corroding green and eventually chipping. Small red crescents formed, one on each cheek, as if branded there with little tongs, all thanks to an acute nickel allergy. The awkward duel between cheeks and frames continued until she painted the metal over with nail polish, an obnoxious red because that was the only color Mother had, and it was hidden away at the back of the second dresser drawer. Glasses were expensive given the family's single income, and these frames were from the "Professional Men's Collection" at Sears, the only ones that would fit such a wide, broad moon face. No dainty red plastic frames, no designer accents in two tones, no brand names alluring to girlish tastes and the expanding materialist imagination. Having frames that fit was blessing enough.

Body Habitus

With her short-cropped hair ("You need to look clean, and short cuts do that," Father advised), men's glasses, lack of neck, and residual Michelin tires of stomach hidden under argyle vests, tight turtlenecks, and tent-like T-shirts (accrued from volunteering at MS races and diabetes society bingos, folk festivals, film festivals, jazz festivals, and various other scholarship-minded extracurricular ventures demonstrating community involvement), it was no wonder an old white man at McDonald's ordered briskly, "Young China boy, pass me that newspaper!" She did not correct him even though "But I'm a girl . . . " lingered under her breath like a lit match that quickly burned itself out. She still passed him the paper with both hands, as she was taught to respect elders, even the rude ones who sipped coffee noisily, littered sugar packs all over the table, and leered at the Sunshine Girl centerfolds of young women sagging confidently out of gaudy bikinis. Not a one had glasses; not a one was Asian. She would understand that the latter were reserved for the late-night porn channels instead, tumbling over lumpy beaded cushions with blunt bangs and lips the color of a red headache. She counted her teeth with her tongue and clenched her jaw in silent annoyance. She hoped these gazing geezers would get diabetes, but only Mother ended up getting it. Years later, the fat kid—now an adult—would climb into the dumpster to find the insulin that had been thrown out by accident, with Mother calling down from the top of the bin, crying and apologizing for the inconvenience. She passed away the next year. The kid's last memory of the body was that its mouth was open, as if to taste a spoonful of sweetness one last time.

For a long while, the kid had the rounded shoulders of the desperately well-fed children of immigrants, used to sitting studiously at a library table or home desk, perhaps munching deftly cut fruit, salty-sweet nuts, or nori-laden rice crackers neurotically across from the "studying so hard" siblings. She was often hunched over a textbook, one leg shaking in nervous tension, tearing at flesh on her hands, fingers, or feet. There was sometimes a sock peeled halfway off the foot for circulation. Or, the shoulders might be curved and sloping from shelling peas or separating twigs, mouse droppings, and other refuse from a sack of dried soybeans at the dining room table after the siblings went to bed. The work was done in an efficient but not entirely invested way. She was aware of the dictum that "One must pay *bap khap*" (or, in literal translation, labor for the privilege of the meal in the household). If something were free and easy, it should invite suspicion, not delight. This is something the immigrant parent knows; this is something Father knew when he won a Fulbright Scholarship to Hawai'i but a corrupt government official had Father's name erased, only to be replaced by that of the official's own daughter. Imagine, thought the teen, I could have been a beautiful Hawaiian. "Fat chance, Fattie," another voice responded in her head. "Maybe they would spit-roast you over the coals and the back fat would sizzle," someone else chimed in. Hearing stories of colonial abuses, war anguish, murdered relatives, government corruption, student protests, unjust incarceration, immigrant humiliations, and dreams deferred—or extinguished altogether—thus prompted the teen to grow up cautious, untrusting, head quick to shrink back into the body turtle-like, self-protective, vigilant, expecting loss or sadness and genuinely surprised by joy when it did come. She knew that the day she was born, her father was not let out of his job because his Ukrainian boss said no ("You did not set up any substitute, so you can't go") so her mother took the cab to the hospital alone. The father always uttered the *chuck* of his boss's surname (Elaschuk or Minchuk or Simenchuk, something along those lines) with particular bitterness. No one remembers when she was born, as Father only comments, "After the workday was over and I arrived there, you were already asleep." Whenever he tells this story, the kid thinks of the day he came home and smashed his thermos on the ground in frustration, shards littering the linoleum like candies from a burst piñata. Mother cleaned it up on her hands and knees.

On picture day, she wore a red oxford button-down shirt, white suspenders, jeans with the bottoms rolled up, and a plastic cameo pin of a fine lady etched in coral plastic. This was Nerd Life. The close-cropped hair was a given, regularly cut while the kids would all kneel naked in the bathtub and Mother clip-clip-clipped black gold down onto the cold white ceramic. Some deft rounds with the curling iron would make for an acceptable mushroom-shaped halo, in a way like a Franciscan brother, sans tonsure but just as manly. "Nice wig," whispered Mike Schwartz at school, slapping his leg in glee. Mike almost killed a twelve-year-old by skiing into him, resulting in egregious head and back injuries for the boy, whose name was never published. He also assaulted a girl in Science 20 by pitching her onto a lab bench with his friend Dwayne Kim, each fondling her and pulling on her splayed legs like they were wrestling a mad calf. Everyone watched but no one said anything. The teacher, who was rumored to watch porn on school computers, was not in the room at the time. The fat kid remembered he had deducted five points on a lab report because she did not underline a heading word with a ruler; she had done so by hand. She retaliated by naming a character after him during creative writing class and having him die at the hands (wings, beaks, claws) of his farm animals. It was a worthy end.

In the school photos, the teen's face is unnaturally pale, soft, and deflatable as a steamed pork bun. Father enforced the short cut rule, since short hair prevented the spread of lice and ensured that undue time would not be spent on frivolous appearance management when one's studies clearly had precedence. Even as an adolescent, she presented the world with the figure of a masculine Asian grandmother, simultaneously young and old, impossibly awkward, solitary, wayward, and seeking.

"The Kongers" (as the white students called them) were a small gaggle of immigrants from Hong Kong who rarely—if ever—spoke in English, laughed loudly in the hallways, and wore shirts with incongruous Chinglish phrases on them like "Absolutely no! A thousand times yes to a Bleu Day Trip." These boys rated her a "one or two" out of ten among the Asian girls in the grade, apparently based on her "Northern peasant" facial features, masculine hairstyle, nonexistent personal style, and unsavory body shape that resembled someone wearing multiple layers of padded fabric to circumvent the countryside cold. The joke was, of course, that the layers were not clothing at all—but fat, ha ha! These revelations were excitedly divulged by one of her Chinese American girlfriends on a cold October day, the sun reflecting against the snow, bright and sharp and blinding. The friend had regretted it immediately upon seeing the teen's stricken face, crying, "I'm sorry, I'm so sorry, I should not have told you!" The friend's apologetic breath blew out in a rush of cold smoke as the teen walked away, smiling and waving to say it was all right but erupting with an internal conflagration that reminded her of the Pepto Bismol ad where a pink rose is lowered into a glass of acid and comes out shriveled and grey. Her whole body felt like wrinkled pigeon's feet resting mutely on a shit-encrusted grate in the rain.

Running the Bully Gauntlet

In spring, crew-cut Robbie Stone accosted the teen, his prodigious belly bouncing like a down pillow under a tight plaid shirt, in the field on the way home. He yelled, "C'mere, I'll beat you up! Do your people really eat rats and cats and dogs?" He let loose a volley of crazed cackles that reminded her of a soldier on television who went insane after a particularly traumatic battle where his buddy was shot in the head but he couldn't stop laughing. She had a vague recollection that maybe they had raped a village woman in the mud before that battle, and the image of the woman's bent legs flapping and squelching there in the darkness lingered in her mind with particular acuity.

English immigrant Mason Crombie had growled at her—growled as would a caged lion or cornered bear—announcing, "I love you . . . I love you, rawr!" in oddly threatening tones to wild laughter all through math class. These antics stopped after she dealt him a succession of stunning blows with the math textbook. Joe Chin, a Chinese American boy with a salamander's bone structure, homely countenance, and the expression of perpetual languor associated with late risers or prolonged substance abuse, was among her worst bullies. He sabotaged her in French class by turning up the volume of her presentation tape to full blast; he instructed her proudly in front of the language arts class, "Go kill yourself already"; he made audible vomiting sounds while pressing himself up against the lockers in mock horror when she passed him in the hallway. Corey Scottsdale thumped like a dinosaur through the dry prairie grass after her one day as she fled the school on a late fall afternoon. In a cavernous voice, he emitted noises aping copulation, groaning, "I want you to have my babies!" while continuing an X-rated monologue about the engorged state of his private parts. She started walking a different route, through some shaded woods, grateful for the sanctuary. Mother caught her eating lunch there after a few months, as the company of trees was preferable to the madness of these sex-crazed young people. A box of cold dumplings, a packet of soy sauce, prairie wildflowers underfoot, silence on a stump: a rare delight, a sanctuary, even in winter.

Again in gym class, the perpetual incubator of youth sadism, Lorenzo DiMangano leaned over and asked her loudly about her private parts (Were they slanted? What kind of hair did they have?) while everyone was sitting obediently in a line awaiting instructions. This thread of discourse was hardly new. Brett Benson had made pointed commentary to the same effect

for the comedic pleasure of the fellow swimmers, surveying her body during the two-week swimming module held at a local pool. Her bulgy shape
was starkly accentuated by the ill-fitting white bathing suit, one that she
had borrowed from a thin sibling because there had been no funds for any
swim gear of her own. One classmate, Kitty Lew, had even called her at
home in the evening, offering to lend her a spare swimsuit because "The
boys are talking about you, making fun—I'm not sure if you know." Kitty
was a size S or XS and had a white boyfriend. Although they were not
friends and not even in the same class, the teen appreciated the sentiment
all the same. It is easy to feel sorry for someone you will never be, after
all, but you still get points for asking.

Now Lorenzo had alarmingly long, camel-like lashes, the angular facial
structure of a Northern pike, and blue eyes the color of moldy veins in
Gorgonzola cheese, but he had baptized himself an "Italian stallion" and
was rumored to have "bit a chick on the tit." The teen had nothing to say
about his gynecological queries or his perverted penchants. She knew that
Lorenzo had asked a classmate named Bettie Pinsent out and Bettie had
accepted, assuming perhaps that he admired her unbridled confidence.
This trait had emerged in her ability to execute a frenetic jazz dance set at
the school talent show in a tight black leotard. Some of the moves had
resembled a seal slipping out of water in pursuit of a joyful rubber ball. She
had worn an assertive red ruffled blouse the color of Bing cherries and lip-
stick to match. Bettie was sorely overweight but with her platinum blonde
hair tied up in a perky side ponytail, she was consistently cheerful and
well-adjusted, never once conveying a sense of illegitimacy based on her
shape. The story goes that Lorenzo willfully stood Bettie up on the designated date night and when queried about his absence directly at school the
next day, shouted out in a stentorian voice, "You think I would actually
EVER go out with someone like you?" The Asian teen was ascending the
steps to the third floor of the building and heard the exchange herself.
Rumor had it that Bettie had looked Lorenzo in those rapacious blue eyes
and stated, "Your loss, asshole."

Later that same gym class, perhaps vexed by her insensitivity to provocation, Lorenzo threw a basketball right into the teen's skull with such
raised-over-the-head force that it knocked the golden glasses clean off her
face and bent the nose pads at a right angle, cutting the top of her nose very
slightly. There was no blood, just a small red C like a slanted smile. Her
right ear, which had been impacted directly by the sudden blow, flushed red

and rang like a siren for a good portion of the afternoon. She stopped its clamor eventually by wetting her pinkie finger and pressing the bottom of the ear canal until a popping sound was heard. This had to be done periodically over a number of hours, obviously an odd situation when picking one's ears is awkward enough in public company, let alone among teenagers. There were no apologies, comments, or questions from witnesses or from teachers. Mr. Perkins was too busy gawking after Elise Hawkes anyhow as she pranced through the skill sets with everything bouncing. Casual brutality was the price of unpopularity. Let the weak fall where they may.

Reiterations
Assault by gym equipment graduated to subtler weapons by the end of junior high. Track meet was an adventure of sorts because of the blazing sun, the busy stands, the excitement of encountering other schools, fried foods at the concession, and sparse supervision. It was a toe being dipped into a space beyond the insularity of a well-manicured school field and the orderly suburban homes beyond, lining the horizon like rows of good Dutch tulips. Enter Adam Murphy, diminutive boy, elfin with large sloppy lips, crusted at the edges from sour, incessant licking, lichen-like impetigo, and teeth reminiscent of the cinematic hillbillies' as they trundled into the city on their wooden wagons. He shot small stones through a straw at the Asian teen in a kind of ingenious aerial acupuncture. One hit the back of the neck, another the upper left quadrant of the torso, one the right thigh (with shorts, it bit somewhat less), another on the right bicep (think a sharp mosquito bite, but with a nail tip instead of a stinger). He and his friends chanted "Fat nerd, fat nerd!" as she rustled by to the shot put and discus events, rubbing the tingling spots in shocked hurt. Corpulent Greek boy Jack Kostas (who flounced through square dance class like a jellyfish through the ocean) and Adam reprised their chant during the awards ceremony that completed the year, jeering the same "Fat nerd" chorus every time she went up to accept an award. She won eight awards ("Like sweeping with a broom" Mother praised), but the photos reflect an untoward ingratitude, her scowling face on stage a commentary on the gauntlet of secret yet public abuse, leaving her devoid of any joy or pride in the year's scholastic achievement. Later in the year, prior to her emancipation to high school, Adam had stopped her on the school steps and asked, point-blank, "Can I ask you something? Do you *know* you are fat?" What a

pathology—the need to be acknowledged, the aggressive entitlement requiring a response. She had walked away, silent, never seeing the boy again but remembering his name and face with diamond acuity, the slant of the steps, the angles of late afternoon light, the weight of words that she never spoke, that old self-censoring clench of teeth and sense of petty torment.

Desperation to earn scholarships to ease the financial burden on the aging parents meant she had launched herself through athletics, including track and field tryouts, knocking down successive hurdles like a stout pony bucking through fences at a country fair. She imitated runner Ben Johnson (prior to his cheating disgrace) with straight hands deftly chopping the air for the hundred-meter dash. She looked longingly at the easy striding of Sunny Haines, a rather neutral-looking girl, straw-colored hair whipping past like a palomino's tail, who wore jeans so tight that they had to be yanked off in the change room by two squealing helpers. Those popular girls never bothered her though. Kristen Needham had laughed at her allergy attacks and commented, "You know you sneeze like a duck?" and made a giddy pantomime of slapping her feet on the hallway linoleum like Donald Duck. Most of these girls were too immersed in their own insecurities, eating disorders, miasmatic family troubles, and traumatic sexual awakenings for any sustained assaults on others. Runty Addie Ho was an exception: she had stolen the fellow Asian's exemplary biology essay (of all things, on the vanishing habitat of pandas) from a bulletin board, citing that the rival scholar needed to be taught a lesson in humility. "She thinks she's so great" was the apparent rationale for the crime, a teacher confided later after the mysterious theft was solved. The teen was truly mystified at this accusation of egotism; she could describe nothing really notable about herself. It was all because of grades; the fat teen had the highest, and that made her a source of supernal jealousy from the narrowly achievement-oriented Oriental. Tiny Addie resembled a devil's doll-baby, decked out in pink ruffled sweaters and ostentatious rhinestone hair barrettes with slim ribbons of various colors, twisted and braided like mini maypoles. Her raucous high-pitched laughter was challenged only by her histrionic crying, which started with a few plangent notes of whimpering and inevitably rose to an industrial wail that summoned the sympathetic ministrations of peers and teachers alike. Addie's sulky expression exuded the emotional power of an agitated Pomeranian when denied a small rubber ball. Jealousy over grades remains a petty but real phenomenon among many Asian

American students, but some buck the trend. There was Jasper Chen who
made such a holy mess of the kitchen in home economics class that the
teacher, Mrs. Wilkes, screamed "GET OUT!" with the same gusto used for
apprehending grizzly bears in the trash bins behind a suburban strip mall.
Mediocre Grace Ko's father insinuated that the fat teen had bribed scholarship officials to win a coveted city-wide award for Korean descendants
because clearly, his daughter (with her B average and small-time swimming
credentials) should have been chosen. Addie eventually married and
became the mother of two generic boys. When the Asian teen—now an
adult—ran into her at the local Staples buying back-to-school supplies,
the young mother, a babbling son swinging his booted legs fitfully in the
shopping cart and another whining offspring trailing behind, looked
intently away.

Summation and Surmises

These memories testify to a youth spent in constant fear of judgment and
ridicule, an enveloping expectation of hurt, shame, and callous commentary that needed to be kept silent, largely out of the assumption that enun-
ciating such troubles would only complicate the life of her parents,
siblings, some kindly teachers, as well as herself. She did not know quite
how to put words to the feelings, understand the hyper-visibility of the so-
called fat and ugly, and how these constraints correlated with the awkward
fit of the young person of color in a white-majority school in a white-
majority city in a white-majority country. She shied away from "bothering"
her teachers because she had been told to keep problems to herself. She
feared retaliation by the bullies, always male at that age, but who would be
joined by a cadre of righteously evil women in later years, women so mean
that even "Fiery Wall of Protection" oil from a hoodoo shop could hardly
keep their bitchery at bay. These were, ironically, other women of color
whom she met at a retreat for activist-minded minority scholars, women
who gave hate stares and did not want her to sit beside them on the bus, all
because she was studying what they said she shouldn't. One even told her
that she was stealing a job from a more legitimate person, someone of the
right color, the preferred background, the "real" woman of color. No one
said a word in her defense, at least in public. There were furtive messages
and sympathetic glances, but that was all. Think of an earthquake in a
glass factory and you will know the serrated opal spectrum of everything
left unsaid.

When she alluded to her troubles while meeting with the high school guidance counselors for college planning, one absent-mindedly handed her a box of tissues and observed drily, "You are upset now but it is an emotional time in a young person's life." He then wished her luck with her studies and announced he had another student coming in five minutes. The next one, a thin older lady named Mrs. Griffith who was as forbidding as her name, told the teen she herself was at fault: "If you want to be liked, you have to make the effort." The teen brought up a racial incident that had occurred while she was volunteering at a local multicultural festival: the teen had been face-painting the public when a young white girl had asked her parent (mid-paint) why Asians "had such flat faces and squinty eyes." The parent had replied, "That's the way they are, honey. They are not like us." Mrs. Griffith had sided with the parent and told the Asian teen that she should not have been angry at the exchange. "You definitely don't know more than a parent," the professional had scolded angrily, "and you should never be rude, especially to a young child." Never be rude indeed. These repeated silencings required the retaliatory weaponry of words, but she did not come to consciousness of this until decades later, already dented and warped with distrust, paranoia, and self-loathing. At home, she had heard the supposedly wise dictum "Silence is golden; empty vessels make the most noise," only here, the silence was inside, as was the emptiness, and the only gold that stayed was the dented men's glasses—and those, too, kept peeling and shedding screws.

After more than twenty years, the Asian American woman can replay these images easily in her mind. It is a reel of film, cut into disparate pieces, heavily edited, and with no special effects. A green screen would have worked wonders had she known of its miraculous capacities. She stares out from different glasses (red and black now, still terribly thick, but women's frames by the grace of God) and surveys the world with her ever-observant, squinting, monolidded slits-in-dough. The dough has since baked and browned, even smoldered into a dead char at the edges. Her mother is still dead but visits occasionally in dreams. Anger about injustice still corks the throat; very infrequently that cork blows off in an explosion of rabid argument, sometimes spraying with invective those who mean the most. Now she lives in a body that has come to know some monstrously delightful and absurd possibilities, as well as its raw capacity to push back, if merely through the learned and savage choreographies of fingers beating down on flat black keys. There are other ways, of course. A man attacked her sibling in the London Tube, and she put a Doc Marten into the back of his knee. A man attacked her in the New York subway but he ended up fleeing, calling her a "gangster bitch" after she unmuzzled that bitch mouth. It was satisfying to fight like that, but most of all, she wished they had just left her alone.

In college biology class, she once researched a parasite that infects fish by infiltrating the gills, eating out the host's tongue, and taking a spot there instead. *Cymothoa exigua* are bullies, consuming everything from that muscular seat of pain, gathering up voice and sound, and swallowing it with side servings of blood and self-respect. The conqueror sat there crowned by the spiky serifs of dead words, fenced in by yellow tombstone teeth, and buoyed up by the stopped stale air. She has slowly cut out that alien tongue year by year, the one sucking letters, the one who fed on numb dumbness. She imagines swimming away from it all, with strange tenderness and righteous anger for all that was felt and known, and for all that was still submerged in the black cosmos of salt water and unforgiving darkness lanced by a single desk lamp at midnight.

· ·

Nancy Kang is Canada Research Chair in Transnational Feminisms and Gender-Based Violence, Tier II at the University of Manitoba. Her creative work appears in such venues as *Stone Canoe, Ricepaper Magazine, Little Patuxent Review,* ARIEL, *Women's Studies Quarterly,* and *Canadian Literature.* She is co-author with Silvio Torres-Saillant of *The Once and Future Muse: The Poetry and Poetics of Rhina P. Espaillat* (2018). The preceding composition was completed, in part, thanks to funding from the Canada Research Chairs Program.

Brooke Lober

Everything's Connected
An Interview with Aurora Levins Morales

Abstract: In this interview, the writer, activist, and well-known woman of color feminist and participant in grassroots left movements Aurora Levins Morales explores the action and language of participatory social change, considered through the lens of her social location and experience. With a focus on intergenerational communication among feminist and Left movement participants, Brooke Lober asks Levins Morales to share her method of writing and activism, based in histories of family and place; to comment on the term and practice of "identity politics"; to assess the current upsurge of feminist movements; and to revisit her historical and contemporary contributions to internationalism, women of color feminism, and Jewish organizing in the Palestine solidarity movement. Levins Morales offers insightful reconsideration of her life, work, and philosophy, with descriptions of the context and motivation of her published writing.

"The body is a storyteller," writes Aurora Levins Morales.[1] Her storytelling merges with and emerges from the body, poetry and prose amassing a life's work crafted over four decades so far—a tour de force of politics and power, of intimacy, family, community history, folktale. This personal and political writing flows through a corpus of self-awareness, sophisticated research, and an ecological approach to knowledge, with a heart open to the always troubled and yet joyful, miraculous world.

A popular participant in the San Francisco Bay Area women of color feminist literary/activist scene of the 1980s, Levins Morales has since been known for her presence in grassroots movements and radical subculture,

MERIDIANS · feminism, race, transnationalism   18:2 October 2019
DOI: 10.1215/15366936-7775784 © 2019 Smith College

and for her entries in *This Bridge Called My Back* (Moraga and Anzaldúa 1981). She coauthored her first book, *Getting Home Alive* (1986), with her mother, Rosario Morales. The classic work oscillates between their voices, distinguished by a change in font as well as a shift in perspective. Rosario, first-generation Puerto Rican, born and raised in immigrant communities in New York, describes her affinity for quotidian women's cultures, for Black and Jewish and Latin American life in the city, for English literature, for communist political ideals—synthesizing a mature but buoyant, leftist, womanist feminism.[2] Aurora, meanwhile, romantically invokes love for the Puerto Rican countryside where her parents raised her and her brother, at a distance from the Red Scare that threatened their well-being in 1950s New York, reaching toward a decolonized sense of home: "Taino, Aruaca, Guaraní . . ." following "the thread of my blood" (55). At the close of this early work, Levins Morales situates her Ashkenazi–Puerto Rican heritage in relation with the Palestinian struggle for survival and freedom in the extended prose piece, "If I Forget Thee, O Jerusalem"; responding to the Israeli invasion of Lebanon with "a buried song" (198), she counterposes Puerto Rican, Ashkenazi Jewish, and Palestinian images of resilience against state violence, drawing a Latin American Ashkenazi Jewish vision of transnational alliance with Palestinian liberation. Followed with "Ending Poem," a revised version of "I Am What I Am," Rosario Morales's entry in *This Bridge Called My Back*, the mother and daughter together elaborate decolonial identity as a holistic, transformative practice.

In the decades following these publications, Levins Morales became a renowned public intellectual and author, increasingly drawn to the role of *curandera*, of healer. Addressing her experience of living with chronic illness and disability while simultaneously incorporating critique of world-historical circumstances of rampant violence, domination, and oppression into her analysis of social life, she exemplifies the practice of writing as a healing modality. Her writing blooms through and beyond the combinations of identity markers that define her position in shorthand; as terms congealed for new liberation movements, Levins Morales joined in advocacy and in self-definition, as bisexual, multiracial, Jew of color, disabled, survivor, marking identity. She recently contributed to the "Ten Principles of Disability Justice" (Berne et al. 2018) coauthored by fellow activists and artists from the performance collective Sins Invalid, bringing her deep-rooted justice politics to a contemporary activist sphere.

Levins Morales has now authored scores of articles and several books on family, culture, movement, and community, producing relational webs of knowledge about the past, routed through the medium of the body. She writes of a life rich with activity: community-based activism, scholarly study, deep, intimate relations, teaching, writing, and spiritual practice, in overlapping spheres of feminism, antiracism, and anticolonialism, transformed through holistic, self-aware approaches to social and political life. As she wrote in her dissertation and, later, the book *Medicine Stories: History, Culture, and the Politics of Integrity* (1998), this is the "historian as curandera," the recognition of one's historical and material position, identity writing that facilitates healing through the act of historicization: telling the untold, contesting dominant narratives, elucidating absences, asking questions, and more techniques for writing as anticolonial transformation (Levins Morales 1998: 23).

Levins Morales's writing from the body draws her work around spheres of health and survival. Years of seizures—which she worked to minimize and endure through a practice not unlike mindfulness—were followed by increasingly debilitating symptoms due to environmental factors. These experiences instigated her disability justice activism and her holistic theory that joins body and ecology to resist an increasingly toxic world. Years after the death of Gloria Anzaldúa, Levins Morales inaugurates the monograph *Kindling* (2013) with a letter to the venerable Chicana feminist theorist and auto-historian. She focuses on Anzaldúa's experience of illness and debilitation, asking the deceased Chicana author "why you refused to identify as a disabled woman, and what illness and pain have to do with what you called the Coatlicue state" (3). Considering this question, Levins Morales addresses Anzaldúa beyond the grave: for Anzaldúa to identify as disabled, "you would have needed a strong, vocal, politically sophisticated movement led by queer working class women and trans people of color who understood your life, and it wasn't there yet" (5). With this, Levins Morales names the disability justice movement in which she participates. Applying Anzaldúa's theory to her experience, she elaborates Anzaldúa's "Coatlicue state" as it arises from bodily pain that "takes me to the core, to the place of new insight" as "the only salvation is to expand, to embrace every revelation of my struggling cells, to resist the impulse to flee, and hold in my awareness both things: the planetary web of life force of which I am part, and the cruel machinery that assaults us" (Anzaldúa 2007: 68, 88–89; Levins Morales 2013: 6).

With Levins Morales, as with Anzaldúa, living with and through pain becomes the portal to greater knowledge and analysis. From the position of the disabled woman of color, understanding (dis)ability as a form of power in the context of contemporary capitalism and colonialism deconstructs the narrative of individual blame and shame otherwise cast through the racialized vector of ability; rather than seeking "inclusion" in a eugenic hierarchy of value, disability justice movements imagine and interact with the world otherwise, proposing a framework of universally inherent worth.

Puerto Rico's cultural history, networks of kin, and contemporary political and economic situation inspire much of Levins Morales's thinking and writing. When Hurricane Maria devastated the island, Levins Morales used her platform as public intellectual, philosopher, and poet for advocacy: on the radio, on blogs, on social media, and at Kehilla, the synagogue she attends—where, during the Jewish high holy days of 5778–79, I rose with hundreds of congregants as Levins Morales stood at the bema and enjoined us to literally turn our bodies, redirect our gaze, to pray toward Puerto Rico, and to mobilize ourselves in solidarity and in care. Since then, she has sparked an initiative to confront white supremacy within and beyond the synagogue; meanwhile, she continues to advocate on behalf of Puerto Rican people, and all Latin Americans who suffer the burden of colonization and its wake.

At every turn, we find Levins Morales healing, writing, telling a story of transformative possibility. On her website, she writes:

> The stories we tell about our lives shape what we're able to imagine, and what we can imagine determines what we can do. My job is to change the stories we tell and help us imagine a world where greed has no power, the earth is cherished and all people get to live safe and satisfying lives. Because once we truly imagine it, the pull to create it becomes irresistible. (Levins Morales 2019)

I met with Levins Morales to ask her about her life, to understand her orientation to antiracist and anti-imperialist politics now, and to find out what she hopes people will learn from her teaching, writing, activism, and healing today. As we sat at a Berkeley kitchen table in the home of a friend, we talked about her life in the rural North Bay, and her plans to take care of her health and to write. That morning, I found her happy, and I was delighted at the chance to query this venerable thinker and to receive her wisdom and vision for transformation.

o o o

BL: Part of your work is that you keep the genealogy of your family, and you show the relations and connections you've found between your mother's and father's family—the "ropes," as you have called them, the bridges.

ALM: I think watching the way that my parents built their alliance was a foundational piece of assuming solidarity as a major force in the world. I've always been fascinated with family histories, and in doing antiracism work with people, I've found that it's often easier for people to see, understand, and face up to legacies of participation in oppressing other people when it's a family story—investigating the specific relationships that people establish over time. If your place in North America is a result of specifically inhabiting this indigenous land, or profiting in this way from slavery or from indentured labor—and where did the fruits of people's own labor end up? Tracing the more personal stories of how structures of power function in family—what I do isn't really genealogy; it's social histories of families. I've found it to be a very powerful tool for people to engage with history differently.

BL: Why are those social histories of families important?

ALM: I think the answer is the same as why story is important overall. My brother [artist Ricardo Levins Morales] likes to say there are two kinds of organizers: the ones who understand it's all based on storytelling, and the ones who haven't figured it out yet. Processes of change have to do with altering the story of how the world works, of what's possible. And while it's really important to have big picture analyses of how systems work, where it comes home to people is in stories. And so, understanding family stories and where that places us in structures is a door into thinking differently about those structures.

So, I was in Puerto Rico doing research for my dissertation, and it was one of these days that I refer to as "ancestor-guided research process" [*laughs*]. I was trying to go to one place, and all of a sudden there were all these cars in the lane, and all of a sudden, I couldn't get off at that exit, and I was stuck on a freeway going west, and suddenly realized I was at my ancestral hometown. So I said, what the heck, I'll go to the church and look at their records, and I found ten generations of my family in a couple of hours, but I also found out that they were slaveholders—which I had not known, because they were working-class people in New York. But it turns out that they were the landed gentry of that town for many generations. And in the baptismal records I found the names of the people who they had held in slavery, and wrote those names down, and began telling their stories as part of my story.

The reason my grandparents were alive to migrate to New York City in 1929 was that the labor of these people had sustained their family. [So I] started looking into the dynamics of slavery in Puerto Rico in a different way, because I had specific stories. There's this woman, this one woman, who, her children show up in the baptismal records, and in the beginning, all her children are enslaved and she's partnered with a man who's free. And you can see, the later children are free, and it's a process of buying the family out. You know, it happened in my town, with my family as the bad guys in the story. So it brings the realities of slavery in Puerto Rico home to me in a different way.

I've had amazing things happen in the workshops that I do. Where people get to think about their family's stories from a different angle, and understand them in a larger context, and it shifts big things about their identities, and their relationships to power structures and systemic oppressions.

BL: It sounds to me like part of what you're talking about is that, in finding our own story, we find what our relationship is to others. And I'm wondering what you think of the term *identity politics*.

ALM: People find all these ways of classifying things and then arguing about them that I find really tedious. It's often used as a put-down for dealing with racism, and with other -isms. But it started out as being about racism. I mean, I remember in the women's movement in the late '60s early '70s, that was, like, the big put-down: "You're not really dealing with—you're not putting class and gender first. You're talking about racism, and that's a distraction. You're an identity feminist."

So often, it's a put-down, meant to exclude certain parts of the conversation. And there's ways that people get so involved in that particular stance—you know, any single-issue politics is gonna be flawed, and is gonna betray somebody. And what interests me is the relationship between all these different types of oppression, and for all of us to be facing the fact that we are both targets and perpetrators of oppression along different vectors. People tend to be much more interested in exploring the vectors in which they have been targeted by oppression, and not so much the ones where we're privileged. And that's another thing about family history, is you follow any thread far back enough and you'll see: "Oh, here's [where] we were burning other peoples' houses; here, our houses were being burned." It goes back. The wheels of history turn our families up and down, up and down, in different ways.

This is what *This Bridge Called My Back* was responding to—the nationalist-oriented identity politics say, you have to put this first, just the way some white feminists say, you have to put this first. And in *This Bridge Called My Back*, we were saying no. You can't actually force us to abandon being people of color, being female. We're not gonna do that. You know, so it's messy. But it's messy in a way that it's always been messy: where peoples' vision of what they're fighting for is too small—inevitably, it leads to betraying alliances, and betraying solidarity.

I'm doing another book of medicine stories. And one of the essays in there is called "Bigger is Better." It's about having the biggest possible vision of liberation, and being of service to that, and then, you figure out what you can do in real circumstances. . . . I remember nationalist men telling me feminism was a white people thing and it was going to divide our movement, and I remember white women telling me, you know, "we're all female and we're all sisters, and it doesn't matter." Easy for them to say. So I'm suspicious of pretty much all the ways identity politics are talked about.

BL: Yeah—the phrase *identity politics* gets interpreted as this narrow thing, narrower and narrower, but when you read the literature of late twentieth-century women of color feminism—it is people doing this deeper, relational identity work. And so I wonder how much of a chance we have to highlight that legacy.

ALM: Well, now it's all being called intersectionality . . . which is actually a term I hate.

BL: Why?

ALM: Because it implies that two separate things intersect, and that is not always true. A class-privileged white woman is still at intersections of race and class and gender and whatever else and is just unaware of the ones in which she is privileged, so there's that. I prefer more organic, ecological kinds of metaphors. But it sort of implies that you can be walking on "Class Street" and take a turn onto "Race"—that these things exist out of relationships with each other, that there's some pure state of gender or pure state of race. All people are somewhere on all of those continuum lines. So it annoys me; it feels glib. I understand its usefulness, but it feels inaccurate in a way that upholds some of the things that we're trying to dismantle. I think words matter, and the language you use is important— it tells a story. So I prefer to talk about complexity, and talk about more dynamic relationships between the different kinds of oppression and to describe the interactions in a less static way.

I tend to think in ecosystem terms, and think about feedback loops, and ways in which things increase and limit each other. I'm very conscious, as a historian, for instance, of the flexibility of racism for the needs of class, and that who gets defined in what ways is always at the service of class privilege, and so there are shifting categories. When identity politics gets essentialist, it erases that. It starts buying into notions of a biological identity that is unchanging.

There's a historical court case somewhere in the Midwest around the racial categorization of Finnish workers, who were doing the bottom-rung work in the timber industry. I mean Finnish people, you can see all their blood vessels through their skin. They are light-skinned people primarily, I believe. And there was a court case where all the race scientists of the day measured heads and did all the weird stuff that they did that they thought was meaningful, and the judge said the evidence suggests that they are white, but common sense tells us they are not—and ruled that they weren't—because the class structure needed to exploit Finnish people at a level that, in their mindset, couldn't be done to white people. So they had to be classified as nonwhite in order to maintain the level of exploitation that was happening there.

And you have, similarly, where they are putting people in two main categories in California at the time of statehood, and because there are still many land-grant, California families that have big properties at that stage, they decide Mexican people are white, and Chinese people are not. Then you come to this moment in history where Asian Americans are targeted in all kinds of ways, but where the mythology is that Asian Americans are the closest to white. Mexican Americans are also very heavily targeted, and it's all rooted in economics. So when you get into essentialist stories it doesn't take that into account. . . . It's so much more complicated than we make it.

BL: So, you share a lot of your own life story as well as family stories in your work. I know that you've participated in a lot of different social moments and identify as a revolutionary. You were in the Chicago Women's Liberation Union. Can you talk about your early politicization?

ALM: I was born into a family. On my father's side, he was a fifth-generation radical. My mom had been radicalized as of her late teens, she'd gone to Hunter College and taken philosophy courses that led to her learning about Marxism, and she said it was like a light went on, like "This makes sense out of my world!"—and she joked about joining the Communist Party when everyone else was fleeing it.

BL: Was this the '50s?

ALM: Late '40s: '48, '49. So my parents were highly politicized and committed in a long-term, lifetime kind of way. My father and I had a conversation in the last few years of his life about the difference between identifying as an activist and a revolutionary. Those words are used in different ways by different people, but it wasn't something you do, it was something you are. So I grew up in a politicized family in which the world was being explained to me in those terms. I don't have the same kind of "aha!" moment stories that other people who found it for themselves have. I do have "aha!" moments, but they're not the same kind.

I would say one critical moment was spending the summer in Cuba. I was fourteen in 1968, which was an amazing year to be there. The excitement and ferment of ideas—and also the fact that I was a fourteen-year-old girl in Cuba, and I was being taken seriously by adults in a way that didn't happen in the states. People wanted to know what I thought Johnson was going to do next in the Vietnam War, and what I thought about the Black Panthers, and the armed resistance versus nonviolence discussions that were happening, and you know, how to have my own analysis and things. That was the summer that my brother and I both had experiences of moving from being children of radicals to being radicals in our own right. I was fourteen, he was twelve.

I was also really fortunate to be in Chicago at a time of tremendous social movement ferment. The Black Panther Party in Chicago: my parents were in support of them, and I was involved in a high school group that was a defense committee for the Panthers. Our family car was used for the breakfast program. We were engaged in alliance with them. And then there were the Young Lords, a Puerto Rican group from the north side. My father taught a course on Puerto Rican history for them.

Then the Chicago Women's Liberation Union: I was the youngest member when I was fifteen. My mother and I went together, joined together, and then I was in a consciousness-raising group from that point until I was about eighteen, and it had a huge impact on my life. I was at that critical point in a young woman's life of becoming sexually active, getting targeted in different ways around sexual stuff and, you know, shaping my independent identity, and I did that within a collective discussion of male domination and sexism and feminism. I was with this group of women, most of them eight to ten years older than me, making decisions about my life in this collective conversation. Watching the process of people telling their own stories and going, "Hey, that happened to me too" and going around the room and thinking—OK, if all of us are experiencing this, there's a different explanation for this particular struggle we're having other than personal character flaws and self-improvement needed. And just watching. I mean, this is what's happening in organizing, is that people get to tell their stories, and understanding suddenly that their personal struggles are actually bigger social struggles that come out of social forces. So, having that experience in such a personal, visceral way, in that particular moment of my teens was hugely important, and it was in the context of big antiwar movements.

The year I was sixteen, my father was part of a scientific delegation to Hanoi of radical scientists from around the world going to say how could we help your side of the war. So not only was my family against the war, we were on the other side. My father got back and started this group, Science for Vietnam, and I was a junior researcher in that group. We were investigating varieties of rice that come to harvest more quickly and have a better shot at escaping herbicides, fish that could be raised in bomb craters to bring down the mosquito population that was causing disease, doing things that would be helpful to the people in Vietnam. So my teens [were] a really tense and formative period.

Then I was in college in New Hampshire and helped create a women's center there, and that was mostly what I was doing while I was in college because I was in remote northern New Hampshire. Then I came to California when I was twenty-two and was involved with the Puerto Rican socialist party and a third world news bureau that was working with KPFA [radio station], so I got to learn a tremendous amount doing that work, the radio work. We didn't have the resources to do national stories, but we could do international stories because we knew people who were from all over the world, who were in exile, who were going back and forth to their countries and so—this is before the internet—we would get faxed stories from behind guerrilla lines in Central America and Zimbabwe. And then we covered local stories, so it was a very fast, deep political education to be part of that at that particular moment—that was like '77,'78, '79. I also became involved with La Peña cultural center, the Chilean exile community. So I was really very fortunate to land in a lot of places of ferment and meet people from lots of different situations who were talking about their lives.

BL: For people who are new to social movement work, it can be hard to understand that all these issues are connected. Can you talk a little bit about being a feminist and being in racial justice movements as a woman of color, and being in women of color feminism, and also, as an internationalist, being involved in revolutionary movements? How do you explain the connections between these movements, and what can we learn from that?

ALM: I feel like, if there's one storyline that I tell in my work over and over and over again it's that everything's connected. Probably comes from growing up with an ecologist father, growing up in a rainforest. Probably comes from having a mother who was deeply and intensely and broadly curious about everything and explored those connections all the time. So I grew up in a family in which that was the conversation. But it's a little hard to answer, because I've never considered anything else.

It's clear to me that when people don't see that the issues are connected, it's because they're not expecting enough. My father said anytime two good causes seem to be in conflict it's because neither side is asking for enough, and he would give an example of loggers versus spotted owl conservationists, that neither side was able to imagine a forestry economy that preserved both people and habitats. They were asking for way smaller things that pitted them against each other. I think part of the reason that I can tell things are connected is because I have a really big vision of what's possible. I'm not looking to put Band-Aids on things; I'm looking to change things from the root. So a solution that improves things locally but causes damage somewhere else has never appealed to me, and understanding that the more about connections we know, the more power we have. It's a little hard to even step out of that perspective enough to even answer your question. I mean, I've seen the failure to do that really gut movements, particularly, failure to incorporate feminism into national liberation struggles and antiracism struggles where feminism could've transformed those struggles and led them to different kinds of victories. To victory at all in some cases. A lot of places where the liberation struggles of the '50s and '60s came to power, [those movements] ended up reproducing a lot of really horrible oppressive stuff and just putting different people on top.

BL: And part of that was the failure to incorporate feminist ethics and forms of relation into the new revolutionary governments and societies.

ALM: Yeah, I mean, feminism is understood as the political nature of things that are deemed to be personal. The wave of revolutionary movements happening in Latin America today has a stronger presence of feminism and women's leadership, and is primarily not armed and not leaving whole populations with PTSD. A lot of those armed struggles depended on the exploited labor of women keeping other things going while the guys went off to the mountains. There's an interesting clip I saw on Bolivia about how they have an executive vice ministry of decolonization and ministry of culture, and someone who was in leadership of that at the time was talking about how some of the reasons why they were focusing on building women's leadership at the grassroots level was not for biological reasons but for historical reasons: women's training was much more about thinking about the whole. Thinking about the whole village, thinking about the family as a whole—the whole community. And they were able to take that kind of leadership far more easily than men, who had tended to, historically, go off to work on their own, and bring resources back to the community, but were not trained by their daily lives to think in "whole organism" ways. There's a lot more to that conversation.

But wherever it's like, "We'll take care of it after the revolution"—what was said a lot during my teens—"Feminism will wait until after we seize state powers"—OK, well, what kind of power will you be creating and seizing? What will you be constructing if you're not including feminism, which deals with half the world's population? And similarly, in nationalist-type movements, we're fighting both colonialism and racism and saying that the women's struggles could wait; and the feminist struggles were saying the real struggle is to overthrow the patriarchy and all the rest will follow.

BL: Do you see that problem of single-issue politics repeated in what people call *white feminism* today?

ALM: I hate that term. There's no such thing as white feminism. There's lots and lots and lots of different kinds of feminists, some of whom are able to think about complex, multi-oppression issues, and some of whom can't. There's not one white feminism just like there's not one women of color feminism. I mean, a lot of things happened to the women's move-ment, the women's liberation movement, and part of it was the profession-alization of the movement into academic disciplines. The beginnings of women's studies were radical. There was a process both of people in that movement professionalizing it, and also, a lot of lateral movement within academia of women in other areas at institutions. They knew they'd get treated better [in women's studies programs] and were moving over, but they didn't necessarily have an activist bent. They loved to do the scholar-ship about women and found a more conducive home to having an intel-lectual life as a woman, but that didn't mean that there was a grassroots activist orientation.

BL: Still true.

ALM: Well that's what I'm saying, is it shifted to that, and became institu-tionalized, but yeah, I hate it when people talk about white feminism as some monolithic thing, because there's lots and lots of white feminists doing lots of different things.

BL: I think what people are often referring to by *white feminism* is feminism that doesn't incorporate racial justice.

ALM: Right. It just needs to be more complex and nuanced. There's also a lot of assumption that that's what the women's liberation movement was like back in the day, and that really pisses me off as a Puerto Rican who was in it up to my neck.

BL: What's your impression of what it was?

ALM: A lot of different things were happening. There were black women involved, and there were Puerto Rican women involved, and there were indigenous women involved, and sure, it was white-dominated, and sure, the organizations that got more visibility were white-led organizations— but we were struggling about all those things. The idea that that movement was white women sitting in their living rooms with class privilege talking about small issues [is just wrong]. We were going door-to-door talking about the need for childcare for working women in working-class neighborhoods and neighborhoods of color in Chicago, or talking about international struggles and having conversations with women in Vietnam and China and Cuba and other places, and exploring the relationships between imperialism and male domination and arguing about the complexities of race, class, gender, sexuality. Yeah, there were homophobic, straight white women and there was class stuff and race, there was all this stuff you would expect there to be, but it was far more complicated. It's part of the rewriting of history and the delegitimizing of that movement to describe it as exclusively that way; it wasn't exclusively that way.

BL: Do you think that we have a chance now to tell that story differently?

ALM: Sure! Do you know the movie *She's Beautiful When She's Angry*?

BL: Yes.

ALM: I love that movie. I think [producer/director Mary Dore] did an extraordinary job of doing a broad sweeping picture that included lots of different pieces of what was happening including the [internal] battles, but also capturing some of the immense excitement of being part of this massive conversation. I remember what it felt like before that movement. It's mostly an emotional feeling, I was young, but the intensity of the contempt for women that could be so openly expressed with no check, looking in the newspapers and jobs were listed under "jobs for women" and "jobs for men." You could be fired for being pregnant, and married women had a really hard time getting jobs because it was assumed that married women were not reliable because our primary commitment would have been to child-rearing. There was open sexual discrimination and harassment with no legal checks whatsoever, and it's not like those things have gone away, but at least there's some pushback.

You know the massive response, the feminist response to Trump—his "Rapist-in-Chief," totally unapologetic grossness—grew directly out of that movement. The shift that happened between that not even being a conversation anywhere on the horizon, and then it being this mass conversation that hundreds of thousands of women are involved in—that was really an extraordinary thing to be a young woman in.

So your question about connecting things: I just keep telling the stories and telling the stories and telling the stories, saying, well, this piece goes with that piece, and this piece goes with this piece. I think that it's only when we're able to look at these interconnected webs that we can really envision the future that we deserve. If you're only looking at one piece at a time, it's really a strategy of hopelessness. . . . The problem is that people have the illusion that they've done their bit, but they're only solving this little itty-bitty problem and they're throwing all those other people overboard. They're saying, "This is enough." So, understanding that anytime what you're asking for is too small, it means that you're betraying somebody and means you're shooting yourself in the foot: getting that principle and then you can say to people, "Ask these questions." Here's a struggle: ask a question. If you go bigger and bigger and bigger in what you want, where will that lead you?

I've been doing a lot more work with disability justice communities. I did a workshop in Seattle at the University of Washington, I was talking to them about going for something a whole lot bigger than access and I said, "Pick an issue, a small local issue, and let's see how big we can make it." People talked about accessible transportation and having more public transportation, and right away you're up against oil companies and the automobile lobby, so who else is up against them? We had a wonderful discussion that connects people who need public transportation for disability reasons with whole webs of people who have other struggles that plug into the same megaproblem.

The other question I ask a lot in a disability context is: how would society need to be different in order for your body not to be disabled in that society? Because of disability being constructed by the society, not the body. We have all different kinds of bodies, and whether something's disabling or not depends on society. In some cases, disabilities wouldn't exist: one thing I talk about is spinal cord injuries from car accidents, that in our capitalistic production spaces and the terrible urban planning that aren't built around people's needs at all, it has become normalized that you travel around at fifty to sixty miles per hour and that's just accepted as the cost of business, and the results are car accidents, and people are killed and injured and disabled as a result. It's not an actual, inherent human need to whiz around that fast, so there are whole realms of disabling injuries and illnesses that are a direct result of the ways that we produce, the kind of economy we have. So you can end up having conversations about extractive economies and the structure of work and disability that are both about how disabilities are created and about how people with disabilities and chronic illnesses actually have bodies that can't comply with capitalism, often; it varies depending on what our bodies are doing, but we have a critique of the nature of work and productivity that the rest of the movement does not. Imagine if people with disabilities led the labor movement! What's being asked for would be very different.

BL: And also the ecology movement, right? In your work, you've connected our understanding of ability, disability, and the body, with the world—the ecosystem.

ALM: Yeah, what I say is that sustainability and inclusion are actually two different angles on the same thing. A society isn't sustainable that excludes large parts of its population from productivity and access. It's not a sustainable way of life. Environmentally unsustainable societies are inherently exclusive of [a lot of people]. You know, people are impacted at different levels and different rates, and what we need to be looking at is a society that is both sustainable and inclusive, and you can't build either one of them independently of the other.

But also, I believe that a lot of what our bodies need is what our planet needs; it's actually the same thing. A great deal of public health, the broad health struggles that humans have, are intimately related to the destruction of the environment—many of them in ways that we don't immediately think about. The Ebola outbreak was very connected to deforestation and to banishing rainforest habitats and the moving of mosquitoes that were carriers into more populated areas. Same thing with Lyme disease: closer proximity of deer and people comes from the deforestation of land for farms, and then the partial reforestation for suburban housing that brings the forest edge, light foliage, close to people—and you get much more transmission back and forth between humans and deer. So many of the things that we are struggling with are directly connected to our relationship with the rest of the planet. That's really the core of what I'm doing right now, is writing about land/water/environmental justice struggles and disability justice struggles and health struggles all woven together. That's the focus of my day-to-day writing.

BL: Before we're done, I want to ask you about the Jewish organizing you're doing in Jewish Voice for Peace, and the history of your thinking and activism about Jewishness and Palestine. You wrote for [the radical Jewish feminist journal] Bridges, and were a part of Jewish feminism in the 1980s; your sense of affinity with Palestinian struggle because of your interest in Puerto Rican decolonization is very clear from that time—you wrote about that in "If I Forget Thee, O Jerusalem" (1986). I think for many Jewish people, the issue of Palestinian liberation was, at best, unclear at that time. What was it like to be a woman of color in the Jewish feminist movement in the '80s, and what does that have to do with your work with Jewish Voice for Peace today?

ALM: That's a long conversation. Where to begin? My great-grandmother was a feminist Jewish labor organizer and worked with Margaret Sanger to deliver birth control information in the tenements back in the day. Her grandmother was the wife of a rabbi who walked out of temple and took her husband with her because she couldn't be a rabbi—she was protesting sexism in the Ukraine in the 1870s or so. So there's a strong Jewish feminist line in my family.

I think the first explicitly Jewish organization that I was involved with was New Jewish Agenda, and there were the Jewish feminist conferences that happened here, not too long after I came to the Bay Area, like '82. I had grown up in a family with a lot of pride in a Jewish identity, but very little knowledge about Jewish ritual, Jewish holidays . . . that other part of Jewish life. Then I landed into this upsurge of feminist seders and liberation Haggadahs of all kinds, and people making the connections between Jewish religious ritual and cultural practices and the political work we were doing, which my father's generation really rejected out of hand. It was very exciting to me. I could see where my father's political principles had roots in Jewish ethical systems of belief, but there was no connection to the religious stuff at all. For me [the Jewish feminist movement of the 1980s] was a discovery of Jewish community that I had never had. We had summer visits to Jewish relatives; but there was a lot of racism in those interactions—it was challenging for me in a lot of ways. And then I started finding Jewish community, and various kinds of groupings of people who were grappling with Jewish rituals as part of Jewish identity for people who are radicals. It was a very lively time, and it was really exciting being a part of Jewish feminism . . . I loved being part of *Bridges* and that community of writers having the conversations we were having. It was really stimulating, and it felt to me like it was a direct descendant of the conversations my great-grandmother was having.

I was really obsessed for a while with early twentieth-century Jewish feminists, especially from New York, and the question of who landed where [ideologically and politically], in terms of their main ground on which they fought—whether it was in terms of Jewishness, class, or gender, and what combinations of those. That was very interesting to me. Being a woman of color in that was challenging, and it remains challenging. Jewish life in the United States is so dominated by assimilated Ashkenazi Jews that have taken on whiteness and don't even know or understand or think about that in relationship to white supremacy. The buying into white supremacy is part of [the] assimilation and upward mobility process for Jews who arrived here and, you know, are super Ashkenazi-centric. I am Ashkenazi, but there's the history of Sephardic and African and other Jews that are so exoticized and marginalized. A lot of people ask me: Well what are you *really*? Are you a Jew or a Puerto Rican? It's amazing that it is still so hard for white U.S. Jews to wrap their minds around the fact that [Jews of color] exist at all. There's a constant "How is that possible?"— literally not getting that it is possible to exist as a Jew of color.

It's the intensity with which that whitening process took place, that's a lot at the center of what I'm doing with Jewish Voice for Peace. The place that most of my energy is going is the Jews of Color and Sephardi/Mizrahi caucus, which is operating independently but in conjunction with JVP.

I'm very excited about that organizing. [In the Jewish feminist movement, the issue of Jewish identity] never stopped being challenging. I met some of my closest long-term friends in the hallways of feminist conferences where there was a room for the Jews to meet and a room for the people of color to meet, and we were standing in the hall dithering over which one we're going to go to today, and finding the others of us who were in that situation.

But in terms of the identification of Palestine: I grew up in a time of decolonization. We were very closely connected to Cuba, we got the posters that came out of the organization of solidarity with Latin America, Asia, Africa. I never really heard much about Israel growing up. It was not a topic of conversation in my family. Palestine was not a topic of extended conversation, but it was obvious that they were part of us: the people who were freeing ourselves. I have a piece in the book that JVP put out on anti-semitism, where I say I see children with stones in their hands, [and] sol-diers shooting at them, and I know what that is, that's Latin America, I've seen it all my life—of course I identify.[3]

There's an upsurge of radical leftist Jews of color right now. What we bring is conversation about what [Jewish] solidarity with Palestine means. We see ourselves as also targets of white supremacist Zionism, not white allies; there's a lot of stuff that's problematic with that entire framework. We come from a different set of motivations, and we come from a recogni-tion of common struggles as well as differences in our positions in rela-tionship to all of that, but the common connections between white supremacy in the U.S. and Zionism is really what we bring to the fore. So [leftist Jewish organizing is] a much more holistic, grounded experience for me now than it was back in the Jewish Agenda days when I was terribly tokenized. I find this too, with Jews of indigenous heritage, that there's such an obvious familiarity with the dispossession of people from their land, and the kinds of suppression that happen, and the destruction of culture and institutions, and the wall building. Of course people identify. What's more complex is understanding the role of antisemitism in all of it and the ways in which Ashkenazi Jews in particular got set up as proxies and middle agents in that situation. You take a people that's oppressed and targeted and terrified, give them guns and money and say, "Go take these people's land," and be our proxy. Not to minimize any of the extreme racism [perpetrated by Ashkenazi Jewish people], but it was a setup.

BL: You're referring to the way that Christian-dominated white supremacy utilizes a form of Jewish supremacy and Zionism as part of a bigger imperialist picture.

ALM: Well, and the European powers who wanted control in the Middle East used European Jews to structure that control. It's classic of the role that Jews played in European society over many centuries, which was to be proxies for the Christian ruling class and to be the targets of resentment and to derail resistance from below, [shifting that resistance] towards Jews and away from the Christian ruling class. The function of antisemitism is [to be] a buffer in class systems. It's a conjuring trick.

BL: I think that when you were talking about the way that disability is constructed, it made me think about the way that Ashkenazi Jews were constructed in the antisemitism that arose and was really institutionalized in the late nineteenth century through the period leading up to the Nazi Holocaust. I guess it made me think . . . maybe there's a way of creating a Jewishness that is decolonizing and is liberatory, because we're trying to transform or annihilate those discourses that turn Jewishness into weakness, or paradoxically, supremacy, within an ableist society.

ALM: There's so much internalized antisemitism in the early Zionist writings, all this stuff about being stereotypically heterogendered and, you know, "We're not like those weakling scholars, we're going to flex our muscles!"

BL: —and be in the sun. Palestine.

ALM: But I think that's one of the pieces of the struggle that most interests me: the shifting U.S. Jewish identity. Part of what happened, following the Holocaust, was a shift away from solidarity orientation and internationalism towards nationalism. There's a wonderful quote someone was circulating from a [European Jewish Socialist] Bundist, written in '47. It's about Zionism being an argument of despair. But we're committed to creating societies that liberate everybody; creating a little armored state won't protect us. He said if we achieve socialism there will be no need to hide, and if we don't, there will be nowhere to hide.

Trying to create a little island and buffer it up with lots of weapons, trying to create a little zone of safety in the midst of a world that's run by oppression, is a policy of despair. It shows a lack of faith in humankind, which is understandable following a genocide, but it dominated the voice of [the] Jewish community ever since. Not that it doesn't have roots from before that, but it's an oppressed community that latched onto colonialism as a way to become real Europeans. It's like, "I'm finally going to be a real German! I'm going to have a colony of my own!" It shows the ways in which antisemitism laid the groundwork for Jews to be drafted into those roles, and the danger of having your own victim's story being the primary commitment. There was a school district in Chicago that tried to expand their genocide curriculum to include other genocides and the Jewish community was up in arms: "You can only tell *our* story! It's diluting the story of the Holocaust to tell the stories of Cambodia and Rwanda." Instead of reconnecting us to the rest of humanity.

o o o

As I left her company, I felt the fabric of history as Levins Morales reveals it: threads of time and culture produce the subject, who in turn produces history, and might revise it—transforming past, present, and future.

From time to time, Levins Morales appears on the radio, on the Bay Area's Pacifica station KPFA. In the wake of September 11, her poem, "Shema: September 12, 2001," introduced her work to new print and radio audiences across the United States. With its title and imagery referring to the most important Jewish daily prayer, the poem presents a sober response to U.S. exceptionalism and military aggression, producing affinities between casualties of empire and a plea for an end to the violence of war. Fifteen years later, in 2016, the poem "Va'ahafta" again gathers the public sphere of activists to prayer: in a sacred manner, Levins Morales invokes Arundhati Roy's popular vision: "Another world is possible," a world free from hunger, from rape, from greed—a world of integrity, a flourishing world, ushered in by a wild and brave, collective imagination.

Aurora Levins Morales is a writer and *curandera*. A new edition of her book, Medicine Stories, was published in 2019. You can assist her livelihood and read her new writing by joining the community of readers and supporters at https://www.patreon.com /auroralevinsmorales.

Brooke Lober is a scholar in residence with the Beatrice Bain Research Group at the University of California, Berkeley, currently researching and writing on feminist, queer, and anti-imperialist movements, and on interactions between late twentieth-century Jewish feminism and the international Palestine solidarity movement. Lober teaches courses in feminist and queer studies at Sonoma State University and California College of the Arts.

Author's Note

This transcript was produced thanks to the work of Sonoma State University undergraduate research assistant, Caeli Matanky.

Notes

1   "Guanakán: 7/9/2017." http://www.auroralevinsmorales.com/blog/guanakan.
2   Aurora Levins Morales calls herself the "family genealogist." Her oral history interview for the Sophia Smith Collection includes detailed elaborations of both Levins and Morales family lines, and Aurora Levins Morales's life story. https://www.smith.edu/libraries/libs/ssc/vof/transcripts/LevinsMorales.pdf.
3   Levins Morales is referring to the following essay: Levins Morales, Aurora. "Who Am I to Speak?" In *On Antisemitism: Solidarity and the Struggle for Justice*, by Jewish Voice for Peace, 103–9. Chicago, IL: Haymarket Books, 2017.

Works Cited

Anderson, Kelly. 2005. "Aurora Levins Morales Oral History Interview." Sophia Smith Collection, Smith College.

Anzaldúa, Gloria. 2007. *Borderlands/La Frontera*. 3rd ed. San Francisco, CA: Aunt Lute Books.

Berne, Patricia, Aurora Levins Morales, David Langstaff, and Sins Invalid. 2018. "Ten Principles of Disability Justice." *WSQ: Women's Studies Quarterly*, 46, nos. 1/2: 227–30.

Levins Morales, Aurora. 1998. *Medicine Stories: History, Culture, and the Politics of Integrity*. Boston, MA: South End Press.

Levins Morales, Aurora. 2001. *Remedios: Stories of Earth and Iron from the History of Puertorriqueñas*. Boston, MA: South End Press.

Levins Morales, Aurora. 2013. *Kindling: Writings on the Body*. Cambridge, MA: Palabrera Press.

Levins Morales, Aurora. 2019. "About Me." Aurora Levins Morales (website). http://www.auroralevinsmorales.com/about-me.html.

Levins Morales, Aurora, and Rosario Morales. 1986. *Getting Home Alive*. Ithaca, NY: Firebrand Books.

Moraga, Cherríe, and Gloria Anzaldúa, eds. 1981. *This Bridge Called My Back: Writings by Radical Women of Color*. Watertown, MA: Persephone Press.

Denisse D. Velázquez

....

Genealogies of Transnational Activism
The Somos Hermanas Project in Central America

In the spring of 1981, public opinion polls revealed that a vast majority of
North Americans overwhelmingly opposed the Reagan administration's
military response to revolutionary activity in Central America (LaFeber
1984: 4). This came mere months after Ronald Reagan had run as a
presidential candidate on a platform that cautioned against a Marxist
Sandinista takeover of Nicaragua, which seemingly threatened neighbor-
ing El Salvador, Guatemala, and Honduras (LaFeber 1984: 1). In response to
the increasing levels of violence by U.S. military–funded death squads, a
multitude of antiwar organizations and collectives emerged throughout
the United States. Many of these groups organized solidarity trips to the
Central American isthmus. One of these included the delegation's trip
Somos Hermanas (We Are Sisters), which formed out of the preexisting
Alliance Against Women's Oppression as a solidarity project.

The Alliance Against Women's Oppression (AAWO) originally formed in
August of 1980, as a successor to the Third World Women's Alliance of the
1970s (Hobson 2012: 9). AAWO was a multiracial coalition of women activists whose mission was rooted in activisms that were women-centered
and intersectional, aimed at improving the material realities of women of
color and working-class white women (Farmer 2017: 190). The Alliance
organized a multiracial delegation of lesbian and straight women that
visited Sandinista Nicaragua in 1984 after receiving an invitation from the

MERIDIANS · feminism, race, transnationalism   18:2 October 2019
DOI: 10.1215/15366936-7775751 © 2019 Smith College

Asociación de Mujeres Nicaragüenses Luisa Amanda Espinosa. Somos Hermanas thus emerged as an organization following this first trip. The group recognized itself as national network of women of multiple oppressed identities who focused on the struggles of Central American and Caribbean women in the midst of intensifying U.S. military intervention. At the height of its organizing activity, Somos Hermanas had chapters in New York, Boston, Louisville, Santa Cruz-Watsonville, and San Francisco (Hobson 2012: 9).

The first delegation of Somos Hermanas members in 1984 coincided with Reagan's reelection, which fueled the group's ideological and personal investment in cultivating this transnational feminist solidarity. A self-identified "veritable rainbow coalition," the delegation reported that the participants consisted of "eighteen Afro-American, Puerto Rican, Chicana, Peruvian, Asian, Arab, and white women" hailing from New York; Boston; Washington, DC; and the Bay Area (Carastathis 2013: 949). Perhaps one of the most exhilarating moments of this delegation's trip was its meeting with Dora María Tellez, popularly known as "Comandante Dos," a central leader of the FSLN (Frente Sandinista de Liberación Nacional) throughout the 1980s and one of the most prolific women leaders of the revolution (Hobson 2012: 7). It is important to note that these participants were largely queer/lesbian-identified women who saw sexual liberation as inherent to revolutionary worldmaking. Somos Hermanas was one of many queer radical collectives that subverted the U.S. Left's internal homophobic tendencies and propensity to conceptualize queerness as incompatible with Third World regions such as Central America.

The documents in this issue include a photograph of Somos Hermanas members at the organization's second delegation to Nicaragua in 1986. The discussion paper "Salvadoran Women: In Search of Peace and Justice" was one of the many publications that emerged from Somos Hermanas in the midst of their solidarity trips to Nicaragua and local community organizing efforts in the United States. Each of the materials elucidates the various ways in which Somos Hermanas sought to both educate their internal membership and spread awareness among their local communities about expanding U.S. interventionism in Central America. All documents are from the Alliance Against Women's Oppression Records, Sophia Smith Collection, Smith College.

Denisse D. Velázquez is a recent graduate of Smith College, where they double majored in Latin American studies and history. They are originally from the San Francisco Bay Area where they hope to return and continue working with local activist communities of color.

Works Cited

Carastathis, Anna. 2013. "Identity Categories as Potential Coalitions." *Signs: Journal of Women in Culture and Society* 38, no. 4: 941–65.

Farmer, Ashley D. 2017. *Remaking Black Power: How Black Women Transformed an Era.* Chapel Hill: University of North Carolina Press.

Hobson, Emily K. 2012. "'Si Nicaragua Venció': Lesbian and Gay Solidarity with the Revolution." *The Journal of Transnational American Studies* 4, no. 2: 2–27.

LaFeber, Walter. 1984. "The Reagan Administration and Revolutions in Central America." *Political Science Quarterly* 99, no. 1: 1–25.

Figure 1. Somos Hermanas delegation to Nicaragua, 1986. Creator: unknown. Alliance Against Women's Oppression Records, Sophia Smith Collection, Smith College, Northampton, Massachusetts.

Salvadoran Women:
In Search of Peace and Justice

By Miriam Louie and Vicki Alexander

A Discussion Paper
Co-Produced By:

**The Alliance
Against
Women's
Oppression
and
Somos
Hermanas**

Figure 2. "Salvadoran Women: In Search of Peace and Justice," by Miriam Louie and Vicki Alexander, May 1987. Discussion paper, p. 1, woman wearing scarf with hand raised in the air on front cover. Creator: Miriam Louie and Vicki Alexander. Alliance Against Women's Oppression Records, Sophia Smith Collection, Smith College, Northampton, Massachusetts.

Miriam Louie and Vicki Alexander are members of Somos Hermanas and the Alliance Against Women's Oppression. This discussion paper was produced as a joint project by both organizations.

"**Somos Hermanas**" means embracing our sisters in solidarity. We are a national, multi-racial organization composed of straight and lesbian women. Somos Hermanas - We Are Sisters - with the women and progressive forces in Central America because we share the burdens of militarism and war, of poverty, racism and sexism. Somos Hermanas takes up educational, organizing, and material aid work concerning our sisters in Central America. We also publish a quarterly bilingual newspaper, the Somos Hermanas News. For further information, contact our National office or any one of our local chapters at the addresses below:

RESISTING REAGAN'S WAR

National Office / Bay Area:
3543 - 18th St., Box 18
San Francisco, CA 94110

Fresno:
P.O. Box 4927
Fresno, CA 93744-4927

Watsonville/Santa Cruz:
P.O. Box 467
Santa Cruz, CA 95061

Louisville, KY:
P.O. Box 3912
Louisville, KY 40201

Boston:
P.O. Box 1091
Jamaica Plain, MA 02130

New York City:
P.O. Box 656
Stuyvesant Station, NY 10009

The **Alliance Against Women's Oppression** (AAWO) is dedicated to the full liberation of women in all aspects of life. We are a national, multi-racial organization of lesbian and straight women with chapters in the San Francisco Bay Area, Boston, New York, and Washington, D.C. The AAWO initiated Somos Hermanas in 1984, and is still active within that organization. AAWO also is involved in the reproductive rights movement, and is active in support of lesbian/gay rights. In 1986, we launched the Dora Tamana Day Care center campaign to benefit the Women's Section of the African National Congress. We also organize annual celebrations of International Women's Day, and publish discussion papers on issues facing the women's movement. We can be contacted at:

c/o The Women's Building
3543 - 18th St., Box # 1
San Francisco, CA 94110

Figure 3. "Salvadoran Women: In Search of Peace and Justice," by Miriam Louie and Vicki Alexander, May 1987. Discussion paper, p. 2. Creator: Miriam Louie and Vicki Alexander. Alliance Against Women's Oppression Records, Sophia Smith Collection, Smith College, Northampton, Massachusetts.

B efore us stood three Salvadoran women dressed in the somber uniform of the mothers of the disappeared. Each wore a red flower symbolizing blood on a white background for innocence, a black dress for mourning, and a white scarf for peace. One of the women held a small baby, as its mother, Maria Teresa Tula, told us of how she had been twice captured and tortured by the police. The first time, after refusing to answer questions about members of the COMADRES (Committee of Mothers of the Disappeared, Assassinated, and Political Prisoners of El Salvador "Archbishop Oscar Arnulfo Romero"), she was raped by three of her captors and beaten in the stomach. The second time she was handcuffed, hooded, threatened, beaten, and left for days with her hands tied to her feet in a tiny, pitch-black cell.

In the auditorium of the Catholic University of Central America in San Salvador, 175 North American and 250 Salvadoran peace delegates listened in angry silence, as she described her second ordeal:

"I was captured again, 20 meters from the COMADRES office. I was going to the market with one of the mothers when suddenly a pickup descended on us...they took us by force with long rifles...those who captured me were hacienda police dressed up as civilians. They took off my clothes and examined me from the tips of my fingers to my toes. They gave me a sheet. Then began my calvary of tortures...I would like you to know that I suffered all of this when I was pregnant. Now my child is here. Thanks to God this child was born. I am not ashamed to say that I have a child from prison."

There was not a dry eye left in the conference hall. Yet Maria Teresa pressed on,

"I want more than your applause and tears. We want your solidarity that is so important for our people to be able to live. You may forget these testimonies, but the repression continues every day...One last thing I want to ask you. I want to go to the U.S. to give this message to those people who don't believe this is happening."

Maria Teresa's story was but one in a string of unrelenting testimonies at the "In Search for Peace" Conference held in November of 1986. Members of human rights, political prisoner, indigenous, peasant, refugee, earthquake victim and trade union organizations gave painful individual ac-

A member of COMADRES describes to U.S. visitors her son's murder by rightwing death squads.
Photo: Mark Warschauer/*Labor Report on Central America*

counts of torture and repression. Yet each ended in a common refrain— even at the risk of their very lives, the Salvadoran people will persist in the struggle for peace and justice against Duarte, the oligarchy, the military and U.S. intervention. They exhorted us to tell the North American people about the crimes being committed in our name in El Salvador.

Under constant threats from Duarte and the rightwing, the largest peace conference ever held on the soil of war-torn El Salvador was organized by the National Unity of Salvadoran Workers (UNTS). Formed in February 1986, the UNTS wields together centrist and left-leaning labor unions, and peasant cooperative organizations, some of whom had signed a social pact with Duarte, a pact that helped him win the 1984 elections. The UNTS also networks many human rights organizations and unemployed workers, as well as the newly organized neighborhood organizations of the *damnificados* (earthquake victims).

On the opening day of the conference, the UNTS led 25,000 people in a march for peace and earthquake relief through the most affected barrios. The breadth of the UNTS revealed how much Duarte's policies of war, economic austerity, and abuse of human rights have alienated all sectors.

The 176 U.S. delegates to the conference included activists from the trade union, church, peace and solidarity movement, minority and other community organizations. Despite grave risks, our Salvadoran hosts spoke openly to us, hoping that this broad cross section of North Americans would bring their message to our different sectors and communities at home. Over the course of the conference, through plenary and workshop discussions, we united on several resolutions. These included an end to all military aid to El Salvador; a dialogue and negotiation for peace amongst all parties and social sectors to resolve the conflict; ending all government repression of unions, cooperatives and the people in general; the unconditional defense of human

Figure 4. "Salvadoran Women: In Search of Peace and Justice," by Miriam Louie and Vicki Alexander, May 1987. Discussion paper, p. 3. Creator: Miriam Louie and Vicki Alexander. Alliance Against Women's Oppression Records, Sophia Smith Collection, Smith College, Northampton, Massachusetts.

rights, freedom for political prisoners, and an end to disappearances; and the immediate meeting by the government of the demands of earthquake victims for food, clothing and shelter.

We from Somos Hermanas gained a vivid appreciation for the conditions, sacrifices and many arenas of struggle taken on by our Salvadoran sisters through the concentrated experience of the conference and visits to refugee camps, prisons and slum areas. The isolation of the Duarte regime, the regeneration of the mass movement for peace in El Salvador, and Reagan's Iran/Contragate predicament now provide valuable opportunities to support our Salvadoran brothers and sisters by stopping

U.S. intervention in El Salvador

WOMEN'S ACTIVISM IN THE MASS MOVEMENTS FOR PEACE AND JUSTICE

Living under military dictatorships for half a century, Salvadoran women have been activated by

---

A Legacy of Oppression, Resistance and Organizing

The troubles of Salvadoran women did not begin with Duarte. His regime is but the latest episode in a long succession of U.S.-backed dictatorships in El Salvador. A quick review of statistics betrays the telltale signs of neo-colonialism in Latin America:

- One in four children dies before the age of five;
- About 75% of all children under five suffer from malnutrition;
- Maternal mortality is five times that in the U.S.;
- Abortion is illegal, but one-third of all the beds in gynecological wards are filled by women suffering complications from botched abortions;
- One-third of all 14 year old girls surveyed in the 1971 census already had at least one pregnancy;
- Fewer than 3 doctors service every 10,000 people;
- Per capita caloric intake is the lowest of any Latin American country;
- 90% of the population earns less than $100 a year;
- Unemployment now exceeds 50%;
- 60% of the population is a illiterate, with women's illiteracy 10% higher than men's;
- Less than 1% of the population owns 40% of the land while over 90% own less than 5% of the land.

Since the days of the Spanish conquest and enslavement of the Indians, El Salvador has been ruled by 14 wealthy families who came to control the coffee, cotton, sugar, export-import industries and the financial system. This oligarchy was backed by a powerful and ruthless military. In 1932 a popular peasant uprising, which the army called an "Indian revolt", was drowned in the blood of 30,000, some 4% of the country's population at the time. General Maximiliano Martinez oversaw the massacre, called La Matanza,

that included the execution of Farabundo Marti, a labor leader and internationalist who had fought alongside Sandino in Nicaragua. With La Mantanza, a generation of dissent was virtually exterminated, Indian culture almost disappeared, and General Martinez rose to power in the first of the military dictatorships which were to last half a century.

An industrialization process that began in the 1950s really took off during the 60s after the Central Ameri-

Photo: Mark Warschauer/*Labor Report on Central America*

Figure 5. "Salvadoran Women: In Search of Peace and Justice," by Miriam Louie and Vicki Alexander, May 1987. Discussion paper, p. 4. Creator: Miriam Louie and Vicki Alexander. Alliance Against Women's Oppression Records, Sophia Smith Collection, Smith College, Northampton, Massachusetts.

the many specific forms of oppression they face as poor people and as women. Their activism has been expressed through the broad united fronts that have developed in pitched battles with the dictatorship. Women were active in the peasant insurrection in 1932, and in the 1944 sit-down strike that led to General Martinez' ouster. In 1961,

the Fraternidad de Mujeres Salvadorenas, a member organization of the World Federation of Democratic Women, together with other organizations, helped remove Colonel Lemus from power. Women's activism reached new levels during the flow in the mass movements of the late 70s, when several of the women's organizations that are now

members of the FDR were initiated. At the same time, human rights, trade union, Christian base cooperatives, student and slumdweller organizations, all with a high proportion of female members, were launched.

The Salvadoran mass movement is characterized by a flair for organization, for base building among

---

can Common Market was formed under U.S. tutelage. The Common Market spurred an unrestricted flow of products, money and labor between Central American nations and deepened their dependency on U.S. multi-national corporations and aid. Other offshoots of the economic transformation were the dislocation of peasants in the countryside and the growth of the urban working and middle classes. By 1975, 40% of the campesinos were without land.

During the 60s and 70s workers and peasants begin to organize again. By the late 70s a plethora of militant mass organizations and coalitions of peasant, tradeunion, Christian-base community cooperatives, professional, student, slum dweller, human rights and women's groups sprang up in opposition to the military dictatorship. Most of the political/military organizations that later evolved into the Farabundo Marti Front for National Liberation (FMLN) also emerged during this period. As Duarte moved to the right, a wing of Christian Democrats, with links to many of the peasant and labor organizations supporting the party, split off in criticism of the dictatorship. These groups and others later united to form the Democratic Revolutionary Front (FDR).

Mass grievances were greeted with a hail of bullets, torture and disappearances by police and rightwing death squads. By the end of 1980 the stage was set for the eruption of civil war. Despite radical changes in Salvadoran society, the oligarchy refused to loosen its grip. However, the people were more organized and, despite repression, the oligarchy could no longer kill off the movement the way it had during La Matanza. The price of these six years of civil war now comes to more than 60,000 dead and 6,000 disappeared.

THE DUARTE PLAN

Jose Napoleon Duarte's election to the presidency in 1984 accomplished at least two things. First, it eased

President Jose Napoleon Duarte is key to the continuation of U.S. domination of El Salvador.   Photo: Time

U.S. Congressional squeamishness about sending millions in military aid to a regime responsible for thousands of disappearances and dismembered bodies strewn through the streets and garbage dumps of El Salvador. Second, as the first centrist candidate allowed to take office from the military in five decades, Duarte was supposed to win broader domestic support for the regime. He promised to stop the economic crisis, grant meaningful reforms, curb human rights abuses, and begin negotiations with the FMLN to end the war.

Having "civilianized" and "democratized" the face of the regime with Duarte, Washington's bottom line objectives were to wipe out the FMLN/FDR and strengthen the regime through an invigorated, all-sided military, political and economic approach to the war. In 1984, the year of Duarte's election, Congress approved $196.5 million military aid, equal to the total amount given during the previous three years. U.S. military and economic aid may well climb to $770 million during 1987. U.S. military strategists are working with their subordinates to up the firepower, efficiency and morale of the Salvadoran army. Utilizing lessons learned from counterinsurgency programs in Vietnam and Guatemala, they seek to destroy the mass political, economic and logistical support for the FMLN and to set up alternate structures to militarize and control the population.

Meanwhile, Duarte stonewalled peace negotiations with the FMLN/FDR at the insistence of the rightwing, who demand military victory over the FMLN. Duarte has also instituted two economic austerity packages to finance the war, placate the International Monetary Fund and stabilize the economy--all at the expense of the workers and peasants.

These policies have neither defeated the FMLN nor broken the spirit of resistance. They have, though, brought untold suffering and misery into the lives of Salvadoran women and the rest of the civilian population. •

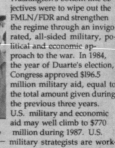

Figure 6. "Salvadoran Women: In Search of Peace and Justice," by Miriam Louie and Vicki Alexander, May 1987. Discussion paper, p. 5. Creator: Miriam Louie and Vicki Alexander. Alliance Against Women's Oppression Records, Sophia Smith Collection, Smith College, Northampton, Massachusetts.

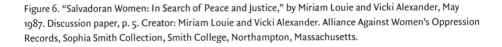

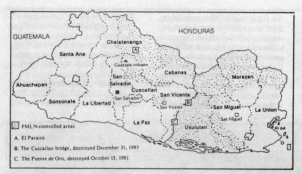

A map showing El Salvador with surrounding countries GUATEMALA and HONDURAS, marked with FMLN-controlled areas and locations.

FMLN-controlled areas

A. El Paraiso
B. The Cuscatlan bridge, destroyed December 31, 1983
C. The Puente de Oro, destroyed October 15, 1981

every possible oppressed sector, and for building broad coalitions of extremely diverse sectors and tendencies even in the midst of repression and war. Women's activism within this broad movement takes many forms. Many mass organizations have a majority female membership because they take up the issues that most impact women's lives, or they bring together a marginalized sector that mainly consists of women. As workers, mothers, campesinas, or guerilla fighters, Salvadoran women have responded to their oppression in all the ways open to them.

Women's lives, and the form of their struggles, are shaped by the war, repression and the balance of forces between the government and the opposition. At any given moment this balance is what determines the initiative that can be exercised by the mass movement as well as the specific demands and tactics required. The form and content of women's activism is impacted by where women are located, as the country, over the past several years, has been divided into three distinct areas or zones: (1) the zones under government control, especially San Salvador; (2) the areas under contention between the government and the FMLN; and (3) the zones controlled by the FMLN (see map). Women's participation in all three zones is striking, but there are several specific issues or areas in which women's activism is especially notable.

WOMEN IN THE STRUGGLE FOR HUMAN RIGHTS

Women from several human rights organizations gave testimonies at the In Search of Peace conference, including Isabel Sanchez of the Non-Governmental Human Rights Commission (CDHES), representatives of the Committee of Political Prisoners of El Salvador (COPPES) of Mariona and Ilopango prisons, and members of COMAD-RES. Women's courageous participation in the many human rights organizations stems from the particular oppression they face as women. Traditional education and social upbringing teaches a woman to feel inferior and that her role is to serve the man and the home.

The struggle of Salvadoran mothers shares a kinship with that of the heroic mothers who stood up to Pinochet in Chile, of the Mothers of the Plaza de Mayo in Argentina, and of the women of AMPRONAC, the predecessor of the Nicaraguan Women's Association(AMNLAE), that confronted the Somoza dictatorship about the deaths and disappearances of their loved ones. CO-MADRES was founded in San Salvador by twelve mothers in 1977 at the suggestion of Monsignor Oscar Romero during a Christmas eve supper. Later, he was assassinated by government death squads for speaking out against injustice, and taking the side of the poor.

COMADRES holds the Vice-Presidency of the Latin-American Federation of Associations of the Relatives of Captured-Missing Persons (FEDEFAM). There are more than 90,000 cases of forced disappearances in Latin America. FEDE-FAM includes 19 associations from various Latin American countries, and is a United Nations non-governmental organization with consultative status. El Salvador has two other family committees, the Committee of Family Members for the Freedom of Political Prisoners and Disappeared of El Salvador "Marianella Garcia Villas"

"Responding to moments of crisis and deterioration of living conditions, women participate massively; as the foundation stone of the home, they defend their families; as the ones who gave life to their children, they demand that their lives be respected.. The defense of women's traditional role is the precondition of women's mobilization: It is not easy for the regime to repress those, who, as mothers, wives, daughters, confront it in the very role which constitute the pillar and foundation of their domination."

—from "Participation of Latin American Women in Social & Political Organizations: Reflections of Salvadoran Women" by the Association of Salvadoran Women (AMES).

Figure 7. "Salvadoran Women: In Search of Peace and Justice," by Miriam Louie and Vicki Alexander, May 1987. Discussion paper, p. 6. Creator: Miriam Louie and Vicki Alexander. Alliance Against Women's Oppression Records, Sophia Smith Collection, Smith College, Northampton, Massachusetts.

(CODEFAM), and the Christian Committee of Mothers and Family Members of the Disappeared, Assassinated and Political Prisoners "Padre Octavio Ortiz-Hermana Silvia" (COMEFAC).

In 1985, Amnesty International noticed a new pattern of short-term detentions by the Salvadoran government, particularly targeting trade unionists and members of human rights organizations. This persecution has continued to date. FEDEFAM had scheduled its VII Congress to be held in El Salvador last November, but Duarte would not allow it, claiming *"This is not the right time for a human rights conference."*

We met with several mothers at the COMADRES office in San Salvador. Sitting together in a small circle we were surrounded by the pictures of their disappeared, imprisoned and assassinated family members. The mothers carry these pictures during their protests and marches. On the wall was a chart that broke down the day-to-day pattern of torture used against victims of Decree 50. Decree 50 allows military tribunals, incommunicado detention up to 15 days and legal admission of "confessions" obtained under torture. The mothers showed us photo albums of tortured corpses and lists of captured people describing their age, sex, occupation, family status, the date, place and military body that captured them and methods of torture applied. Families search through the gruesome albums and lists hoping someone has recorded the fate of their loved ones. At the end of our visit we embraced each of the women and left the office with many images flooding our hearts and minds.

Only through the meticulous debriefing of families, witnesses, victims and prisoners by the human rights organizations is it possible not only to survive the terror, help families find out what happened to their loves ones, support them in their grief, and piece together the new methods in the regime's madness, but prevent the people from becoming immobilized and defeated by the dictatorship. It is through the works of such groups as COMADRES that the Salvadoran people find the strength to continue the struggle.

This fact has not escaped the regime's attention, and has made acting as a mother's conscience perilous. The captures of COMADRES members Maria Luisa Tula and Laura Pinto are testimony to this. So is the brutal rape and murder of Dr. Marinella Garcias Villas, President of the CDHES and Vice-President of the FEDEFAM, attacked while in the countryside gathering evidence of government use of chemical weapons against the civilian population. Last year the entire leadership of the CDHES was captured and tortured after the departure of international delegations that had visited them.

Yet the mothers and families of the disappeared continue to embarrass and pressure the regime with their pictures and placards, and their demand that *"Vivos se los llevaron, vivos los queremos!"* "Alive they took them, alive we want them back!"

Figure 8. "Salvadoran Women: In Search of Peace and Justice," by Miriam Louie and Vicki Alexander, May 1987. Discussion paper, p. 7. Creator: Miriam Louie and Vicki Alexander. Alliance Against Women's Oppression Records, Sophia Smith Collection, Smith College, Northampton, Massachusetts.

WOMEN POLITICAL PRISONERS

The Women's Section of the Committee of Political Prisoners of El Salvador (COPPES) works closely with the Committees of Mothers and other human rights organizations to get news of the prisoners to the outside world. It has also won major concessions from prison authorities. Founded in September 1980, COPPES acts as the elected representative body of all the political prisoners, and has won virtual autonomy within the prison. Visiting international delegations are amazed when guards turn them over to the prisoners once inside. The COPPES arranges the daily schedule, handles disputes,

administration of Ilopango Women's Prison demanding better treatment and an end to human rights violations.

Sister Carla Barr was one of the five people allowed to enter the Ilopango Women's Prison from our delegation. Summarizing her impressions, she said:

"The women prisoners were a mixture of such courage and such strength when they could be utterly devastated because Decree 50 allows the government to pick up anyone and hold them incommunicado for 15 days. During those 15 days the women recounted such horrors, it was enough to turn your stomach. They told stories of brutality, both physical and emotional, and of rape. So many babies were born in

know'...

"If the women live through the 15 days, they will make it. Their children under 5 stay with them in the prison. They get a minimal provision for bedding and food, but nothing for medicine. If the kids get sick, you're out of luck. Such courage of these women in the prison, they organize courses for each other to keep up each other's spirits...They have a whole network of grassroots leadership."

ACTIVISM OF THE CAMPESINAS AND THE DISPLACED

In the countryside women work from sunup to sundown to grind corn for tortillas, feed, clothe and shelter their families, to secure fuel and fresh drinking water. Only 30% of the rural population have access to safe drinking water, and diseases from bad water are one of the biggest killers. Because of many men migrating to the cities in search of work, women make up a growing proportion of the rural labor force, especially in the coffee, tobacco and fish industries. Landless campesinas are employed only two or three months per year, picking coffee, tobacco or cotton with their children on the plantations, earning a third less wages than men for the same work.

Economic instability and the war have made it difficult to stabilize poor families. El Salvador has one of the lowest marriage rates in the hemisphere. It is not unusual for rural women to have eight or ten children. A large number of children are raised by single mothers. Sex education and contraception are available in the cities, but the program is promoted by the Salvadoran Population Association, headed by North American advisers whose sole antidote to social unrest in the developing world is "population control."

UNTS conference delegates visited the Calle Real Refugee Camp near San Salvador administered by

Duarte has done little to curb death squad activities, as assassins continue to target human rights activists.

collectively prepares the food shared by all, and organizes educational and social support activities for the prisoners. The women and their children rely on food, supplies, and medicines from visitors since the prison budget still only allows ten cents a day per person. Prisoners also nurse new arrivals suffering from torture, multiple rapes, and prolonged periods in clandestine prisons. In 1985, twenty-two political prisoners seized the

the prison. I think it was 18 the previous year out of 80 prisoners. What struck me most was when one woman told us, 'You know, the gringos talk with an accent. You can tell that it is a gringo, with his hood on. He didn't think that we would know where he was from but you could tell he was a gringo. And he was one of the worst ones, telling us he was going to kill our families, our children. Why he was there, who sent him, I do not

Figure 9. "Salvadoran Women: In Search of Peace and Justice," by Miriam Louie and Vicki Alexander, May 1987. Discussion paper, p. 8. Creator: Miriam Louie and Vicki Alexander. Alliance Against Women's Oppression Records, Sophia Smith Collection, Smith College, Northampton, Massachusetts.

the Catholic Church, and Tenancingo, a bombed out village in a zone of conflict just 15 miles northeast of the capital. Delegates also journeyed to Las Hojas in Sonsonate, headquarters of the National Association of Indigenous Salvadorans (ANIS), where in 1983 the military massacred 74 villagers. Recently ANIS offices were invaded and turned over to a pro-government union affiliated with the American Institute of Free Labor Development (AIFLD of the AFL-CIO). These visits clearly revealed how peasants have become the prime targets of U.S. counterinsurgency programs.

Aerial bombings of the civilian population using "scorched earth" tactics pioneered in Vietnam are driving peasants from their ancestral lands. The newest U.S. program, euphemistically called "United to Rebuild," militarizes civilian life down to the grassroots level through forced military service, local civic action units, systematic bombings of the zones sympathetic to the FMLN, and forces relocation of the civilian population. The program began with "Operation Phoenix" in January 1986 when combined military forces carried out "search and destroy" missions to drive out the people living on the Guazapa volcano.

Thirty-one percent of the entire population has been displaced by the war. An estimated 700,000 refugees live within El Salvador, with 500,000 in the U.S., and tens of thousands in Honduran refugee camps, or in Costa Rica, Mexico and Nicaragua. In El Salvador, 70% of the displaced are children, and the rest are women and old people. All live in a state of extreme deprivation and with deep emotional scars because of the brutality they have witnessed and suffered.

Maria of the Calle Real Refugee Camp told how government bombs had killed 500 villagers:

"Mothers lay dead with babies still trying to suckle from their breasts. It was so bad that some mothers prefered to kill their babies by suffocation rather than have their cries be heard by the

In El Salvador, 70% of the displaced are children, and the rest are women and old people. All live in a state of extreme deprivation and with deep emotional scars because of the brutality they have witnessed and suffered.

military and give away the hiding place."

Peasants and displaced people have both organized. Many rural women were involved in the Christian base cooperatives encouraged by the popular Church before the murder of Archbishop Romero, and are now active in peasant associations and organizations of the displaced. Rosa Ramirez, a campesina from Las Brisas Cooperative, told how the army took away three

cooperative members, calling them subversives because they wanted to go back to their native land. Other cooperative members were forced to sleep in the mountains to avoid capture.

Luisa Guadalupe Fuentes of the National Coordinating Committee for Repopulation described how her village of Antonio de Chalatenango was invaded by the army and National Guard. They captured and killed nine people, including her

Figure 10. "Salvadoran Women: In Search of Peace and Justice," by Miriam Louie and Vicki Alexander, May 1987. Discussion paper, p. 9. Creator: Miriam Louie and Vicki Alexander. Alliance Against Women's Oppression Records, Sophia Smith Collection, Smith College, Northampton, Massachusetts.

pregnant cousin with her four children. As Luisa Guadalupe watched silently from a hiding place, she heard soldiers laugh as they smashed the children's fingers, cut off the men's testicles, raped the women, beheaded the one year-old baby and cut open the stomach of her pregnant cousin, ripping out the fetus and dismembering it with their machetes. Ending her testimony, she told us:

"There are thousands and thousands of people in El Salvador who have suffered at the hands of Duarte and foreign intervention...One e thing convinces us Salvadorans to keep going, and that is international solidarity. We will struggle hand in hand, shoulder to shoulder to rid ourselves of the yoke the U.S. wants to keep on us. We hope that you will work to stop the war and tell your people that their taxes and money which is being sent by Reagan is used to kill our people."

dents said that the only aid they'd received came from the Catholic Church and the UNTS. International aid was trapped in warehouses or siphoned off by the corrupt bureaucracy. Many feared that the $50 million promised by Secretary of State Shultz for earthquake relief would be diverted into the military and private sector and never trickle down to the victims.

The UNTS moved decisively to promote the self-organization of the damnificados. Neighborhoods were encouraged to elect a *barrio junta directiva* so that equitable

and earthquake through collective efforts. Speaking on behalf of the 200,000 earthquake victims, Irene Dominguez told conference participants,

"I don't bring a written statement because pain cannot be written on a piece of paper. The earthquake left us with nothing but tragedy, with more victims in a worse situation. What are the causes of the social injustices? It is the war. I know about what is going on with the aid...there is a question I would have liked to ask Mr. President had he been here. Where is our food, our clothing? Don't you hear the cries of our children? How can you call yourself a government? The damnificados demand more food, more than inhuman housing because they believe that not only the upper class and the military are Salvadorans. I would like for our brothers and sisters to take this message back home so that sometime we can find an answer to these questions, to these problems, and find a way to get the peace that we want so much."

Salvadoran women have a long and proud legacy of militant trade union organizing.
Photo: Mark Warschauer/*Labor Report on Central America*

WOMEN OF THE BARRIOS AND OF THE DAMNIFICADOS

The devastating earthquake that rocked El Salvador last October 10 created 200,000 victims and destroyed 80% of the housing in San Salvador. It also increased misery in the slums of the poor and displaced, and brought the atmosphere of war and destruction into the heart of the capital. We visited some of the neighborhoods most heavily affected by the earthquake, such as San Jacinto. Resi-

distribution plans could be developed. Committees are functioning in 86 neighborhoods representing 114,000 people. An estimated 50% of the participants in the November 22 march were from the newly organized barrios.

Some of the barrios have historical links to the slum dweller organizations of the 70s. Like the women of the shantytowns of Santiago, Chile and in the Black townships of South Africa, women play a central role in the organization of the "tugurios" or slumdwellers. Activists hope to form Committees of Women to lessen the impact of war

WOMEN OF THE TRADE UNION MOVEMENT

Because of the abominable conditions in the countryside, women often migrate to the cities. Many become street vendors, as seen by the fact that 33.5% of female workers are self-employed. Taking their children with them, they search for a space on the street to sell their goods, and are extorted and jailed by the police. Other unskilled

Figure 11. "Salvadoran Women: In Search of Peace and Justice," by Miriam Louie and Vicki Alexander, May 1987. Discussion paper, p. 10. Creator: Miriam Louie and Vicki Alexander. Alliance Against Women's Oppression Records, Sophia Smith Collection, Smith College, Northampton, Massachusetts.

women work as domestics for long hours and little pay, subject to abuse and sexual harassment by their male employers.

In 1980 an estimated 206,124 women worked as domestics for middle and upper class families. Women also work in handicraft centers making clothes and shoes in cottage industry style conditions for low wages. Before the civil war broke out, women worked in the garment, food processing and electronics industries of the "Free Trade Zone". Transnational corporations, such as Texas Instruments, Maidenform, and ARIS were allowed to operate free from taxes and union organizing, exploiting Salvadoran women's labor as another link in of the "global assembly line" of women workers that stretches from Latin America and the Caribbean to Asia to "Silicon Valley" in California.

During the late 70s women workers increased their activism in the militant trade union movement. In 1979 women workers from Fabrica Medusa in the Free Trade Zone took over the factory when the company tried to close shop and return to the U.S. This example was then followed by women workers at the Diana, Confiteria Americana, Delicia factory and then at Pan Lido.

In 1979 the Association of Market Vendors and Workers (ASUTRAMES) was formed to unite the women market vendors of the barrios of San Jacinto, Modelo and the Central Market of San Salvador. These tough fighters succeeded in winning many of their demands during spirited strikes and marketplace occupations.

Women with the privilege of an education are mainly employed as secretaries, salesclerks, nurses and teachers, all jobs considered to be "women's work," and all getting less pay than their male counterparts. However, strikes by the National Association of Salvadoran Teachers (ANDES), 85% of whose members are women, have played an important role in the resurgence of the Salvadoran trade union movement. Despite tremendous repression, ANDES continues to play a leading

40% of the national budget goes to the war machine, while workers and peasants foot the bill through wage freezes and higher taxes.

The UNTS has staged massive demonstrations against Duarte's austerity policies and his continuation of the war.
Photo: Ivan Montecinos

role in the UNTS.

Elizabeth "Febe" Velasquez, the woman heading the powerful Union of Textile Industry Workers (STITAS) delivered the UNTS report on the current situation of Salvadoran workers. She criticized Duarte's first social austerity *paquetazo* (packet), in which 40% of the national budget goes to the war machine, while workers and peasants foot the bill through wage freezes and higher taxes. Febe herself was recently captured and tortured by the regime last July. She was only released after intense pressure by her Salvadoran fellow workers and international unions, including U.S. trade unionists.

Around the city we saw "*Libertad Para Febe!*" spray painted on the walls. In a clear message to the regime that the trade union movement refuses to be intimidated, Febe was promoted on her release to general secretary of FENASTRAS, a union federation within the UNTS.

At the conference, Febe testified, "*I would like to tell you what it is truly like in our country, for anyone who talks to the workers, who tells the truth. From that moment on their destiny is guaranteed. If they are lucky, they get a ticket to government prisons. For the unlucky, for the 60,000 dead and disappeared, it means death.*"

WOMEN IN THE ZONES OF CONTROL

Several women's organizations were formed during the mass upsurge of the late 70s to increase women's activism in the overall struggle and to fight for the specific rights of women. In 1984 representatives of six women's organizations came together to develop the Constitutive Committee of the Federation of Salvadoran Women. These organizations also belong to the FDR, and include:

Figure 12. "Salvadoran Women: In Search of Peace and Justice," by Miriam Louie and Vicki Alexander, May 1987. Discussion paper, p. 11. Creator: Miriam Louie and Vicki Alexander. Alliance Against Women's Oppression Records, Sophia Smith Collection, Smith College, Northampton, Massachusetts.

> "Reports from rebel-controlled zones note a major effort to change sex roles. Men cook and wash clothes; and women fight, direct economic development projects, and do construction work. Women are routinely put in command positions, and not surprisingly that has created problems when men are commanded by women for the first time. The rebels' commitment to the issue is indicated by their devoting a page of the literacy primer to the status of women as well as their coining the phrase, `A real revolutionary is a man who doesn't beat his wife.' So far, one stumbling block in sexual equality has been tortilla making. Reports indicate that it has remained a female task."
>
> --from El Salvador in Crisis, by Philip L. Russell

- Association of Women of El Salvador (AMES)
- Progressive Women's Association of El Salvador (AMPES)
- Unified Committee of Salvadoran Women (CUMS)
- Salvadoran Women's Association (ASUMUSA)
- Salvadoran Women's Association "Lil Milagro Ramirez" (AMS-LMR)
- Organization of Salvadoran Women for Peace (ORMUSA)

Especially since the civil war, any association with the FMLN/FDR runs the risk of certain death. The women's organizations work primarily in the zones controlled by the FMLN, where a pro-people, pro-women program can be implemented. Women's associations are represented in the Local Popular Governments elected by villagers to coordinate housing, health, production, education and self-defense.

The women's organizations also bring news of Salvadoran women's struggles to international women. For example, members of the Constitutive Committee of the Federation of Salvadoran Women spoke on panels at the United Nations Decade of Women Forum in Nairobi, Kenya in 1985. They also have offices in major cities in the U.S., Mexico, Canada, and Western Europe.

Women's work in the zones of control has suffered some setbacks since

the U.S. and Salvadoran military began massive aerial bombing of the civilian population to destroy the FMLN's base. In 1984 the FMLN

FMLN women in the zones of control take up defense, production, education and other necessary tasks.
Photo: ALERT

made a strategic shift to thwart U.S. plans. Decreasing its obvious presense in the zones of control, the FMLN has dispersed its forces into smaller battalions and accelerated the integration of the people into clandestine militia and guerrilla units. The recent FMLN operation against the El Paraiso military garrison is a clear example of the

strength and effectiveness of these new tactics. The women's organizations have adapted their work accordingly.

Women's work also extends to combat. Women play a leading role in the rank and file of the FMLN/FDR. Approximately 40% of the commanders of the People's Revolutionary Army are women. In recent years special training courses have been offered to women joining FMLN military ranks. Some areas now have all-woman squadrons and militias. Commandante Ileana of the Fuerzas Armadas de Liberacion (FAL) heads the all-woman Sylvia Battalion which forced the retreat of crack U.S.-trained battalions in February 1982.

Women active in the FMLN/FDR are products of the teacher, student, peasant, trade union and slumd-weller movements of the 70s. The women of the FMLN represent all sectors of Salvadoran society, and many have made the ultimate sacrifice in the struggle against the dictatorship--they have given their lives for the future of their people.

One of those is Dr. Melida Anaya Montes, who headed the ANDES during the stormy years leading to

Figure 13. "Salvadoran Women: In Search of Peace and Justice," by Miriam Louie and Vicki Alexander, May 1987. Discussion paper, p. 12. Creator: Miriam Louie and Vicki Alexander. Alliance Against Women's Oppression Records, Sophia Smith Collection, Smith College, Northampton, Massachusetts.

the civil war. Affectionately known as Comandante Ana Maria, she also played a leading role in forging together trade unions and peasant organizations into the People's Revolutionary Block (BPR), a mass organization. As second in command of the Popular Forces of Liberation (FPL), one of the organizations of the FMLN-FDR, she was a key strategist of the Salvadoran liberation struggle, and a dedicated promoter of unity in the FMLN-FDR.

Lilian Mercedes Letona, "Comandante Clelia," was a leader of one of the organizations of the FMLN. Neither capture, torture nor imprisonment were enough to stop this courageous woman. In 1981 she led a hunger strike of political prisoners to demand improvement in the treatment of prisoners. She was finally stopped by a bullet in combat.

Lil Milagros Ramirez was a teacher and leader of the National Resistance(RN), an organization of the FMLN-FDR. Government troops "disappeared" her in 1967 and held her for years in one of the many clandestine jails of El Salvador. She was raped, beaten, starved, and forced to undergo medically unattended abortions. She was finally assassinated by her jailers.

Women like "Comandante Susa-

Comandante Ana Maria is one of many FMLN women who have given their lives to the struggle.

Photo: Christian Poveda

na" continue to carry out their work, despite tremendous sacrifices. Both Comandante Susana's brother and sister were killed by the regime. Her parents, living in exile, did not know for years whether their remaining daughter was alive or dead. It was only on reading a newspaper interview with her and two other women combatants in charge of a liberated zone that they found out she was alive and well.

DUARTE'S ISOLATION, REAGAN'S CONTRAGATE AND OUR RESPONSIBILITY

The UNTS conference and subsequent events show that the Duarte/Reagan project is unraveling. Duarte was supposed to deliver social support to the oligarchy and open up the pipeline of military aid from a U.S. Congress that had grown squeamish about the trail of corpses left by rightwing death squads. Yet reliance on U.S. counterinsurgency and economic austerity programs have not won the war, brought economic recovery nor satisfied popular demands for reform. Duarte has even lost the oligarchy's support, heightening the possibility of another rightwing coup. In January, conservative businessmen led a 90% effective one-day work stoppage to protest the second economic package. Rightwing parties have also led boycotts of the National Assembly in order to strengthen their hand in the regime's crisis.

The FMLN/FDR issued another peace proposal last July that calls on all social sectors and parties to negotiate a peaceful political settlement and to initiate a govern-

Training of local militias in the zones of control.

Figure 14. "Salvadoran Women: In Search of Peace and Justice," by Miriam Louie and Vicki Alexander, May 1987. Discussion paper, p. 13. Creator: Miriam Louie and Vicki Alexander. Alliance Against Women's Oppression Records, Sophia Smith Collection, Smith College, Northampton, Massachusetts.

ment of broad participation. The UNTS, representing the broadest popular coalition, has now added its powerful voice to the call for a peaceful negotiated settlement to the war, an end to human rights violations, and an end to U.S. military aid and interference.

Without massive U.S. support, the Salvadoran oligarchy and military could not continue its dictatorship over the majority of Salvadorans who want peace. But a pro-U.S. regime in El Salvador is central to U.S. strategy in Central America. Since the days of the Monroe Doctrine, the U.S. has considered Central America its "backyard," and used economic blackmail and military force to ensure that it remains so. After the Nicaraguan people's triumph against Somoza in 1979, the

Reagan Administration was determined not to let another Latin nation slip out of its clutches. Military advisors, sophisticated aerial weaponry, bombs, chemical weapons, and billions in military aid were pumped into El Salvador. Honduras was transformed into a giant base to launch military aggression against the people of Nicaragua and the progressive forces of EL Salvador. Guatemala was earlier "pacified" in an attempt to surgically silence the dissent of its largely indigenous population.

For the past several years the American public has been bombarded with Reagan's diatribes accusing Nicaragua of being a "terrorist state", supposedly arming the Salvadoran rebels and acting as a base for Soviet and Cuban intervention in

Central America. With the downing of the plane loaded with U.S. arms for the contras, the testimony of mercenary Eugene Hasenfus and now the revelations of the Iran/Contragate scandal, the true story of what is going on in Central America has turned out to be the opposite of the official White House version. Instead of the Soviet-Cuban-Nicaraguan-FMLN conspiracy, we now have "smoking gun" evidence of the Reagan-National Security Council-CIA-Contra conspiracy which extensively uses military facilities in El Salvador and Honduras to carry out its attacks against Nicaragua.

Between Duarte's isolation in El Salvador and the cracks in Reagan's "teflon coating" as a result of the Iran/Contragate scandal we now have a new opportunity to stop U.S. aid to the contras and the Salvadoran regime. As women we must join the rest of the anti-intervention movement in organizing to pressure Congress to cut off aid.

We must take every opportunity to make connections between our struggles and those of our Salvadoran sisters. There is much to share. As mothers, we identify with the tears and anger of Salvadoran mothers who are fighting the dictatorship because of the loss of their precious loved ones. As women of color and the descendants of indigenous people, slaves and immigrants, we share the fate of Salvadoran refugee and displaced women who have been driven from their native lands by the war and U.S. counter-insurgency programs.

Women working in low-paying, dead-end jobs in the U.S. can identify with the struggles of Salvadoran women trade unionists, be they teachers, garment workers or market vendors. As we struggle for decent housing, healthcare and nutrition in the U.S., our work links us to our Salvadoran sisters active in organizations of slumdwellers, unemployed and earthquake victims. Religious women of all faiths, while continuing to provide sanctuary for Central American and other refugees, can deepen the ties with Sal-

U.S. military advisor training a Salvadoran soldier. U.S. military aid to El Salvador amounts to more than $1.5 million per day. Photo: Philippot-Sygma

Figure 15. "Salvadoran Women: In Search of Peace and Justice," by Miriam Louie and Vicki Alexander, May 1987. Discussion paper, p. 14. Creator: Miriam Louie and Vicki Alexander. Alliance Against Women's Oppression Records, Sophia Smith Collection, Smith College, Northampton, Massachusetts.

vadoran women by pressuring the Church to stand unwaveringly for justice.

Those of us working for women's rights in the U.S. are fully united with the efforts of the Salvadoran women's organizations devoted to integrating women into the struggle for peace, justice, and equality. As the relatives, friends, and lovers of the young men who died as cannon fodder in the jungles of Vietnam, we will not allow more youth to kill or be killed by our brothers and sisters in Central America. As poor and working women, we can see better ways of using our tax money than to send $1.5 million per day to El Salvador to perfect the methods of killers, rapists and torturers of women and children.

Speaking tours, material aid projects, Congressional lobbying, mass rallies and marches, postcard and telegram campaigns to release po-

litical prsioners -- we must employ these tactics and more to help bring peace and justice to El Salvador. A long struggle lies ahead. The U.S. government and Salvadoran oligarchy stubbornly refuse to "let El Salvador go" from the dictatorship to the people, from domination and repres-

sion to self-determination and liberation. But our Salvadoran sisters are organized now in every sector, and there is no turning back. Our responsibility is to match the level of organization they have achieved, under difficult conditions, with our own to stop U.S. intervention in El Salvador and win peace in Central America. •

In writing this paper, in addition to testimonies and interviews from the "In Search For Peace" Conference, we also drew information from a number of excellent sources.

1. Women and War - El Salvador, Women's International Resource Exchange (WIRE), 2700 Broadway, NY, NY 10025. An excellent new book published by ZED Press.
2. "La Mujer y la Revolucion en El Salvador," El Salvador, Informacion y Analisis Politico, Vol. 1, March/April 1986.
3. Women of El Salvador, The Price of Freedom, Marilyn Thompson, Institute for the Study of Human Issues, 1986.
4. Fact Sheet, El Salvador, by SHARE Foundation, P.O. Box 53372, Washington, D.C. 20009, September, 1986.
5. "El Salvador Revisited: Why Duarte is in Trouble," by Kenneth E. Sharpe. From the World Policy Journal, Summer, 1986.
6. El Salvador in Crisis, Philip L. Russell, Colorado River Press, 1984.
7. El Salvador's Link, P.O. Box 11555, Madison Square Station, New York, NY 10159.

Other Publications Featuring El Salvador include:

1. NACLA Report on the Americas, 151 W. 19th St., NY, NY 10011.
2. Alert!, Committee in Solidarity with the People of El Salvador (CISPES), P.O. Box 50139, Washington, D.C. 20004.
3. For Peace and Solidarity, P.O. Box 20555, Oakland, CA 94620.
4. Labor Report on Central America, P.O. Box 28014, Oakland, CA 94604.
5. El Salvador, The Face of Revolution, Robert Armstrong

and Janet Shank, South End Press, 1982.

For those who want to hook up with different groups in this country doing solidarity work with the women of El Salvador, there are both Salvadoran groups with offices in this country, as well as organizations of North Americans. A partial listing is provided below:

Salvadoran groups include:

1. COMADRES is an independent organization of more than 500 Salvadoran women, established in order to support the mothers and relatives of persons captured, disappeared, or assasinated for political motives. P.O. Box 21299, Washington, D.C. 20009.

2. Constitutive Committee of the Federation of Salvadoran Women is a committee that unites six Salvadoran women's organizations with the FDR.

North American groups (primarily focused on women) include:
1. Somos Hermanas, National Office, 3543 - 18th Street, San Francisco, CA 94110.

2. MADRE is a friendship association between women and mothers in the U.S. and Central America. MADRE organizes material aid campaigns and frequent fact-finding delegations. 853 Broadway, #301, New York, NY 10003.

3. Woman to Woman organizes campaigns to support the women of El Salvador and Nicaragua. 5825 Telegraph Ave., Box A, Oakland, CA 94609.

Figure 16. "Salvadoran Women: In Search of Peace and Justice," by Miriam Louie and Vicki Alexander, May 1987. Discussion paper, p. 15. Creator: Miriam Louie and Vicki Alexander. Alliance Against Women's Oppression Records, Sophia Smith Collection, Smith College, Northampton, Massachusetts.

Somos Hermanas
National Office / Bay Area:
3543 - 18th St., Box 18
San Francisco, CA 94110

Bulk Rate
U.S. Postage
PAID
Permit No. 10579
San Francisco, CA

ADDRESS CORRECTION REQUESTED

The Alliance Against Women's Oppression / Somos Hermanas is a sponsored project of the San Francisco Women's Building / Women's Center.

Figure 17. "Salvadoran Women: In Search of Peace and Justice," by Miriam Louie and Vicki Alexander, May 1987. Discussion paper, p. 16. Creator: Miriam Louie and Vicki Alexander. Alliance Against Women's Oppression Records, Sophia Smith Collection, Smith College, Northampton, Massachusetts.

Tara Daly

Claudia Coca's Chola Power
Pop Art as Decolonial Critique

Abstract: This essay showcases the work of Claudia Coca, a contemporary pop artist from Lima, Peru whose paintings and drawings critique the links between race, gender, and class in a decolonial, transnational frame. First, the essay explores the way Coca celebrates the Peruvian chola by presenting herself as an empowered subject instead of as an insulted object in her paintings. While the term chola has historically been used derogatorily, Coca reappropriates her chola identity and reclaims it as her own, consequently subverting its prejudicial, racist origins. Second, the essay studies the critiques she performs of the "afterlives of colonialism" on the natural and cultural environment in her most recent series of drawings from 2017. She demonstrates that not only human bodies, but other natural materials are tangled up with the project of cultural colonization. Throughout the article, the work of Chela Sandoval is drawn on to argue that Coca practices an oppositional aesthetic that makes sensible the perspectives of subjects whose voices and bodies have been disparaged instead of valued within an uneven global capitalist system.

Claudia Coca is a contemporary artist and activist from Peru whose pop art makes visible the gender, race, and class differences that adversely impact daily life in and beyond Lima. Figure 1 initially captivates viewers with its enticing cartoon appearance and its buoyant blue colors: the azure sky and the indigo streaks in the subject's hair. The female in the image is a representation of Coca herself: youthful, healthy, in a patterned blouse, and with a hip hairstyle. Her mouth is slightly open, as if she is on the verge of responding to something or someone, contributing to the viewer's

MERIDIANS · feminism, race, transnationalism   18:2 October 2019
DOI: 10.1215/15366936-7775773 © 2019 Smith College

Figure 1. *Strange Fruit*, 2007

curiosity. The flat depth to the image lends a contemporary feel to it, add-
ing to the lightness of the mood it sets, which is initially enhanced by the
jaunty music notation to the right of the subject. Yet, once viewers are
drawn into the image, the original levity of the bright palette and the starry
night fade into the background. Viewers quickly see that the protagonist is
either listening to, or recalling internally, the lyrics to "Strange Fruit," the
most haunted of songs about slavery, lynching, and the eerie images associated with both. The subject of the painting's eyes well with tears, indi-
cating a sadness or bewilderment. Her hair, which previously seemed to
move in an innocuous wind, becomes sinister when juxtaposed with the
same "breeze" of the "Strange Fruit" lyrics. Coca's borrowing of the
"Strange Fruit" lyrics is complex. She appropriates the lyrics but invents;
she repeats but with difference; and she visualizes inferred alliances

between women across geographic, racial, and temporal boundaries through her transnational reference to Billie Holiday, the poplar trees, and the deep historical violence that emanates from an otherwise accessible portrait. The tension between a digestible medium and an uncanny message about historical violence is where the power of her art lies. She jars viewers to consider the layers of social injustices that underlie the shiny screens of late capitalism.

This image is the synthesis of a complex politics of representation, repetition, and difference that conditioned its existence. Billie Holiday's song is in fact already a few times removed from its "original" source. Holiday, born in 1915, "did not write 'Strange Fruit,' as she claimed in her unreliable but immensely readable memoir, Lady Sings the Blues. But she made it her own" (Als 2001: xvi). "Strange Fruit" has been described as a song about "the deepest shame of racist America," and Holiday first sang it in 1939 in New York, when she was on the verge of entering Café Society (Margolick 2001: 6). The "song," however, was not "hers." It was written by a Jewish schoolteacher from New York City, Abel Meeropol, who wrote under the pen name "Lewis Allan." As Meeropol recounts it, he came across a photograph of a particularly ghastly lynching in a civil rights magazine that haunted him for days. So he wrote a poem about it, one that the Communist journal The New Masses agreed to publish in early 1936 but that first saw print—as "Bitter Fruit"—in the January 1937 issue of the New York Teacher, a union publication (Margolick 2001: 21). This backstory serves to demonstrate the way that class and race issues as well as Jewish and black identity intersected well before Coca's own reframing of intersectionality in her pop art.[1]

The lyrics Coca includes in her image stand in for the violence the African American population endured in the United States under slavery but simultaneously refer to the legacies of slavery in Peru, which occurred from the sixteenth century to its official abolishment in 1854. Coca intertwines at least two different histories in the same image. She designs the Billie Holiday image to link disparate moments in history, spaces, and bodies in order to engage with broader questions of continuities and discontinuities in contemporary local and global decolonial artistic movements. Her work counters the glossing over of historical violence and serves instead as a witness to the persistence of racism and its legacies as the foundation upon which nations have been constructed. Additionally, by using her own body as a starting point, she draws attention to the material conditions that differentiate subjects and the ways in which the "marked" body can be a site of connection between dominated subjects, women being one such group.

Coca's feminist intervention recalls decolonial theorist Chela Sandoval's work. Sandoval has made the case that while 1968 served as a landmark year for Western feminism, after 1968 new alliances formed that were differentiated by nation, ethnicity, race, gender, and class, but that were still "allied nonetheless by their similar sociohistorical, racial, and colonial relationships to dominant powers" (Sandoval 1998: 355–56). While Frederic Jameson has theorized that during the postmodern era, an "oppositional" subject to hegemonic norms no longer exists because postmodernity results in a shattering of "the original" or "the normative," Sandoval builds on but challenges Jameson's arguments, demonstrating that due to third world social movements and women of color feminisms, an oppositional consciousness to Jameson's reading of history had already developed out of the 1968 context and continues to evolve as a creative, mutating pattern of differentiation vis-à-vis hegemonic forms of history (Sandoval 2000: 104–5). Likewise, decolonial feminist theorist María Lugones writes that at the core of the movement toward women of color feminisms is a shift from a logic of oppression to a logic of resistance. She writes: "As Women of Color we need to emphasize intersectional subject positions and the superimposition of both intersecting and intermeshing oppressions as we work towards the formation of bridges that transform less complex resistant circles into polymorphous affiliations" (Lugones 2014: 80).

Coca, Meeropol, Holiday, and Sandoval—while very different—share a common outsider status to their trade: art, culture, music, and theory. But it is out of these differences that a creative oppositional consciousness can emerge from collective practices of resistance. This first image incites us to think about potential alliances between oppressed subjects as they navigate transnational spaces as part of a broader decolonial feminist aesthetic. Historically, the racial, gendered, sexual, and class "other" to the white, male, heterosexual subject has not been he, she, or they who perceive(s), but instead, he, she, or they who is or are perceived. Coca's art prompts transnational alliances between oppressed subjects by linking disparate historical moments through a recognizable and accessible artistic form. Coca's alluring art enables viewers to access an oppositional consciousness under the "neocolonial postmodern" conditions that shape chola subjects in the Americas as they live with the legacies of physical wars and their ongoing psychological impacts.[2]

Collective Action and Popular Protest

Claudia Coca was born in Lima, Peru in 1970 to a working-class family and grew up with a relative set of privileges—especially with regards to education—to which the average citizen does not have access.[3] Although she did not consider art as a career path early on, she eventually went on to study art formally at the School of Fine Arts in Lima (Escuela de Bellas Artes). There, she made connections within the art world and learned about the more formal and theoretical aspects of art history. Coca was in the midst of taking art classes during the most politically unstable period of Peru's recent history: the years of the internal war (1980–2000), a period that would shape the first phase of her work. To briefly summarize, in 1980 the terrorist Maoist group Shining Path (Sendero Luminoso), under the leadership of Abimael Guzmán, initiated an invasive and violent campaign that began in Ayacucho (about nine hours southeast from Lima by bus) and spread outward in all directions. During the nearly twenty-year period of internal guerrilla warfare that plagued Peru, a latent racism bubbled up to the surface and pervaded the nation, contributing to a contentious political divide in Lima about how to most effectively resolve the situation.

By 1991, Shining Path had control of most of the Ayacucho region and was increasingly encroaching upon the outskirts of Lima. Many people, especially indigenous peasants, were forced from their homes in the highlands to the periphery of the city to escape the violence. This influx of indigenous peoples to Lima resulted in renewed racial and class awareness in an already diverse city as demographic changes due to the war affected everything from the economy to housing to public safety. By the end of the conflict, an estimated sixty thousand people had been killed and another ten thousand disappeared.[4] As Laurietz Seda has observed, because the most impacted were poor indigenous people and peasants who were largely displaced, it is clear that race played and continues to play a role in the tragedy that was the civil war.[5] Recognizing the racial component to the war, the official obfuscation of the role of the Peruvian military in the violence, and the initial denial of a thorough investigation, many activists, artists, and everyday citizens took issue with what some perceived as public indifference toward the internal conflict. Coca and a group of her peers chose to confront the complicity of such indifference, a testament to her and their ethical commitment to art that catalyzes reflection and prompts action in the name of those disappeared.[6]

When we talked about this period in an interview I conducted with her, Coca explained: "When I started in the Fine Arts department officially in 1989, the university was going through a period of political cleansing because of supposed groups of students that followed Shining Path. When I first began studying, no one really even talked about politics anymore. But then, we began to talk and hear about potential overthrows of the State and of the Constitution. By the 1995 elections, my work was being colored by all that I was seeing."[7] It was from this charged climate of fear and with the desire to raise national and transnational awareness of the situation in Peru that the Colectivo Sociedad Civil (CSC) coalesced and responded to the aforementioned political and military violence as it continued into the late 1990s under Alberto Fujimori's ten-year regime (1990–2000). The CSC, initially made up of art students, began to crystallize in 2000, before the April 9 presidential elections. It was then, on the night of the elections, that

> Armed with veils, black ropes, crucifixes and even a coffin in the center, a group of folks from the plastic arts community including Susana Torres, Gustavo Buntinx, Emilio Santiestevan, Claudia Coca, Jorge Salazar, Abel Valdivia, Luis García Zapatero, Sandro Venturo, and Natalia Iguiñiz acted out the burial of the ONPE (National Office of Electoral Processes) in a solemn ceremony that, in front of the Palace of Justice, marked the death of Fujimori's regime. . . . This first performance marked the emergence of the Civil Society Collective that, over the course of the next few months, would have an unprecedented political impact. (Vich 2008)

The left-leaning population of the community in Lima was incensed with the corrupt "politics as usual" under Alberto Fujimori and the reality that the government was not doing enough to investigate the pervasive violence of the past ten years.[8] The general consensus among the Left was that Fujimori's dictatorship would continue, regardless of the semblance of elections, because of entrenched corruption. Therefore, as a response to a seemingly intractable political atmosphere, the CSC strategized and subsequently occupied highly visible public spaces, like the Plaza de Armas in Lima, with the goal of raising public awareness and reanimating civil society as a political agent.

As a founding member of the collective, Coca and the approximately ten other core members initiated a national movement to stimulate a collective "washing" of the Peruvian flag. Well covered by the media, the "Wash the

Flag" ("Lava la bandera") event was first performed during the Democracy Fair, May 20–21, 2000 in the centrally located Campo de Marte. This ritual act aimed to metaphorically cleanse Peru's collective conscience of past mistakes. For example, one of the posters announcing the event read: "Bring your flag for a ritual of electoral cleansing."[9] After the success of the event in the Campo de Marte, on May 24 the CSC revived the event, this time in the Plaza de Armas of Lima, and without the safety of being diffused as part of the multifaceted Democracy Fair. The flag-cleansing event was not confined to Lima, but spread to many different parts of Peru, and to diasporic Peruvian communities.[10] The event was so simple both in action and message that it reignited a participatory politics in Peru's civil society. Due to the first event's success, when Fujimori fled Peru in November 2000, the CSC initiated another flag-centered event that brought people together in the Plaza de Armas, the central hub of the Peruvian government, to sew together a massive black-and-white flag that symbolized the number of civilian deaths at the hands of the Peruvian government. This event was described by one local newspaper as a symbolic act to compensate for the harm inflicted on thousands of Peruvians during the past decade. This second event also served to push the government to form the Truth and Reconciliation Commission and undertake a systematic investigation into the events of 1980–2000. The final report of the Truth and Reconciliation Committee was made public on August 28, 2003 (see TRCP 2003).

In the performance art produced by the Civil Society Collective, the line between politics and art, aesthetics and ethics was purposefully blurred via the actions of ordinary citizens. As a result of this conjuncture, a collective subject emerged that was concerned with the obligation that a community and its government have to reconcile the violence of the past, and has catalyzed a turn toward remembering. The tactic used by the group demonstrated the power of taking up public space in a peaceful, participatory way, to help embody an oppositional movement and consciousness within the nation and transnationally to Peruvians around the globe who came to form alliances in opposition to both Shining Path and the state military at once. This example of an oppositional aesthetic project speaks to the power of collective action via a peaceful act built on love and respect for difference within a nation. It also was a display of the rights of citizens to remember violent histories in order to potentially avoid their repetition in the future.

"I Am Not Your Chola": Self-Portraits and *Cholaje*

I was initially struck by Coca's work when I was in Lima a number of years ago. While there, I visited the National University of San Marcos, chartered in 1551, where I saw her retrospective exhibit, *Revelada e Indeleble* (*Revealed and Indelible*), an assemblage of works she completed between 2001–11.[11] This exhibit combined works she produced in her earlier exhibits about race, gender, and beauty including *Que tal raza* (2002), *Peruvian Beauty* (2004, with Susana Torres) and *Globo Pop* (2007), and reflected her trajectory since her work with the CSC. The work that Coca did as part of the CSC led to her direct engagement with race and gendered social inequities, which prompted her to interrogate her own identity in a body of work involving self-portraits, a theme that carried through her work until the 2007 exhibit. When I asked her about the incorporation of herself into her art, Coca explained that "suddenly with the self-portrait genre, I could filter my social and political discourse. I began to say things myself, without intermediaries. . . . People identify with it. . . . 'She experiences the same things that I do' or 'she thinks like I do,' they comment" (Gonzales and Coca 2011). Coca's use of self-representation enables her to connect to people through empathy, and to avoid speaking "for" others, but rather as herself alongside peers. In that *Revelada e indeleble* exhibit, I was able to see a key part of the evolution of her work, specifically around the theme of race, particularly as it functions in Peru under the terms of *mestizaje* and *cholaje*.

In their recent article, one of the most significant critical pieces on Coca, Mihaela Radulescu de Barrio de Mendoza and Rosa Gonzales Mendiburu trace the way that Coca uses self-portrait to link her body to "mestizaje, hybridity, and transculturation" within a Latin American context. As they interpret it, "La obra de Claudia Coca define el racismo como un problema estructural de la sociedad peruana, cuyo origen se da en la época de la Colonia, pero al mismo tiempo ubica al 'otro,' en términos generales, en el campo de la exclusión con respecto a los códigos de la sociedad" [Claudia Coca's works defines racism as a structural problem in Peruvian society, whose origin takes root during the colonial era, but at the same time locates the "other," in general terms, in a field of exclusion with respect to the codes of society]. They go on to observe that when Coca recognizes herself as a mestiza, she questions stereotypes and the internal racism that plagues a subject who does not conform to a racial ideal portrayed in popular media (Radulescu de Barrio de Mendoza and Gonzales Mendiburu

2016: 60). In works like *Mestiza*, which shows Coca as an elegant woman in heels with straightened loose hair, next to another version of herself with a much simpler dress, flat shoes, and braids, she speaks to stereotypes associated with ways of dressing matched to race: the elegant version of self is the same as the braided version, but on the surface, almost seems like a different person. Both versions of Coca stare out at us with a penetrating gaze, seemingly daring the viewer to challenge either one of these persons. Coca's juxtaposition of these two versions of self emphasizes duality or multiplicity *as* identity, not as problems to be resolved.[12]

While Radulescu de Barrio de Mendoza and Gonzales Mendiburu describe Coca's work under the rubric of *mestizaje* and hybridity, Coca also uses the term *cholo/a* to describe her and other Peruvians' identity. As she explains in an interview in *La República* about her exhibit *Mejorando la raza* (*Improving the Race*, 2000), it grew out of "the popular jargon: it is better to get married to a gringo. That way of growing up, it's very common, from which the Peruvian begins to marginalize other Peruvians. The cholo is the other, that's a way of putting ourselves down. That chip is so ingrained that we're afraid to recognize ourselves as Andean." Coca goes on to explain that because she was raised to deny her indigenous blood, "I did not perceive myself as chola. In high school, I felt ugly because people made me feel it or note this difference in various ways, and it turns out, that wasn't how it was; in reality, I was chola" (Gonzales and Coca 2011). It is in response to that feeling and the recognition of their chola identity that Coca and Susana Torres, a fellow member of the CSC, coproduced the installation *Peruvian Beauty*, with the intent of "taking on the theme of the ideals of beauty that we did not meet" (Gonzales and Coca 2011). The exhibit emphasizes the subjective nature of beauty and with its English-language title also insinuates the ways that products and images from the outside can influence self-perception in Peru. The exhibit is an ironic take on the way that standards of beauty have been constructed in visual art, whether via formal art or popular practices. In order to critique the types of women painted by canonical male artists, the exhibit consisted of a series of diptychs, or side-by-side images, that revised recognizable paintings of male "masters" from abroad and within Peru with an ironic twist.

As one example, in the painting *Après Durero*, Coca reinterprets Albrecht Dürer's etching *The Four Witches* (1497) and Peter Paul Rubens's *The Three Graces* (1639). In Coca's version of the original, the three female "graces" or "witches" are painted in sepia tones that recall late nineteenth- and early

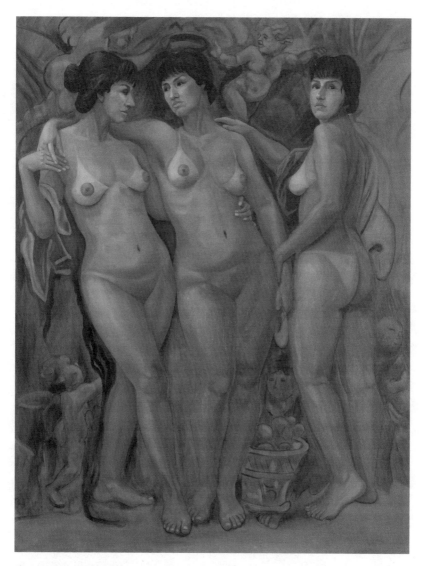

Figure 2. *Aprés Durero*, 2002

twentieth-century photographs and travelogues that visually represented indigenous peoples as objects of the anthropologists' gaze. However, this time, Coca has turned the lens around by representing herself as the three graces, thus subverting the dynamic between the object of the painting, the subject in the painting, and the painter herself. Coca alters Dürer according to her own way of seeing, providing a new perspective on an entrenched image within the art canon. Because Coca chooses herself as artistic muse, she eliminates the power dynamic between "painter" and "painted," or anthropologist and object of study, by collapsing the two and flipping the relationship between outsider and insider and the directionality of the male gaze. In the figuration farthest to the right, "she" gazes steadfastly out, challenging the viewer to see her as she is also caught seeing. The way that she distorts the original for her own use is part of her tactical methodology of referencing multiple historical moments at once and gesturing toward an established art canon while reinventing it as she goes.

As she did in the Billie Holiday image, she mixes the contemporary with, in this case, a distant past, as a Renaissance image is displaced into the present; likewise, white women are transformed into chola women; that is, women of both indigenous and European origin who have been socially disparaged. This transformation empowers viewers to see, tell, or represent history according to their own point of view. Coca demonstrates that in a global capitalist market, consumers are not passive but inventive and tactical. By drawing attention to the dissimilarity between the bodies of the original and those of the reproduction, Coca makes the differences between imported images and her perception of embodied reality sensible. Her figure in the painting is naked but demonstrates a bathing suit line, subverting the myth of the naked savage, again through the temporal tension between a nineteenth-century color scheme and a twenty-first-century female, mestiza body. It also multiplies Coca's body into three, which furthers the idea of a multiple subject in flux, rather than a unified individual. But this multiplicity is not paralyzing like the schizophrenic, fragmented subject of capitalism that Jameson describes; rather, it is nomadic and crafty, as Chela Sandoval argues in her revisionist take on Jameson's "lost" subject in the postmodern era of late capitalism.

As part of this same diptych, Susana Torres transforms an image from the famous indigenous chronicler and illustrator of the Incas, Felipe Guamán Poma de Ayala, and his *Nueva corónica y buen gobierno del reino deste Perú*. Guamán Poma de Ayala's work traces the conquest of Atahualpa, the last Inca king, at the hands of the Spanish. Torres paints herself in the likeness of a hand-drawn Incan princess by Guamán Poma. Torres's gesture glorifies and recuperates indigenous and chola identity because she creates a lineage between herself and the Incas, reframing a canonical "internal" image to Peru as a complement to Coca's European borrowing.

Torres emphasizes the presence of the Incas today: their survival and persistence in the contemporary era. As Torres explains of the exhibit, "Just as
is the case with the mass media, our art history has not liberated itself from
aesthetic ideologies based on racist stereotypes, and yet we are always
mixed by a reality that goes beyond us. Peruvian beauty runs the gamut
from the alienated to the appropriated."[13] The title of Coca's and Torres's
exhibit is ironic because the artists implicitly pose the question of what
constitutes "Peruvian Beauty" to their audience, leaving the answer to
emerge from the provocation the exhibit performs. The question invites
the direct participation of others in the exhibit as part of a collective
reflection that contributes to a reconsideration of beauty as an ongoing
aesthetic and personal project, not an imported look to attain.[14]

Of course, Torres and Coca are not the first to incorporate their own
bodies into their art as a challenge to the types of bodies represented in
an art canon. Jamaican American artist Renee Cox has done the same,
by creating revisions of recognizable paintings. Art historian Peg Brand
describes how Renee Cox "caught the attention of former mayor of New
York City Rudolph Giuliani, prompting him to seek to create a censorship
panel in the city to control what he called 'indecent' art" based on Cox's
rendering of Leonardo da Vinci's *Last Supper* (Brand 2006: 178). Cox's pho-
tographic version of the original, entitled *Yo Mama's Last Supper*, shows herself, pictured naked, with twelve clothed black men. I bring up Cox to point
out that the idea of feminist artists redoing canonical images is a named
phenomenon, one that Brand has aptly called feminist visual parodies
(Brand 2006: 166). In these women's work, their images do more than just
parody the original, but showcase the ways that dominant patterns of gender and racial hierarchies play out within visual culture. These recastings
of established images contribute to the formation of an oppositional consciousness, through a critique of the art history canon as it has operated
through the exclusions of brown and black bodies. And in another famous
example, Chicana activist, performer, and artist Judith F. Baca produced
Las tres Marías in 1976, which includes two colored pencil images of herself but then included a mirror in the center. The mirror emphasizes the
viewer's participation directly in the art, and again, the collective and
shifting nature of identity as it comes to be in relationship to others
(Gabara 2018: 14, 29).

As we continue with the concept of chola identity, a more elaborate discussion of the term will help to explain its unstable and shifting socially

constructed meanings. The term *cholo/a* (or *cholx*) is an unstable racial and social category that is acutely dependent on context, and reflects a cultural dynamism that is, at its worst, racially and culturally derogatory, and at its best, celebratory in its symbolization of an emerging, new identity. In its most basic and general sense, the word refers to someone who is in the midst of racial and cultural transition, usually referring to someone who identifies as indigenous or mestizo, but is in the process of becoming "whitened" by taking up the perceived cultural habits of the criollo/a culture—including language, dress, types of jobs, and cultural practices. Aníbal Quijano comprehensively traces the term as it emerged in the colonial era and evolved up until 1964, when he published his most extensive work on it. During the period of colonization and the first century of the Republic, Quijano explains that the "cholification" process of mestizos and Indians was a process of acculturation, in which the cholo/a was an in-between category that was usually later subsumed into that of *criollo*, at least culturally (Quijano [1969] 1980: 78). The process of cholification was exacerbated during industrialization, when economic opportunity and material accessibility in cities become advantageous to indigenous peoples, and consequently led to their increased migration to urban areas. As a result of internal migration practices in 1960s Peru, Quijano observes that the category changed in such a way that "right in the capital of the Republic, one can observe what may be described as an urban culture notably distinct from Western urban culture because it is made up of a combination of rural Indian and chola culture, as well as certain elements from Western urban culture" (Quijano [1969] 1980: 111). When Quijano concluded his initial discussion of the processes of cultural cholification, published as his doctoral thesis in 1964 and later in book form in 1969, the process was ongoing, as it is today.[15]

Many critics have expanded Quijano's work on the complicated topic of *cholaje*. Milagros Zapata Swerdlow and David Swerdlow, in their essay "Framing the Peruvian Cholo," continue to describe the term as a floating signifier: "Cholos are in constant transit because they are of a social class conceptually based on an individual's or family's supposed movement from or between categories, rather than membership in one category" (Swerdlow and Swerdlow 1998: 111). In the Andes, the term *cholo/a* has tended to carry a negative connotation considered to refer to a person who is "more indigenous" than white, versus *mestizo/a*, which tends to refer to someone who is more white than indigenous (Swerdlow and Swerdlow 1998: 110). At the beginning of the twentieth century, some Andean authors inscribed the category of cholo/a with the hope of the unified nation, under the broader project of Indigenismo. In novels like *La Chaska-ñawi* by Carlos Medinacelli (Bolivia 1947), Jorge Icaza's *Huasipungo* (Ecuador 1934), or even earlier, in Clorinda Matto de Turner's *Aves sin nido* (Peru 1889), a national project was often tied to the salvation of the cholo/a through education, marriage, modernization, and the imposition of criollo/a values. However, in the latter half of the twentieth century the category of cholo/a has also been applied derogatorily or, at best, ambiguously, in a range of media from telenovelas that feature criollo/a characters dressed up as "cholos," to newspaper articles that present blatantly racist comments about those deemed inferior due to race, cultural standing, or both.[16]

Coca embraces the term *chola* now, but as cited above, she struggled with her identity until well after high school. Today, she recasts the term in a way that speaks outward from Lima to an audience that is situated beyond the geographic nation in order to create partial alliances with women who identify as racially other than the white subject. Coca uses the category as a source of pride and creative force, rather than a negative characteristic. Further linking Coca's work to the question of *cholaje*, Marco Avilés, in his highly readable 2017 book *No soy tu cholo* (*I'm Not Your Cholo*), uses Claudia Coca's image, *Luchadora* (*Fighter*, shown below) on the cover. His book is accessible and entertaining, as he attempts to trace the complicated origins, permutations, evolutions, and becomings of the noun *cholo/a*, the active verb *cholear*, and the passive verb *ser choleado*, in the contemporary context of Peru. As he talks about the different usages of the word in Mexico and Peru, he concludes that—somewhat like Octavio Paz argued years ago about *La Chingada* and *chingear*—"los peruanos de hoy hemos construido nuestro país alrededor de esa palabra. El Perú es el amor-odio entre blancos y cholos" [today's Peruvians have constructed our country around that word. Peru is constructed from that love-hate relationship between whites and cholos] (Avilés 2017, 10). And one thing that Avilés points out is that both in Mexico and Peru the word is usually an insult, a "tool for segregating" (Avilés 2017: 10).

Avilés's title, *No soy tu cholo*, captures the point of his discussion. The term is insulting if used by one person to put the other person down

Figure 3. *Luchadora*, 2007

because of an inferred racial superiority, thereby converting the "cholo" into an object. Annelou Ypeij echoes this sentiment in the article "Cholos, incas y fusionistas: El nuevo Perú y la globalización de lo andino" ("Cholos, Incas, and fusionists: New Peru and the Globalization of the Andean") as she writes, "cholear es humillar al otro adoptando una actitud de superioridad y desdén" [to cholo-ize is to humiliate the other, adopting a superior and disdaining attitude] (Ypeij 2016: 74). And yet, as both Avilés and Coca do, reclaiming the term for oneself and in solidarity with other "cholos" tells an altogether different story: one about self-empowerment, self-actualization, and social critique. Javier Sanjinés also recently revisited the theme of "cholification" in a presentation in Bolivia. Echoing the fluidity of the term in the Bolivian context like Avilés does in Peru, he says, echoing back to Quijano, "Este proceso de choloificación fue un fluir, como dije en mi conferencia, un 'devenir' social que no pudo ser tenido por una identidad inmutable. El cholaje no fue, ni es, una estructura fija ni está sujeto a fronteras duras. Antes bien, es una estructura porosa, blanda, que se transforma, se cambia" [This process of cholification was fluid, like I said in my conference talk, a social "becoming" that could not be considered as an immutable identity. *Cholaje* was not, nor is it, a fixed structure; nor is it subject to hard and fast borders. Rather, it is a porous, soft structure that transforms, that changes] (Sanjinés 2017).

Coca's choice of pop art to engage with the theme of *cholaje* also reflects today's broader global context. Pop art, as a hemispheric and global project, has been undergoing a critical renaissance, exactly fifty years after its peak in 1968. For example, in 2015 the Tate Modern in London opened the exhibit *The World Goes Pop*, a show that presents pop art as a constellation of movements produced all over the world from the 1950s through the 70s, from Asia to Europe to the Americas (Tate Modern 2015). In the same year, the Walker Art Center in Minneapolis organized an exhibit titled *International Pop*, also highlighting the expansive geographic scope of pop art produced from 1950–1970. And, as recently as the fall of 2018, Esther Gabara curated an exhibit and produced an extensive catalog titled *Pop América* with the sponsorship of two museums: the Nasher Museum of Art at Duke University and the McNay Art Museum in San Antonio, Texas. In the case of *Pop América*, the geographic configuration of the exhibit and the catalog is hemispheric, featuring a broad array of pop art produced from 1965–1975 in North, Central, and South America.[17]

Figure 4. *Globo Pop*, 2007

The title of the exhibit at the Tate features the word *pop* as a verb, not just an adjective, to emphasize the action that the word performs; pop art "pops" that which went before it—stylistically, abstraction and expressionism; and culturally, the notion that art could not be inspired by graphics associated with mass production, like Campbell's soup cans or the Sunday comics. Furthermore, it pops open viewers' subconscious thoughts, quite literally represented by the cartoon text clouds associated with this genre that visually convey the internal monologues or anxieties of their subjects. In Gabara's *Pop América* exhibit, the title is also ambiguous, as *pop* could be read as an adjective or a verb. As such, Gabara begins her own article in the catalog, "Contesting Freedom," by quoting the artist whose image appears as the catalog cover and shares the exhibit's title, Chilean artist Hugo Rivera-Scott. Rivera-Scott explains, "we always thought about it [pop] as . . . explode América, blow up América, in that sense. Pop as an onomatopoeia." As Gabara summarizes, then, "Pop is an action" as much as a descriptor (Gabara 2018: 10).

In her installation *Globo Pop* (2007), Coca plays on the verbal form of the word as well.[18] In figure 4, the subject in Coca's painting is about to pop a bubble of gum.[19] However, the title of the exhibit also references the world itself with the word *globo*, or globe. I propose two central questions to guide our discussion as we further explore *pop* as a verb and a genre of art in the context of Coca. First, how does she "pop" racial and gendered stereotypes and form alliances within and beyond national borders via her art? And second, how does she more broadly "pop" colonial legacies projected onto the landscape? It is from this discordant aesthetic that an oppositional consciousness emerges as a reminder of the unresolved contradictions of uneven global capitalism as they cut across race, gender, class, and the environment.

Coca takes up *cholaje* particularly in the exhibits *Plebeya* and *Globo Pop*, both of which are based on cartoon-like images. As a concrete illustration of this, in figure 5, she is inspired by and directly cites Felipe Pinglo, known as the founder of the popular criollo genre of music in Peru. Because Pinglo was a member of the APRA (American Popular Revolutionary Alliance) political party during José Carlos Mariátegui and Víctor Raúl Haya de la Torre's era, his popular music was banned from radio play under the second conservative presidency of Oscar Benavides (1933–39).[20] By revisiting his lyrics, Coca makes a connection between her own generation's post–internal conflict political flight and class struggles from the past. She also returns to the anachronistic term *plebeyo* in the contemporary, again recalling that the unresolved class struggle of the past continues to inform today's social injustices. The lyrics, now part of a bold visual field, foreground the continued class and race divisions in Peru and link oppositional movements together.

Figure 5, *Plebeya* (2005–6), presents an edgy-looking, beautiful woman with mestiza coloring and rock star–inspired hair who thinks to herself in a cartoon bubble, "Mi sangre aunque plebeya también tiñe de rojo" ("My blood, even though plebeian, is also red," from Pinglo's lyrics). The image, like the Strange Fruit image, is alluring in its color scheme. The black and indigo-blue hair jumps out at us, as it takes up almost half of the left side of the canvas. The lighter blue-green sky behind the subject is

Figure 5. *Plebeya 1*, 2005–6

starry, as in the image with the Holiday lyrics, perhaps implying that it is night, but a night that is now illuminated. In both images, Coca illuminates the dark, making visible the invisible to a popular audience. This image draws attention to the racial prejudices that have shaped contemporary Peru, especially during the aforementioned years under Shining Path. By referencing blood, Coca elicits a consideration of the difference between who counts as fully human and who is considered less than human based on race, gender, class, and/or their intersections, criticizing positivist-era racial exclusions based on blood. The phrase "even though plebeian" (*aunque plebeya*) insinuates that this subject considers herself less-than to an implied "non-plebeian" subject, even though what runs inside them is the same: their red, human blood. The figure's head is held high, communicating her pride, despite the tears in her eyes. The physical positioning of her body is a site of resistance to those that would put her or others down as she stands firm and vulnerable before the exclusivity of the assumed community.

In figure 6, the woman, identical to the one in the previous image, cries. However, the tears do not represent emotional weakness but beseech

Figure 6. *Plebeya 2*, 2005–6

that precarious subjects be seen, and by extension heard, within society. The position of the subject is vulnerable, as she is shown lying down on a pillow or bed, as if defeated. At the same time, she considers privately the lyrics from Pinglo, lyrics that highlight the contradictions inherent in considering someone else "different" on the outside when they are completely the same on the inside. Paul Preciado, in his reconceptualization of the body in reaction to the mandates of modernity, argues that part of decolonization means "making corporeal vulnerability a platform for action and common resistance" (Preciado 2011). This vulnerability is not just Coca's to experience, but is shared—going back to her work with the CSC—by the collective community that came together in an act of refusal of complicity with Peru's past. This vulnerability was shared by the workers-based and class-based movements of 1968, but as Chela Sandoval traces, it is from 1968 that third world movements and alliances were formed. In both cases above, the women represented in Coca's art are likenesses of herself and are visualized as part of the "plebeian masses." This equation draws attention to historical blind spots of class-based movements in not recognizing the particular experiences of women, and moreover, women of color. But Coca also uses her image to stand in for an "everywoman" of the masses who is politically vulnerable and symbolically unaccompanied, as the "crying woman" or the superheroine is either alone or with a child in this series. In Coca's case she brings a vulnerable chola subject to the forefront of the popular conscience. She mixes the contexts in which one usually thinks of *cholaje*—as a folkloric or kitschy genre—by making her subject chic, and linking her to past class-based movements in the name of creating alliances.

In a subsequent image from the series *Globo Pop* (figure 7), Coca includes a cartoon bubble that asks, " . . . Por qué nos odian tanto?" (Why do they/all of you hate us so much?). This cartoon-like version of Coca as Wonder Woman shows her with hand placed on her head in anguish as she poses her question to the viewers. The image of the superheroine icon with tears in her eyes and looking depleted of energy is visually located in front of the brightly colored canvas background, bursting with shooting stars and colorful stripes. The rainbow-colored stars and stripes behind her are not just the red, white, and blue of the U.S. flag, but appear to allude to it, leading viewers to question who the subject of the verb *odian* (you all/they hate, the Spanish works in either voice) is. Is it Coca's North American neighbors, internal ones, both, or beyond?

Coca translates hidden thoughts into the cartoon bubble to grant her audience access to latent worries internal to her subject. The colorful and eye-catching background also contributes to the perception that Coca is a local and vulnerable heroine, if only because she poses a question that many others might already be thinking.[21] At the same time the subject is seen as "in strife," she is, after all, Wonder Woman. This further emphasizes her power and strength alongside her vulnerability.

Coca draws attention to the fact that strife is not commonly represented in pop art, even though the affective experience of anxiety associated with social prejudice might be one of the most popular shared experiences that people undergo in the public sphere. Coca makes sensible what is invisible publicly, but might be hyper visible internally to citizens: the doubt within as to why someone else might hate "us" so much. It is not just the particular woman (who is an invocation of Coca herself) who asks this question. The *nos* invites a collective "us" to share or identify with Coca's experience. Such a collective identification contributes to the potential development of an oppositional consciousness to an unspecified "they." The tears in the

Figure 7. *Mujer maravilla 1*, 2007

painting symbolize the historical legacies of colonization, especially as they have played out on the female chola body, while also drawing attention to the underlying hatred that can exist between subjects—whether conscious or subconscious. However, in response to an externally imposed hatred, and the tears that seem to energetically pop out of the subject's eyes, Coca's image confronts the audience with her own suffering but more emphatically, her determination. If hate is the result of neocolonial prejudices, then love is that of decolonial alliance. Sandoval explains the concept of love as a method as "the experience of 'the originality of the relation' between two actors that inspire new powers" (Sandoval 2000: 142). By leaving the "why" behind the hate unanswered, Coca brings viewers into the fold, leaving them to contemplate a postponed answer: the question raises consciousness before differences. Figure 8 also uses the popular Japanese comic form of manga to invoke another "luchadora," or fighter, the geisha. As Coca explains it, this heroine has survived the "lluvia negra," the black, radiation-filled rain, from Hiroshima and Nagasaki. But, she keeps fighting.

In reference to Coca's exhibit *Globo Pop*, Gustavo Buntinx described the metaphoric punch of "*cholo power*" (Buntinx 2007), an inspiration for my

Figure 8. *Lluvia negra*, 2007

essay's title. It is through the figure of the chola that Coca activates an oppositional consciousness through the expression and depiction of marginalized racial and gendered subjects. By identifying as a chola, Coca helps lift the pejorative stigma from this term, mobilizing it in a way that connects the more neutral category of mestizo/a to cholo/a identity as well. The chola, as envisioned by Coca, is a quotidian hero transformed into pop icon via color, gloss, and repeatability. What Coca asks in her art is "Why do they hate us so much?" And yet, as viewers she challenges us to reflect on the opposite question: "Why don't we love each other and ourselves?"

Returning to Avilés's book *No soy tu cholo*, he begins his text with a quote from James Baldwin, antislavery writer and advocate for social change. Baldwin said, "Any writer, upon looking back . . . understands that the things that hurt him and the things that helped him cannot be divorced from each other" (quoted in Avilés 2017: 8). Coca's art invokes such a tension: viewers look at the beauty of the art and the creative power and are hurt by the hate or marginalization that inspires them, but simultaneously empowered through their reaction. That tension contributes to the ongoing call for oppositional consciousness to the smoothing over of difference. Coca is able to "develop modes of perceiving, making sense of, and acting

upon reality that are the basis for effective forms of oppositional consciousness in the postmodern world" (Sandoval 2000: 35). Coca's *Luchadora*
(*Fighter*) uses her body and difference to convey her strength: "No soy tu
chola." Her literal stance of opposition, with fists up and gaze focused, is
the perfect cover to Avilés's book. Together they take back *cholaje* for and
by themselves.

Beyond Cholaje: Decolonizing the Exploitation of Nature

On a final note, colonization has impacted the body, but it has also
impacted the earth. In addition to thinking about an oppositional consciousness in relationship to the female and chola body, Coca's most recent
works perform a broader critique of the concepts upon which the historical
project of colonialism in the Americas has hinged in a series of charcoal
and pencil drawings. Figure 9 brings nature and culture together, through
the imposition of the word (culture) upon the ocean (nature), drawing
attention to the tensions between the two as well as their mutual constitution. In this image, *Colonizados*, the black-and-white thrashing ocean
becomes less a symbol of pristine and neutral nature, and more that of a
force inscribed with the arrival of a project that transforms the ocean from
a shared resource to a privileged imperial space. What is striking about the
image is that it is not site specific and instead speaks to the violence of a
colonialism that cannot be located. Therefore, its hidden "agent" is more
dangerous in its diffuseness and ambiguity. As Slavoj Žižek lays out in *Violence*, his book-length, scathing critique of late capitalism, we are missing
the point if we think that subjective violence is the pressing societal concern of our times. Instead, he argues that it is the much deeper and more
complex systemic violence that fades from our discourse as we point the
finger and blame individuals for the symptomatic issues of a diseased system. Coca's collection, *Cuentos bárbaros*, critiques these broad patterns of
coloniality and neocoloniality through its effective abstraction.

As part of the same series, Coca turns the lens on *National Geographic* on
her canvas, in a clever representational inversion. Coca draws a *National
Geographic* cover, putting a subjective hand into the flagship journal of
"objective" images of nature and culture. Her choice of pencil as well as
black-and-white images enables her to problematize the concept of a per-
manent archive, implying that it is under erasure (the letters in *National
Geographic* fade in the upper right corner). She demonstrates that nature
can overtake representation, as the wild jungle seems to take over the

Figure 9. *Colonizados*, 2015

"cultured" letters. In another image from the same series, not included here, the artist writes the words *cuerpos bárbaros* (savage bodies) on the ocean, again diffusing the blame for colonization into an unnamed and unassigned source that seems to arrive onshore as if it were a natural force, as formidable as the ocean. Of course, the irony is that in her invocation of nature Coca both denaturalizes colonization and reinstates the centrality of nonhuman nature as a necessary part of sustainable human life.

The ways that Coca draws attention to abstract nature itself return us to the beginning of the article, and a recent observation that Esther Gabara makes in her catalog from the exhibit *Pop América*. Gabara writes, "The Pop liberation of America involved its air, land, and water as much as its people, natural formations that unite a continent in defiance of the political borders that divide them" (Gabara 2018: 17). While the terms *cuerpos bárbaros* or *colonizados* are written in Spanish, the reference to natural formations like the ocean or the shore lack geographic specificity, insinuating that the project of colonization has impacted people, but moreover places that exist beyond national boundaries. Coca's newest work from the exhibit *Cuentos bárbaros* is more abstract than her previous work but equally indicative of "the afterlife of colonialism" as it continues to play out at a cosmopolitical level (Sandoval 2002: 21). The "barbaric" subject in these images is not the

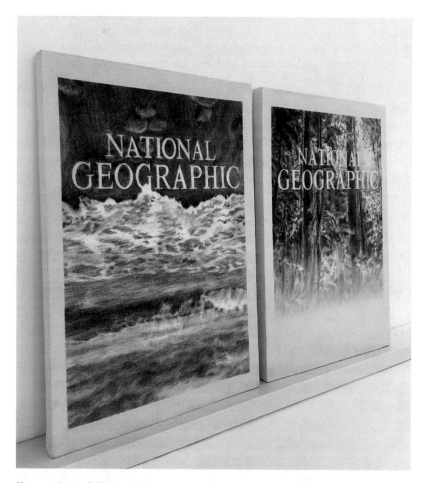

Figure 10. *Cuentos bárbaros*, details, 2015

colonized, but rather the disembodied colonizer who "discovers" and exploits others, whether in the 1500s, the 1900s, or today. Our material relationships, across race, gender, sexuality, and even species, are sites of oppositional movement to the tide of exploitative economic and social practices that develop out of empires. Her art brings invisible subjects, human and otherwise, forward to focus on subjugated points of view—the chola, the colonized, nature itself—that can converge to challenge insularity, individuality, and binary differences and instead prioritize plurality and creative alliances as ongoing oppositional movements to hegemonic patterns of exploitation: a cosmopolitics that considers humans as only part of the broader ecosystem.

Tara Daly is assistant professor of Spanish at Marquette University. She is the author of *Beyond Human: Vital Materialisms in the Andean Avant-Gardes* (2019) and co-editor of *Decolonial Approaches to Latin American Literatures and Cultures* (2016).

Author's Note

I am grateful to the multiple readers of this manuscript whose careful editing and suggestions improved the piece immensely.

Notes

1   The song was performed regularly in left-wing circles—by Meeropol's wife, by progressive friends at gatherings in hotels and bungalow colonies around New York, by members of the local teachers' union, by a black vocalist named Laura Duncan, and by a quartet of black singers at a fundraiser for the antifascists during the Spanish Civil War. The club owner of Café Society in New York, Barney Josephson, first heard the song and introduced it to Holiday, who had already sung on various occasions at the Café Society club. Holiday started singing the song fairly regularly, and by October 1939 the *New York Sun* was describing the singer and the song as "practically inseparable" (Margolick 2001: 24).

2   With the phrase "physical wars," I refer to the internal conflict under Sendero Luminoso (Shining Path) in Peru (1980–2000) as well as the physical legacies of slavery in South and North America. Shining Path was a terrorist group that operated under Communist Maoist doctrine and the leadership of Abimael Guzmán. The Peruvian military was also an active participant in the war, contributing as well to the death count.

3   As she explains in an interview in *La República*, "Mi papá es contador y mi mamá es estilista; quizás mi interés por la plástica viene de ella"; "My Dad is an accountant and my Mom is a stylist; perhaps my interest in the plastic arts comes from her" (Gonzales and Coca 2011). My translation.

4   *Informe final de la Comisión de verdad y reconciliación*, Annex 2, estimates 69, 280 victims total (2003).

5   Seda writes: "If we take into consideration that . . . the most affected were poor indigenous peoples and peasants, with little education, residents of rural Andean or forest regions, it stands out that the racial component of the war played, and continues playing, a principal role with respect to the attitude of indifference with which the majority of the Peruvian population has responded to these tragic events" (Seda 2012: 94). My translation.

6   Coca is only one example of many artists and activists who have spoken out and participated in documenting the tumultuous years under Shining Path and their impacts on a collective Peruvian memory. The most well-known exhibit has been the photography exhibit *Yuyanapaq* (*To Remember* in Quechua). Vich 2010 looks at the way that popular street performers were able to bring to light

the violence incurred during the Shining Path period through their engagement with everyday citizens.

7   I have translated all excerpts from my interview with Claudia Coca (2013).

8   Alberto Fujimori fled Peru for Japan in November 2000, where he remained in self-exile for five years, after a corruption scandal led by his chief staff member Vladimir Montesinos had been caught on tape. While he wanted to resign from the presidency, he was instead impeached by the state. While he is credited with eliminating Shining Path, he is also known, and was convicted for, having committed human rights abuses to realize such an outcome. Fujimori was extradited from Japan and is now in a Peruvian prison.

9   This information comes from a packet that Coca shared with me about the work she had done with the Collective Civil Society Group. This packet included a range of newspaper and magazine articles about the group's work.

10   A map ran in El *Comercio* in July 2000 of the various places that this event was carried out. Basically, it took place in almost twenty different cities in Peru. Also, Peruvians in other cities like Buenos Aires, New York, Madrid, Geneva, and Santiago participated.

11   See Peralta Berríos 2011. Coca has since produced additional art on *mestizaje*, for instance the clay-based *Mestizaje sin paraíso* shown in the exhibit *Mestiza* in 2014 at Museo de Arte Contemporáneo (Museum of Contemporary Art), Lima.

12   Another image on *mestizaje* that makes fun of the desire to "whiten" oneself or one's family is titled *Mejorando la raza* (*Improving the Race*). It shows Coca donning a cape that features what appears to be a picture of her parents. The implication is that their marriage resulted in the "improvement" of racial status through an implied generational dissolving of indigenous blood. This image is ironic, attempting to draw attention to the absurdity of the discourse.

13   The Spanish reads, "Al igual que los medios masivos, nuestra historia del arte no se ha librado de ideologías estéticas con estereotipos racistas, y sin embargo siempre amestizados por una realidad que los supera. La belleza peruana va desde lo alienado a lo apropiado" (*Peruvian Beauty* catalog). See also Torres 2013.

14   The topic of beauty merits deeper discussion with respect to the role of the media and particularly advertising in the employment of models who do not match the sizes, races, ethnicities, and bodies of a given population. This topic stretches well beyond Peru. Paula Black's work on the beauty industry is a good starting point for a nuanced reading of the positive female bonds that can be forged in the beauty salon. While salons may at first seem to impose standards on women, they also can empower them to define their own standards as well as to build community through storytelling and conversation with their communities. See Black 2004 and Jeffreys 2005.

15   The term *cholo/a* is not only specific to South America. In Los Angeles in the 1950s and 60s, a form of cholo writing emerged, described as the following: "Latino gangs would tag buildings in their neighborhoods to claim their territory. Unlike the bright cartoon-style murals of the East Coast graffiti, cholo writing features stark black-and-white lettering that pays homage to traditional

typefaces. The artist Charles 'Chaz' Bojórquez created his own style of cholo writing," characterized by "sharp lines and accents. Now 67, Bojórquez continues to work and considers himself one of the oldest living graffiti artists" (*Tampa Review* 2017: 26). In other contexts, the term is used to refer to those that dwell in the border between Mexico and the United States, to refer to a cholo community that feels neither quite Mexican nor quite U.S. American. See Powers 2011.

16   In Ecuador, for instance, the telenovela *El Cholito*, which ran from 2006–8, is about a cholo character who lives in Quito. This program presents an example of the somewhat mixed attitude toward cholos who are both inferior but also somewhat "beloved" as part of a national consciousness. In December 2015, in Bolivia, the president of the Senate dressed in a *pollera*, or as *una cholita*, in solidarity with Aymara women after the community of Caquiaviri forced a questionably serving mayor to dress as a *cholita*, attesting to the disrespectful view of this classification as well as its redemption. For a very comprehensive study on the term in the Peruvian context, see Vargas Benavente 2016.

17   In the Directors' foreword to Gabara's *Pop América*, Sarah Schroth and Richard Aste explain that in San Antonio in 1968 there was a fair titled "HemisFair" that promoted the visual arts across the Americas (Schroth and Aste 2018: 6). It was there that the McNay Museum first put together an exhibit called *Confluence of Civilizations in the Americas*, based on the fair's theme. The McNay Museum, this is to say, has a long history of promoting broad geographic approaches to hemispheric art and that continues in Gabara's exhibit.

18   Coca has said of her interest in pop art that "the language of pop is of the masses, and therefore permits a more direct communication with the spectator. Mass media and popular language has always been of interest to me, and so I've started increasingly working with popular song lyrics, with popular myths and sayings" (Daly and Coca 2013).

19   Gustavo Buntinx (2007), a well-known art critic in Lima, writes a great analysis of the exhibit in the *Globo Pop* catalog: "*Globo Pop* puede así ser el nombre comercial de una barata golosina trasnacional y al mismo tiempo el título artístico de una exposición a su manera altermundista, donde los signos exteriores de diferencia étnica friccionan la rutilancia festiva de formas y colores cosmopolitas" (*Globo Pop* can as such be the commercial name of a cheap transnational sweet and at the same time the artistic title of, in its way, an alter-global world, where exterior signs from different ethnicities create friction with the festive sparkle of cosmopolitan forms and colors; my translation).

20   Felipe Pinglo Alva, "El Plebeyo" ("The Plebeian"), video, 3:24, https://www.youtube.com/watch?v=Y8If7hiF000.

21   In her interview with María Isabel Gonzales, Coca says that in 2007 she wanted to "go beyond the national. For that reason, the *globo* of global and the *pop* of popular. I use the most well-known global icons, Wonder Woman, or the Geisha Lluvia Negra, who cries because of the radioactive rain of Hiroshima" (Gonzales and Coca 2011).

Works Cited

Als, Hilton. 2001. Foreword to *Strange Fruit: The Biography of a Song*. New York: HarperCollins.

Avilés, Marco. 2017. *No soy tu cholo*. Lima, Peru: Debate.

Black, Paula. 2004. *The Beauty Industry: Gender, Culture, Pleasure*. New York: Routledge.

Brand, Peg Zellin. 2006. "Feminist Art Epistemologies: Understanding Feminist Art." *Hypatia* 21, no. 3: 166–89.

Buntinx, Gustavo. 2007. "Cholo pink, cholo pop, cholo power." Lima: Galería Vértice. http://ccglobopop.blogspot.com/2009/03/texto.html.

Daly, Tara, and Claudia Coca. 2013. Unpublished interview over email.

Gabara, Esther. 2018. Introduction to *Pop América*. Durham, NC: Duke University Press.

Gonzales, María Isabel, and Claudia Coca. 2011. "Trabajo con las cosas que me agarran las entrañas." *La República*, May 22. https://larepublica.pe/archivo/542677–trabajo-con-las-cosas-que-me-agarran-las-entranas.

Jeffreys, Sheila. 2005. *Beauty and Misogyny: Harmful Cultural Practices in the West*. New York: Routledge.

Lugones, María. 2014. "Radical Multiculturalism and Women of Color Feminisms." *Journal for Cultural and Religious Theory* 13, no. 1: 68–80.

Margolick, David. 2001. *Strange Fruit: The Biography of a Song*. New York: HarperCollins.

Peralta Berríos, Juan. 2011. Prologue to *Antología: Revelada e indeleble de Claudia Coca*. Lima, Peru: Museo de Arte de San Marcos.

Powers, Melinda. 2011. "Syncretic Sites in Luis Alfaro's *Electricidad*." *Helios* 38, no. 2: 193–206.

Preciado, Beatriz [Paul Preciado]. 2014. "Cuerpo Improprio." *Parole de queer* (blog), November. http://paroledequeer.blogspot.com/2014/11/cuerpo-impropio-guia-de-modelos.html.

Quijano, Aníbal. (1969) 1980. *Dominación y cultura: Lo cholo y el conflicto cultural en el Perú*. Lima: Mosca Azul Editores.

Sandoval, Chela. 1998. "Mestizaje as Method: Feminists of Color Challenge the Canon." In *Living Chicana Theory*, edited by Carla Trujillo, 352–70. Berkeley, CA: Third Woman Press.

Sandoval, Chela. 2000. *The Methodology of the Oppressed*. Minneapolis: University of Minnesota Press.

Sandoval, Chela. 2002. "Dissident Globalizations, Emancipatory Methods, Social-Erotics." In *Queer Globalizations: Citizenship and the Afterlife of Colonialism*, edited by Arnaldo Cruz-Malavé and Martin F. Manalansan IV, 20–32. New York: New York University Press.

Sanjinés, Javier. 2017. "El cholaje no es una estructura fija." *El Deber*, April 6. https://www.eldeber.com.bo/brujula/Javier-Sanjines-El-cholaje-no-es-una-estructura-fija-20170406-0047.html.

Schroth, Sarah, and Richard Aste. 2018. Directors' foreword to *Pop América*, edited by Esther Gabara, 6–7. Durham, NC: Nasher Museum of Art at Duke University.

Seda, Laurietz. 2012. "Para no olvidar: Teatro y guerra sucia en Argentina y Perú." *Latin American Theatre Review* 46, no. 1: 91–102.

Swerdlow, Milagros, and David Swerdlow. 1998. "Framing the Peruvian *Cholo*: Popular Art by Unpopular People." In *Imagination beyond Nation: Latin American Popular Culture*, edited by Eva P. Bueno and Terry Caesar, 109–28. Pittsburgh: University of Pittsburgh Press.

Tampa Review. 2017. "Charles 'Chaz' Bojórquez (bio)." 53: 26.

TMAG (Tate Modern Art Gallery). 2015. "Art Term: Pop Art." https://www.tate.org.uk /art/art-terms/p/pop-art.

Torres, Susana. 2013. "Es momento de volver a crear una cara para el arte en Lima." *El Comercio*, April 17. http://archivo.elcomercio.pe/art-lima/noticia/susana-torres -momento-volver-crear-cara-arte-lima-noticia-1565120.

TRCP (Truth and Reconciliation Commission of Peru). 2003. *Informe final de la Comisión de Verdad y Reconciliación.* http://www.cverdad.org.pe/ifinal/.

Vargas Benavente, Raphael. 2016. "Del cholo de mierda al cholo power. Discriminación, prototipos y cambio semántico en el español del Perú." PhD diss., University of Montreal. https://papyrus.bib.umontreal.ca/xmlui/bitstream/handle/1866 /19038/Vargas_Benavente_Raphael_2016_these.pdf?sequence=2.

Vich, Victor. 2004. "Desobediencia simbólica: Performance, participación y política al final de la dictadura fujimorista." *Emisferica* 1, no. 1. https: //hemisphericinstitute.org/en/emisferica-1-1-enacting-democracy/desobediencia -simbo-lica-performance-participacio-n-y-poli-tica-al-final-de-la-dictadura -fujimorista.html.

Vich, Victor. 2010. *El discurso de la calle: Los cómicos ambulantes y las tensiones de la modernidad en el Perú.* Lima: Fondo Editorial Pontificia Universidad Católica del Perú.

Ypeij, Annelou. 2013. "Cholos, incas y fusionistas: El nuevo Perú y la globalización de lo andino." *European Review of Latin American and Caribbean Studies* 94: 67–82.

Žižek, Slavoj. 2007. *Violence: Six Sideways Reflections.* New York: Picador Books.

Rosamond S. King

Radical Interdisciplinarity

A New Iteration of a Woman of Color Methodology

Abstract: This essay delineates the concept of radical interdisciplinarity, the use of methodologies that combine traditional scholarship with that which is not traditionally considered either scholarship or even part of an academic discipline—specifically poetry and other creative arts. The author describes radical interdisciplinarity as building on the hybrid methodologies of women of color authors such as Gloria Anzaldúa, Audre Lorde, Leslie Marmon Silko, and Michelle Cliff, who often combined memoir with fiction or poetry. The essay itself includes examples of radical interdisciplinarity in the form of a critical biomythography that weaves together scholarly analysis and poetry related to the author's current research on the jamette women of nineteenth-century Trinidad.

This essay will delineate how I have come to be writing a *critical biomythography*, a type of hybrid text that is an example of *radical interdisciplinarity*, which is the use of methodologies that combine traditional scholarship with that which is not traditionally considered either scholarship or even part of an academic discipline—specifically poetry and other creative arts. I will describe radical interdisciplinarity as building on the hybrid methodologies of women of color authors such as Gloria Anzaldúa, Audre Lorde, Leslie Marmon Silko, and Michelle Cliff, who often combined memoir with fiction or poetry. While the focus of this piece is methodology, the essay itself does include examples of radical interdisciplinarity in the form of an excerpted critical biomythography that weaves together

MERIDIANS · feminism, race, transnationalism   18:2 October 2019
DOI: 10.1215/15366936-7775652 © 2019 Smith College

scholarly analysis and poetry related to my current research on jamette women in nineteenth-century Trinidad.

I am a trained comparativist,[1] and have been comfortably using those strategies for my entire scholarly career. Methodology only became a question and a problem for me when my work shifted from the analysis of contemporary literary texts to a reliance on archival sources. My current project examines the interventions that jamette women made in nineteenth-century Trinidadian society, culture, law, and policy. The term *jamette* (from the French *diamètre*) originally referred to those who, in the late 1800s, were considered below the "diameter" of respectable society. This group was comprised of poor Afro-Trinidadians who worked in marginal or illegal sectors such as domestic work, manual labor, prostitution, and gambling. Elites proclaimed jamettes—especially jamette women's participation in protests and carnival performances—the bane of the colony, exhibiting immorality and criminality. In reality, though, the plantocracy was targeting black people who refused to continue to work in the fields after emancipation, and who would not restrict their sexuality to legal marriage.

Jamette women in particular became infamous for behavior that scandalized the colonial upper classes, including their leadership of social protests and the ways they celebrated carnival—especially the crossdressing some of them engaged in (King 2011). It is these behaviors and interactions that I am analyzing. The problem this work presents is that a trail of writing by or from the perspective of nineteenth-century Afro-Trinidadian women is not readily available. I have been unable to locate books, memoirs, pamphlets, or diaries written by black women in that space and time. And the texts that do mention them—mostly newspapers, legal and government documents, and travel memoirs—were largely created by middle-class or wealthy white men, whose vested interest in keeping Afro-Trinidadians as close to impoverished servitude and sexual availability as possible is evident in their writing. David V. Trotman notes that black women were regularly singled out as beyond the pale; he writes that "They were viewed not merely as immoral but more often as amoral" (Trotman 1986: 246).

> not woman but
> fe-male, meaning
> one who can be fucked.[2]

My research depends on and builds upon Trotman's singular work on women and crime in nineteenth-century Trinidad, and on the work of John Cowley (1996), Susan Campbell (1988), Andrew Pearse (1956), and Daniel J. Crowley (1956) on early carnival, as well as the pioneer scholars of women and gender in Trinidadian history, head among them Bridget Brereton (1975, 1979, 1981, 1994). Unfortunately, none of this work features writing by nineteenth-century black Trinidadian women.[3] My search for information about Afro-Trinidadian women's participation in nineteenth-century protests and carnival reveals what many of us already know: the traditional colonial archive is a contested—even a hostile—place when you are looking for information about black people. In such a situation, traditional methodologies cannot suffice. The question of how to read, consider, and use archives is one of the central questions within Africana and black feminist studies today, and has been addressed by a number of scholars, the most well-known being Saidiya Hartman. I agree with Hartman on the importance of critically reading and interpreting archives, and neither of us is satisfied with that project alone. As I will detail later, Hartman arrives at critical fabulation as her methodology, while I have chosen radical interdisciplinarity realized through critical biomythography as mine.

Why do I consider this lack of primary resources created by black women a problem? Why not leave silence as silence? Why not describe the silence, but let it stand as a testimony to the physical and epistemological violence done to these women? I cannot and do not wish to erase the fact of the silence, which itself reflects jamette women's reality. But neither do I wish to leave it as the only material in my writing about these women. While I must contend with archival silence, I cannot let this silence stand alone and uncontested because it is not natural, but enforced. Nineteenth-century black Trinidadian women did not fail to leave a substantial written archive by happenstance. While it is true that during slavery black literacy was often a crime, the time of the jamettes was more than a generation beyond emancipation. I am convinced, in fact, that some Afro-Trinidadian women must have kept diaries, must have written letters, must have recorded in writing their thoughts and experiences. These texts—those that survive—await discovery by someone who will both look for them and value them. For so long black Caribbean women's writing was not considered of value to the archives, just as they were not considered qualified or appropriate writers for the newspapers that so often mentioned them disparagingly.

I cannot leave this silence to endure alone, furthermore, because there is already something in place of the silence; what is in that place is racist, heteropatriarchal propaganda. I am aware of, but less willing "to respect the limits of what cannot be known" (Hartman 2008: 4) than some other scholars because I do not want to let the silence stand as the final record. If violently enforced silence is left as erasure and not rendered as a scream, it is as if the horror did not happen.

Radical Interdisciplinarity

I noted above that methodology became a problem and a question for me when I became subsumed in researching jamette women. Ironically, in *Webster's Third New International Unabridged Dictionary* (1981), the second definition of methodology is "the processes, techniques, or approaches employed in the solution of a problem or in doing something." Thinking along these lines, I realized that methodology could solve my problem with methodology.

The solution was always in front of me. From the first time I began researching the jamettes, I have always known that the work would include poetry. Initially, I guarded that information, hiding it from academic proposals and essays out of fear that the project would not be seen as scholarly, and would be less likely to receive such funding as is available. But no other strategy, no other *methodology*, made sense. As historian Marisa Fuentes, who uses nontraditional methods in her own work on seventeenth-century Barbadian women, writes: "A legible and linear narrative cannot sufficiently account for the palimpsest of material and meaning embedded in the lives of people shaped by the intimacies and ubiquity of violence" (Fuentes 2016: 6).[4] Whenever I tried to write narrative, linear, scholarly prose about these women—the kind of scholarship I've been comfortable writing for years—poetry would interrupt me and temporarily take over the page.

Once I decided to accept this and keep the poetry and academic writing together, I needed a way to describe this methodology. In fact, although colleagues at the Caribbean Studies Association and the West Indian Literature conferences seemed to neither question nor seek explanation of my methodology (at least not from me), when I have presented this hybrid work in U.S. American settings, there is always a substantive contingent interested in an explanation of my methodology. These queries, and the interest of my colleagues in the "Radical Transnational Feminisms" Research Seminar provided the encouragement to write an essay delineating my method.[5]

While hybrid critical-creative methodologies are still rarely seen in the most highly rated and respected academic journals or in books published by university presses,[6] hybrid methodologies are not so unusual in women of color feminist writing at the edge or outside of the academy. Thus, as I consider how to evidence my research on jamette women's protests and performances, it is important that the hybrid methodology that I have arrived at—and the strategy of the critical biomythography that I will discuss below—exist within an activist, artistic, and intellectual tradition. Marisa Fuentes describes her groundbreaking scholarship as within a tradition of academics who "use analyses of race and gender to destabilize the power of dominant knowledge and representations of women of the African diaspora" (Fuentes 2016: 11), and I believe my work builds on a similar tradition not only of black women, but of women of color, and not only by those embraced by the academy, but by those who largely wrote outside of it.

I define radical interdisciplinarity as the use of methodologies that combine traditional scholarship with that which is not traditionally considered either scholarship or even part of an academic discipline. As I conceive of it, one aspect of radical interdisciplinarity entails accepted methods of scholarly research and writing, and the other aspect is creative work, such as poetry, performance, or film. Because of this incorporation of the creative arts, and because its best use is to address that which traditional scholarship cannot adequately access, radical interdisciplinarity is in part a *subjunctive* practice. Its goal is to imagine, to suppose. Its artistic aspect is informed and informing, but not reliable; grounded and contextualized, but neither factual nor verifiable. Radical interdisciplinarity is an articulation of activism that builds on radical women of color traditions that seek to make visible the lives, experiences, thoughts, and perspectives of people who have been othered and silenced.

Radical interdisciplinarity is a direct descendent of the works of a number of feminists of color—women of multiple races and ethnic and linguistic heritages, most of whom were immigrants or the children of immigrants. Gloria Anzaldúa's autohistorias in *Borderlands/La Frontera: The New Mestiza* (2008); Audre Lorde's biomythography *Zami: A New Spelling of My Name* (1982); and the unnamed styles of Michelle Cliff in *Claiming an Identity They Taught Me to Despise* (1980), which also combines memoir and fiction, and Leslie Marmon Silko, whose *Sacred Water* (1993) combines poetry and photographs, all are hybrid works that have inspired me. The primary difference between what they produced and my manifestation of radical interdisciplinarity is that I am using critical scholarship and not memoir, which all of these earlier authors integrated into their work.

Critical Biomythography

If my methodology for my jamette project is radical interdisciplinarity, then the manifestation of that methodology is a hybrid text, a critical biomythography that weaves together scholarly analysis and poetry (as this essay does). This form will turn the limits and absences of the available archive into an opportunity to paint a fuller picture of what jamette women's lives *might* have been like. At the same time, this strategy is an opportunity to subvert the genres and academic conventions that have historically misrepresented communities such as the jamettes.

What is a critical biomythography? It includes both research and poetry (though another scholar might use film, performance, or another artistic medium). And just as radical interdisciplinarity can be seen as activism, the critical biomythography is itself protest: not only against traditional methodologies, but also against colonialism and the racist heteropatriarchies that established methodologies and the disciplines that discipline them. Lorde wrote that her biomythography was "a new spelling of [her] name," and in the same vein, a critical biomythography makes something that is new both in content and in form. Through its methodology of radical interdisciplinarity, it also has the potential to create new understanding.

The term biomythography comes, of course, from Lorde's description of *Zami: A New Spelling of My Name.* Lorde did not codify an exact definition of the biomythography. She may have done this deliberately to leave the form as an open signifier available to other writers. Her intention seems to have been to create a text that utilized her own biography and a mythmaking of her own design, combining them in such a way that the distinctions are not always apparent.

Lorde's choice to employ the word *myth* rather than *fiction* (e.g. biofictography) is significant. The *Oxford English Dictionary* defines *myth* as "A traditional story, typically involving supernatural beings or forces, which embodies and provides an explanation, aetiology, or justification for something." In this case, the "something" being detailed is her own existence.[7] Lorde's use of myth suggests that she wanted to create a narrative so powerful that it would linger for generations. And she might have refused *autobiography* to emphasize that one person's story could be, as one scholar suggests, "a fabulated strategy for community survival."[8] Similarly, though any given poem I include might embody a single voice or experience, the overall focus of my critical biomythography is presenting the archival and subjunctive experiences of jamette women *as a group* in a way that might linger for as long as the formal archive.

A *critical* biomythography draws on the structure of Lorde's *Zami*—and that of other women of color feminists, as described above—but it also includes academic research. The addition of the word *critical* does not imply that there is no rigor or analysis in creative literature. Rather, it signifies the inclusion of research-based analytical writing and strategies generally attributed to academic publications. In my critical biomythography, the scholarship analyzing jamette presence and traces in the formal archive, and building on existing scholarship on nineteenth-century Trinidad, both exists on its own and informs the poetry, just as the possibilities imagined within the poetry benefit the scholarly writing. Saidiya Hartman asks about her own work examining the under-archived lives of enslaved African American women: "How can narrative embody life in words and at the same time respect what we cannot know?" (Hartman 2008: 3). I answer the question she poses not with narrative, but with poetry.

Poetry can resolve this seeming incongruency in a way that is more difficult with traditional narrative criticism. Whereas historical scholarship attempts to declaratively state what *was*, poetry can be subjunctive, exploring *what might have been*, and making statements that do not claim to be fact even as they are informed by academic research and intellectual and visceral reactions to that research. In order to discuss the importance of poetry, it is helpful, of course, to turn to the venerable essay by Lorde, "Poetry Is Not a Luxury," in which she writes that "poetry is the way we help give name to the nameless so it can be thought" and "where that language does not yet exist, it is our poetry which helps to fashion it" (Lorde 1977: 372). In my work on/with jamette women, poetry helps name and describe details not included in the archive, so that both I and my readers can imagine, think, and fashion a fuller sense of what their lives might have been like.

In the introduction to this essay, I wrote that poetry "interrupted" my scholarly writing in ways that have resulted in radical interdisciplinarity. Indeed, poetry is useful as both an interrupter and a disrupter. One instance of interruption came while I was writing about Trinidad's Contagious Diseases Ordinance (CDO) of 1869, which forced women accused of being "common prostitutes" to submit to exams searching for venereal disease which, if found, would result in the women being imprisoned in a hospital until cured. The problems with this law were many; the threat of being registered as a "common prostitute" was used by some police officers as leverage to rape non-elite women who would have a hard time either proving the rape or proving that they were not prostitutes. And black women in Trinidad and elsewhere were considered unrapeable because of "the idea that all these women of non-European stock were sexually promiscuous, inveterate liars, and devoid of what Police Inspector Fraser called 'any womanly sense of shame'" (Trotman 1986: 179). Indeed, in 1881 jamette women protested against the ordinance while a Sergeant Holder was on trial—*for the twentieth time*—for using his power to extort sex from a woman.

> Holder
> Hold her!
> Hold her like a claw
> It would tear out your humanity if
> it thought you had any
> Holds a badge like a claw
> to make your dignity bleed
> to make you gag
> this claw digs its blunt
> into you—*swallow it*
> or else
> the badge tells you to get
> naked and like it
> torchlight pricks your belly
> then pitch grinds your knees
> gun tells you to like it
> so you like it better than prison
> better than more Holders more
> badges more guns[9]

In writing about jamette women, about women who were treated as though neither their lives nor their deaths were of any consequence, who were violated in ways ranging from insult to rape to murder, the interruption of a visceral, often more emotional voice, into the supposedly objective academic one, reminds us that what we are reading about *happened to actual people*, even though we are reading it on a smooth page with clear type. Poetry, especially poetry that is based on research, offers the opportunity to see events from a different, inside perspective, and does not refuse the subjective, emotional response. In "Poetry Is Not a Luxury," Lorde writes "our feelings were not meant to survive," and Toni Morrison similarly states that one inspiration for writing about enslaved people in *Beloved* was "to find and expose a truth about the interior life of people who didn't write it (which doesn't mean that they didn't have it)" (Lorde 1977: 373; Morrison [1987] 1995: 93). The archive tells us the number of women—twenty—who brought rape charges against Sergeant Holder, but only names one survivor, Elizabeth Walcott. Nor are details, such as what words *might* have been said, how the women *might* have felt, or how they *might* have chosen survival, available in the archive.[10]

The inclusion of poetry in the critical biomythography was not a decision that I took lightly or made as some kind of escape from the difficult work of archival research. As both a serious scholar and a serious poet, I know that each genre requires a great deal of effort for the best results. The poetic voice included in my jamette research is an invention based on existing actual research and informed by contemporary realities, and as it is here, the poetry will be presented in a different physical format from the narrative text.

The intention is not at all to trick or mislead the reader, but to explicitly acknowledge the inventive and subjunctive voice. The goal is to address the spectral archive while refusing to let biased perspectives be the only voices that are heard. Furthermore, while here, in an essay focused on elucidating methodology, there is some commentary on the poems, in the larger work the poems will not be accompanied by commentary. They will remain interruptions and disruptions of both the archive's screaming silence and of the more traditional scholarly analysis of those archives.

"another day"

sometimes you just get tired
carrying all the things in your hands
all the people on your back and
you stumble
keep going
you cannot fall you
cannot   cannot

fall[11]

The traditional archive of documents carefully held in secure buildings is not the only archive. Spectral archives also exist, and these present questions traditional archives do not answer, and propose subjunctive statements that create enough space for full humanity. In my research with the jamettes, I use both the traditional archive and the spectral archive. In search of a "truth" that is more inaccessible than usual because of the absence of the voices I most wish to hear, I plan to do my best to deliberately tell my research in a different way, one that is both critical and creative, gesturing toward truth without claiming it.

Authors such as Anzaldúa, Lorde, Marmon Silko, and Cliff challenge(d) fundamental understandings and assumptions of race, gender, sexuality, ethnicity, writing, and theory. Precisely because not every methodology is appropriate for every project, we need to use and acknowledge more ways of learning, knowing, and doing. In particular, if we want to have in our collective body of knowledge the most robust sense of the world and everyone in it, then methods, strategies, and theories created by people outside of hegemonic groups and power must be recognized as not only viable and legitimate, but as useful and necessary, *even if they do not resemble traditional methods, strategies, and theories.*

A great deal is at stake in the elucidation of hybrid creative-critical methodologies such as radical interdisciplinarity and their origin within women of color feminist traditions.[12] As Harney and Moten write, "to be a critical academic in the university is to be against the university, and to be against the university is always to recognize it and be recognized by it" (Harney and Moten 2013: 31). I have created and published both scholarly writing and creative work (and will continue to do so). Why should I risk my position in both of these worlds to engage and describe a process that will be seen by many as not quite academic (enough) to warrant reading or teaching it, and which might be seen by others as too scholarly to be engaged by the poetry world?

The answer is because this work—one might even say the jamette women themselves—requires it. Examining the remnant strands of their lives compelled me to create a richer, more complicated representation of them, one that acknowledges that they were full human beings and not one-dimensional stereotypes. And since I'm sure there are other situations—other work—that call out for radical interdisciplinarity, this contribution and its gesturing beyond traditional scholarship might be useful to some of those who are doing that work.

Rosamond S. King's book *Island Bodies: Transgressive Sexualities in the Caribbean Imagination* received the Caribbean Studies Association best book award, and her poetry includes the Lambda Award–winning *Rock | Salt | Stone*. King is associate professor of English and director of the Institute for the Humanities at Brooklyn College.

Notes

1   Note, however, that the comparative literature I both learned and practice are focused on the Global South, not centered in the countries and concerns of postwar Europe that originated the field.

2   All text appearing in sans serif is original poetry by Rosamond S. King; this poem appears in *Rock | Salt | Stone* (2017).

3   Many years ago, Gayatri Spivak (1985) reminded us that speech need not be confined to writing. And though only biased descriptions exist of them, there are references to jamette women's physical behavior and other types of "speech" and protest that will be examined in my longer work.

4   Fuentes is referring to the "many configurations [of violence]: physical, archival, and epistemic" (Fuentes 2016: 6).

5   I am especially appreciative of Working Group members Maile Arvin, Karen J. Leong, Judy Tzu-Chun Wu, and Laura Briggs, who provided substantive feedback on earlier drafts of this essay.

6   Some recent interesting exceptions include Alexis Pauline Gumbs's *Spill: Scenes of Feminist Black Fugitivity* (2016), Omise'eke Natasha Tinsley's *Ezili's Mirrors: Imagining Black Queer Genders* (2018), Lyndon K. Gill's *Erotic Islands: Art and Queer Activism in the Caribbean* (2018)—all published by Duke University Press.

7   Lorde's work simultaneously utilizes this first definition of myth, while also countering the second definition, "A widespread but untrue or erroneous story or belief; a widely held misconception; a misrepresentation of the truth. Also: something existing only in myth; a fictitious or imaginary person or thing." In relationship to Lorde's work, this second definition refers not to her biomythography, but to the stereotypes and other negative myths that misrepresent the truth of black women, of lesbians, and of black lesbians.

8   Anne McClintock as quoted in Crichlow (2004: 188).

9   The poem excerpted here is previously unpublished.

10   I emphasize the conditional tense to underscore that these poems are speculative, and meant to suggest but neither to report nor to make claims about the women's actual experiences.

11   Poem "another day" excerpted from King (2017).

12   There is more than one women of color feminism, so I use the word *tradition* to encompass them.

Works Cited

Anzaldúa, Gloria. 2007. *Borderlands/La Frontera: The New Mestiza*. 3rd ed. San Francisco, CA: Aunt Lute Books.

Brereton, Bridget. 1975. "The Development of an Identity: The Negro Middle Class of Trinidad in the Late Nineteenth Century." In *Social Groups and Institutions in the History of the Caribbean*, 50–65. Mayagüez: Association of Caribbean Historians.

Brereton, Bridget. 1979. *Race Relations in Colonial Trinidad, 1870–1990*. Cambridge: Cambridge University Press.

Brereton, Bridget. 1981. *A History of Modern Trinidad, 1783–1962*. Port of Spain, Trinidad: Heinemann Educational Books.

Brereton, Bridget. 1994. *Gendered Testimony: Autobiographies, Diaries, and Letters by Women as Sources for Caribbean History*. Mona: University of the West Indies Department of History.

Campbell, Susan. 1988. "Carnival, Calypso, and Class Struggle in Nineteenth Century Trinidad." *History Workshop*, no. 26: 1–27.

Cliff, Michelle. 1980. *Claiming an Identity They Taught Me to Despise*. Watertown, MA: Persephone Press.

Cowley, John. 1996. *Carnival, Canboulay and Calypso: Traditions in the Making*. Cambridge: Cambridge University Press.

Crichlow, Wesley E. A. 2004. "History, (Re)Memory, Testimony, and Biomythography: Charting a Buller Man's Trinidadian Past." In *Interrogating Caribbean Masculinities: Theoretical and Empirical Analyses*, edited by Rhoda E. Reddock, 185–222. Mona: University of the West Indies Press.

Crowley, Daniel J. 1956. "The Traditional Masques of Carnival." *Caribbean Quarterly* 4, no. 3/4: 194–223.

Fuentes, Marisa J. 2016. *Dispossessed Lives: Enslaved Women, Violence, and the Archive*. Philadelphia: University of Pennsylvania Press.

Harney, Stefano, and Fred Moten. 2013. *The Undercommons: Fugitive Planning and Black Study*. Wivenhoe, UK: Minor Compositions.

Hartman, Saidiya. 2008. "Venus in Two Acts." *Small Axe*, no. 26: 1–14.

King, Rosamond S. 2011. "New Citizens, New Sexualities—Nineteenth Century Jamettes." In *Sex and the Citizen: Interrogating the Caribbean*, edited by Faith Smith, 214–23. Charlottesville: University of Virginia Press.

King, Rosamond S. 2017. *Rock | Salt | Stone*. New York: Nightboat.

Lorde, Audre. 1977. "Poetry Is Not a Luxury." In *Women's Voices, Feminist Visions: Classic and Contemporary Readings*, edited by Susan M. Shaw and Janet Lee, 371–73. New York: McGraw-Hill Education.

Lorde, Audre. 1982. *Zami: A New Spelling of My Name*. New York: Crossing Press.

Morrison, Toni. (1987) 1995. "The Site of Memory." In *Inventing the Truth: The Art and Craft of Memoir*, edited by William Zinsser, 83–102. Boston: Houghton Mifflin.

Pearse, Andrew. 1956. "Carnival in Nineteenth Century Trinidad." *Caribbean Quarterly* 4, no. 3/4: 175–93.

Marmon Silko, Leslie. 1993. *Sacred Water*. Tucson, AZ: Flood Plain Press.

Spivak, Gayatri. 1985. "Can the Subaltern Speak? Speculations on Widow Sacrifice." *Wedge* 7/8: 120–30.

Trotman, David V. 1986. *Crime in Trinidad: Conflict and Control in a Plantation Society, 1838–1900*. Knoxville: University of Tennessee Press.

Deema Kaedbey and Nadine Naber

....

Reflections on Feminist Interventions within the 2015 Anticorruption Protests in Lebanon

Abstract: This essay reflects upon the themes of collaborative research, intersectional feminist activism, and social movements against corruption and sectarianism in the context of Lebanon. The authors focus on the summer of 2015 when protesters filled the streets in response to the government's mismanagement of garbage in what they called the "You Stink" movement. Feminists, primarily through the formation the "Feminist Bloc," joined in the protests and presented nuanced frameworks for understanding the problem and mobilizing against the state with a gendered lens. In the pages that follow, the authors historicize the conditions that inspired feminist participation in these protests in order to present the perspectives of a few feminist activists voicing their own analysis of this period. In addition, they reflect upon what it means to write and research collaboratively, between the United States (Nadine) and Lebanon (Deema).

We began this research in 2015, when Nadine initiated a discussion about what it could look like to produce collaborative research that would contribute to both transnational feminism, and to a feminism in Beirut that was putting forward a critical intersectional framework to theorize and engage with issues in Lebanon. At that time, it was only a few months after the end of a public movement in Beirut often referred to as the "You Stink" movement, in which many feminists participated. This movement brought to the surface of our conversations many of the issues central to the work of feminists in Beirut. Emerging while the revolutions in Tunisia, Egypt,

MERIDIANS · feminism, race, transnationalism   18:2 October 2019
DOI: 10.1215/15366936-7789750 © 2019 Smith College

and Syria were still on our minds, the You Stink movement brought up
questions of regional solidarity; but there was also a feminist discourse
and a mobilization on the ground that we believed presented a very valuable contribution to feminist praxis.

Lebanon, Summer 2015: the country witnessed a captivating movement
against corruption, epitomized by a crisis that tellingly concerned the government's mismanagement of garbage collection. As garbage filled the
streets and neighborhoods across the country, activists led protests against
the mismanagement of this crisis and the government's disregard for
people's lives. Feminists joined in the protests and presented nuanced
frameworks for understanding the problem and mobilizing against
the state with a gendered lens.

These events took place three years after the revolutions of 2011–12 that
swept over countries such as Tunisia and Egypt. Even though Lebanon
did not witness similar mass mobilizations, there were demonstrations
around capitalism and sectarianism, as well as visible feminist activities
within and separate from these mobilizations. In 2015, activists, including
feminist activists, made links to and drew inspiration from the revolutions of the Middle East and North Africa (MENA).

This piece captures some of the conversations we had with feminists
about the 2015 protests, many of whom evoked the earlier protests of
2011–12 as inspiration. It is not meant to be a research paper or to present
our own exploration of the feminist discourse around the period of the
organizing. What we do is provide a brief historical context followed by the
perspectives of a few feminist activists voicing their own analysis.

The Background

In July 2015, hills of garbage began filling the streets of Lebanon, from
major streets in Beirut to neighborhoods outside the capital city (Mavropoulos 2017). Activists thus mobilized to announce unapologetically to
their government: "You Stink." What came to be known as the You Stink
movement (which was in fact the name of one of its leading groups) saw the
"rottenness" and "smell" that people in Lebanon were breathing as the
embodiment of a corrupt government and an entire political class that
had been ruling with no accountability for decades. Some factions in the
movement called for the decentralization of services and new parliamen-
tary elections. There were also calls for alternative solutions to manage
the garbage crisis (Atallah 2015; CSKC).

The protests inspired new discussions about regime change in Lebanon, as well as regional solidarity—with comparisons or connections being made to the revolutions in the MENA region. The movement also mobilized feminists, as we saw a revived discourse with a noticeable presence on the ground. We believe this feminist mobilization presented important and innovative contributions to critical feminist praxis in Lebanon.

Women activists were very prominent in the You Stink protests, especially within alliances that were antisectarian, antiracist, leftist, and/or feminist. Yet this presence became even more visible when feminists worked to unify their voices under the "Feminist Bloc," a coalition of feminists who marched during the protests under the banner "The Patriarchal Regime is Lethal." The bloc included feminist collectives like Sawt al Niswa (which called for the formation of the bloc), feminist groups, feminist co-ops, and feminist student clubs representing campuses from the public Lebanese University to the private American University of Beirut. There were also feminists from the antiracism movement and from leftist groups and coalitions, mainly from the coalition Al Sha'ib Yurid [The People Want].

Despite this presence, most scholarship and public discourse obscures the queer and feminist work and its distinct political contributions within the You Stink movement. At the same time, dominant movement discourses subsume and erase women's demands and fail to consider one of the key feminist critiques within the movement: that patriarchy is at the root of the violent sectarian regime, so entrenched that it even impacts the activist organizing of progressive men.

The work of feminist activists involved in the You Stink movement operated within, beside, between, and sometimes even in opposition to some social movement discourse.[1] Because of this position, the Feminist Bloc brought a series of distinct interventions to the antisectarian movements of Lebanon by highlighting the interconnected nature of sectarianism and patriarchy and how they operate violently; but they also showed how racism and structural racial hierarchies divided women in Lebanon, and how nonconforming gender and sexual identities were often violently marginalized. By working to merge multiple political struggles and multiple points of view through their work, these activists are striving to remain accountable to the struggles of all women (not only heteronormative Lebanese middle- and upper-class women). Therefore, the positions of migrant workers, refugees, and LGBT people were included in the discourse and in the organizing.

What activists defined as the You Stink movement in the context of the national garbage crisis generally relegated concerns related to gender justice and sexual rights to the status of a secondary priority or even deemed them irrelevant. However, it is these very moments, especially within mobilizations by civil society and leftist movements, that bring the visions and agendas of these feminist and queer feminist activists to the surface, opening up possibilities for bringing their work to bear on various social justice movements and pushing the critiques, frameworks, and networks feminist and queer activists have created and re-created over the years into new spaces.

In 2011–12, for example, feminists mobilized on multiple fronts, including organizing against sexual harassment within political marches and protests. They insisted that leftist movements must integrate resistance against gendered racism impacting migrant domestic workers. In 2012, feminist activists involved in these mass protests created an anti–sexual harassment campaign called the "Adventures of Salwa" to publicize the problem of sexual harassment within political movements in Lebanon and simultaneously organized the first antirape protest in Lebanon. Some of the feminists we talked to about the 2015 protests (such as Jo, whom Nadine interviewed in February 2017) spoke about these earlier mobilizations. They also talked about the ways the feminist activism that coconstituted the revolutions of the MENA region inspired their own integration of feminist and queer politics into movements for regime change in Lebanon.

The Research

A few months after the You Stink movement came to an end, Nadine initiated a discussion with Deema about whether conducting collaborative research that maps urgent feminist interventions could contribute to the struggle of feminist activists to theorize, articulate, and assert a critical intersectional feminist politics in Lebanon. Inspired by the visible antiracist queer and feminist vision that was mobilized within the antisectarian/anticorruption You Stink movement in Beirut, we agreed that this is an exceptionally important moment to both document and contribute to discussions about feminist and LGBTQ possibilities, especially in relation to movements committed to ending capitalism, racism, and sectarianism in Lebanon.

We conducted our research in the summer and fall of 2016, through interviews and participant observation with self-identified feminists whom we knew participated in the 2015 protests, many of them in the Feminist Bloc, and we identified activists whose work and politics are intersectional. While it would certainly be interesting and valuable to interview women and queer people who do not identify with feminist politics but were present during the protests, or who are in different movements, this research focuses on highlighting, analyzing, and building on the work of self-identified feminists with an intersectional lens in order to understand the possibilities that emerge when feminist activists and protests for regime change share political space. We call this feminism that we are zooming in on in this piece "queer feminist politics," which is not about sexual or gender identity, but about practicing a politics that is antisectarian as well as antiheteropatriachal, and that is committed to gender justice as it also intersects with ending racism, capitalism, and sectarianism.

Also based on Deema and Nadine's conversations, we decided to give our interview material back to the Knowledge Workshop (KW), the feminist organization that Deema cofounded, which is working on building a feminist archive, including an archive of women's participation in social movements in Lebanon, both historical and current. Rather than serving only the purpose of our research project, we wanted these interviews to be available for use by researchers, students, and activists interested in the feminist movement and women's mobilization for years to come. This research thus turned out to be very helpful for the KW's archival work. And in reaching out to feminists from different age groups, ethnicities, and experiences, our research also reflected the intentional politics of the KW to be inclusive of all women mobilizing in Lebanon, and to interconnect communities, individuals, and movements.

Complementing the use of stories and oral histories that combine the personal with the political and present alternative narratives to mainstream discourse, a practice that Deema and the KW adhere to, Nadine has been working with a similar methodology that she developed in her book *Arab America: Gender, Cultural Politics, and Activism* (2012) and calls "documenting activist stories." This methodology looks at individual stories within the context of a collective movement, and the historical/political conditions that gave rise to the ways activists discuss and theorize the stories they tell and the politics they adopt. In both cases, we have been paying attention to the interconnection of collective political struggles and identities and acknowledging the complex power dynamics and layers of both injustice and possibility that shape the stories we include. Moreover, our methodology critiques the power dynamics between researcher and researched as we affirm that we do not hold the authoritative theoretical voice. Our aim is to center our interlocutors as the theorists of their own stories and activism.

Feminist Visions within the You Stink Movement

In their coauthored essay, "What's Feminism Got to Do with It? Is There a Need for Feminism in the Current Protests in Lebanon?," Lamia Moghnie and Stephanie Gaspais (both active within feminist movements in Lebanon) succinctly capture the feminist vision and politics that we highlight in this paper, which was consolidated on the streets of Beirut in the summer of 2015 and captures the distinct perspectives of many of the feminists we talked to:

> Because a feminist reading can shed a light on relations and dynamics of power; on violence and discrimination from the state. This analysis is not secondary or parallel to other demands, but is at the heart of understanding the patriarchal practices of the violent state on different groups.

> Because feminism contains tools that make visible the social/cultural violence against women in the streets, manifested in the masculinist slogans that are more an expression of state power than the demands of the protest.

> Because feminism allows us to read better the practices of violence and harassment that some marginalized women face in Lebanon, among other minority groups.

> Because feminism gives us the ability to better reflect the streets and the demands and rights of women, whether they are Lebanese or not. (Moghnie and Gaspais 2015)

As Moghnie and Gaspais show, feminists have developed the framework to understand the crisis and the mobilization around it through looking at intersecting power structures and systems. Below we introduce feminist activists whose analysis and praxis further illustrate the feminist visions that Moghnie and Gaspais outlined.

The first interview we feature is with Lebanese feminist activist Maya

Ammar, who at that time was working as the communications officer in KAFA (Enough Violence and Exploitation), a large nongovernmental organization that mainly focuses on violence against women and trafficking. Maya was also at the time a member of the feminist collective Sawt al Niswa, and was thus part of the conversations in the Feminist Bloc. We met Maya at KAFA's offices in Beirut in February 2017, and we asked her about her reflections on the protests, as well as on the connections between her activist work and feminist activism in South West Asia and North Africa. In response, she reflected on the violence that she witnessed, the reason she participated in the protests, and the experiences of women in them.

On the topic of violence during the protests, and how the Feminist Bloc viewed it, Maya said:

> The police violence actually was very shocking. . . . Really I didn't expect it. . . . I think we all went through this, we all were hit with gas and water. . . . Now as a Feminist Bloc, when things were no longer limited to the question of garbage, . . . in my opinion, things start to unfold and you want to talk about everything, because really when you want to deal with the garbage issue then you have to deal with the corruption issue, then you have to deal with the political confessional, sectarian system in Lebanon and then you find yourself dealing with everything, with the whole system at once.

Maya also explained the link between sectarianism and patriarchy:

> This [the sectarian system] is the root of all our problems, of course related to other elements, definitely. So what we brought to the discourse was this word: *patriarchy*. As groups, we were all talking about the system and everything: OK it's capitalist, corrupt, inefficient. But don't forget that it's patriarchal. And then there was this shift in discourse I guess when the Feminist Bloc was created, it emerged in the middle of the protests—and it actually helped a lot of women talk about their experiences in the movement, while they were protesting, while they were organizing, or while they were in the meeting. And they were being silenced, some of them were subjected to sexual harassment in the streets while protesting, so this Bloc really helped them have a voice and highlight what was happening also inside the movement. So, it's not like we waited for it until it ended and then we were critical about it. We were critical about it while it was happening, which I think is a very strong point.

And she continued to analyze women's positions in this sectarian system:

> We're also saying that women have been dealing with this structure, with this system, for decades, for years. We know it by heart. We know how the sectarian system affects us because it actually governs our personal affairs, and we know how the courts can be biased and unfair towards women. We know the police, a lot of women have already tried filing complaints before and have witnessed harassment from police officers, so you know, women already know that, OK. And we deal with shit and garbage every day. [It's] our mothers' daily lives. That's what our mothers do, they clean our fathers' shit.

Furthermore, Maya spoke about women and feminists organizing in male-dominated spaces, and the sexual harassment they faced:

> And during meetings I know, and we know, we heard our friends saying that they weren't able to continue a phrase and they were constantly interrupted by their male comrades, inside the meetings, so I think the women used this, the platforms they were present in to actually make that point. There's much more awareness among women activists I think. I saw a lot of strength, and also challenging the discourse of priority: what's more important what's less important.
>
> The sexual harassment cases are documented. Some of them were actually direct physical assault, and the women who talked about it were very discouraged but kept going, and they usually happened when people started to leave the protests, or when you know you're just crossing the other street to go to another corner so just one of the protesters follows her and grabs her. Others were, one of them was a police officer, the harasser. In my case, it was a group of boys protesting. And the interesting part of it is that I was very confused about what to do, because, you know the boys were the ones facing the police. The people who are throwing stones are the boys who feel they have nothing to lose, they are desperate boys, they don't care about anything, and maybe they have gone through prisons, and there are of course young people and maybe we were brave to go forward, but the most boys who climbed the shields or face the police are those young men from Khanda' el Ghamee' [a poor/economically marginalized neighborhood in Beirut]. So these boys who are facing the police and who I would defend if the police did something to them, this boy [is the] one who harasses me.

When we asked about transregional collaborations, Maya responded:

[The protests] also brought people [from the region] together. There was a need for people to benefit from each other, you know. When you create this need, the need is the drive I think to connect, to see someone who understands what you're saying, even if they are not living it. And that's what I think a lot of the feminists were trying to find, someone who understands them a bit in this. So, we all used to meet and understand each other. . . . Maybe with the [male] comrade you understand and he understands you on the topic of the system and how it is hurting us. But the comrade will not understand my position in my work and my family and on the streets, as much as I understand it. So you want feminists to talk to in this matter, to understand you. And sometimes, you share with them mechanisms of what you are doing to go out, so that you can go on.

It was the following day after meeting Maya that we headed to the Migrant Community Center (MCC), also in Beirut, and we sat down to interview Jane, a Filipina domestic migrant worker and a veteran activist for the rights of domestic migrant workers, as well as for labor rights and feminism in Lebanon in general. With us in the interview was also Farah, an antiracist feminist from Lebanon who was part of founding the MCC and the antiracism movement. Jane and Farah explained and analyzed how racism against migrant domestic workers is part of the institutional, social, and individual relations in Lebanon, leaving workers vulnerable to exploitation and abuse.

Farah summarized what migrant domestic workers in Lebanon face:

The main things domestic migrant women face is the nonpayment of wages (which are already ridiculous) all over the country—whenever the employer feels like it. But racism is not simple. There are levels—like yes she can swim at the beach but she has to sit under the tree. Yes she will be paid but not what they agreed. Then there is physical abuse, sexual abuse, thousands of stories—whether by visitors to the employers, the agency, the consul, the Lebanese honorary consul. . . . There is the confiscation of passports, even by the most decent employer, as well as confinement at work and no days off. And whatever sort of abuse she has been getting for a year, there is no mechanism to complain about it. Zero. If this person hasn't been paid for six months, is sick and tired of fake promises, or if this person has been harassed, raped, or impregnated by the rape and then says, "That's it, I'm leaving"—the minute she's out of the house, she's the criminal—before they hear her story, before they see her bruises. There is one death a week among female domestic workers. And those are the ones that are in newspapers. The question is, why are so many domestic workers killing themselves here and if they're not suicide, then what are they?

Farah also explained what the Migrant Community Center (MCC) is and does; and she continued to explain about the antiracism movement:

We are in the Migrant Community Center of Beirut now, and there are two other centers, one in Jounieh, one in Saida. The organization has been working for five years on issues of racism and discrimination with the migrant communities and domestic workers in Lebanon—mostly women, because migrant domestic workers in Lebanon, worldwide too— and their children and families. The centers do school work, university work, educational sessions. Members (rather than Lebanese people or staff) prepare to go and lead the sessions. We have someone who leads trainings on public speaking, how to handle a class, how to deal with children, how to share your story. Sometimes volunteers come and offer piano, yoga, dance, Zumba, therapy sessions, drawing, and language or computer classes. We do case work, supporting people writing their letters, appeals, with UNHCR, with their files, taking video testimonies, organizing cultural events, celebrations, and birthdays. In the summer many of the migrant workers who are part of the center bring their children when they are at work and children don't have school in the summer, so a few children are here and somebody's taking care of them.

As a part of the antiracism movement, we never do lobbying. We focus on key issues in our messaging and all our work, which is the sponsorship system, the exclusion of domestic workers from Lebanese labor law and the lack of a protection mechanism and no basic rights. We are talking about 250,000 women or 8 percent of the country. These are the basic concerns and demands of migrant workers taken up year after year on Workers' Day, International Migrants Day, International Day of Domestic Workers—abolishing the sponsorship system, protection mechanisms, and remove the article that excludes domestic workers from Lebanese labor law.

Jane reflected on her experiences of organizing in Lebanon, going back about a decade prior to the 2015 garbage protests:

I started my activism in 1995 with my Filipino embassy as a community mobilizer, volunteer, and then it happened once when in the war of 2006 between Lebanon and Israel—I was part of the rescue team and I found out that a lot of migrant workers needed help and there's none. When we rescue Filipinos and other communities, we take them with us and we call their respective consulate or agencies. That was when I decided to say, "Let me go and advocate for the Filipino community"—when I started participating nationally and internationally. I became a volunteer of Caritas and all the NGOs here, Insan, Kafa, and also [the] antiracism movement. Me and other women activists developed a lot of material and guidelines for this movement. We were the founding members of the Domestic Workers Union [no longer active]. I now contribute to the alliance for domestic migrant workers in the area of advocacy and promoting rights.

After that, both Jane and Farah explained how race separates women in Lebanon, and how Lebanese women contribute to the oppression of migrant women. They also talked about the importance of solidarity:

> **Farah:** [Lebanese] women here who are facing a lot, society-wise, policy-wise, can themselves be so actively oppressive of other women and this cycle can regenerate itself. The idea is that you are tackling racism with people who don't know what the word even means. We use a tool kit that talks about six countries, those six countries are the main countries where migrant domestic workers are coming from—talking about Bangladesh, Nepal, Philippines, Sri Lanka, Madagascar, Ethiopia.

> **Jane:** There is a need to create solidarity among women—for Lebanese women to realize the domestic worker is a migrant woman, but a woman like me. And about having our periods every month, doesn't she think that if she herself is sick once a month, that once a month, I cannot lift the bottle of water because I have pain? Like, they criticize migrant domestic workers when they dress up on their day off. Doesn't the employer, the madame, think that this migrant worker is a woman too?

> **Farah:** The Feminist Bloc [during the You Stink protests] was one of those spaces that allowed for inclusion for all people who are excluded by the rest. So, if you don't feel safe at the beginning or the end of a march, the Feminist Bloc is a place that is by default, people can just

join it on their own and realize that it's welcoming. It's the mini impossible dream.

Farah: [on regional networks for domestic workers] There are great networks all over the world, there's Migrant Forum Asia doing great work, by people from the origin countries, but the Arab world, nothing regional whatsoever. So this network came in a few years ago with the hope that it will bridge the gaps especially between here, Lebanon, Egypt, Jordan and the Gulf. A few meetings happened.

Jane: And we have the coalition of Women Human Rights Defenders [WHRD].

The WHRD-MENA coalition is a coalition of women human rights defenders, women activists who work on community as well as regional levels, using different tools for solidarity and protection against abuses, including UN and other international mechanisms. Being supported by the WHRD-MENA coalition acknowledges that domestic migrant workers are part of the MENA society, and as activists, they are at risk of what many women human rights defenders face in oppressive and deeply discriminatory societies; it also provides the activists with platforms and networks to seek to mobilize local, regional, and international tools to end such discrimination and oppression.

As we went through the interviews and some of the feminist writings that came out during the 2015 protests, we both felt how important it was to affirm these milestones of feminist organizing. The Feminist Bloc, for example, which was initiated in 2015 during the protests, continues to operate and grow in different forms today. And as Farah, one of the activists we interviewed told us, so much is always happening that we forget events, we block things out. We often live in a crisis of memory because there is always something going on, a violation to respond to, so many things to do. But to have this opportunity to remember, to connect then and now, can be an important contribution to the work of activists who are putting forth important analysis of their situation. In addition, our research opened up conversations about what it means to have this collaboration between a feminist based in Lebanon (Deema) and an activist academic based in the United States (Nadine) who is ultrasensitive to the ways feminist research emanating from the United States is intertwined with imperial and colonial domination in the MENA region.

Therefore, in order to stay accountable to the feminist interlocutors we were talking to, we committed to a decolonizing methodology based upon the following four principles:

First, the importance of our collaboration: Deema and Nadine conducted most of the research together. Nadine knew about feminist activism in Lebanon through her previous research, but also ongoing relations she has with feminists in or from the country, including Deema. Deema and Nadine continuously talked about how this research would align with the relationships and activist histories she belonged to.

Secondly, we were intentional from the beginning that our research will not focus on Lebanese women's voices, but will also include migrant women workers, and Palestinian feminists in Lebanon, for example, who are part of its feminist movements. Our methodology therefore also adheres to a framework that many feminists in Lebanon have developed, and our research highlights this framework rather than superimposing an exclusionary nationalist approach.

Thirdly, we wanted our research and our analysis to grow and change with the feedback from movement activists. We organized a discussion at the KW, for example, where feminist activist attendees shared their feedback and helped shape our analysis and the future of the project. When Nadine first approached Deema about the project, she expressed her desire for research that would listen to and serve the need of the feminist movements we were talking about. We decided that since so much research material and interviews often remain inaccessible to the public, and since Deema was already working on building the KW's feminist archives, it made sense to have the interviews also support the KW's work.

Thus, the interviews went to the KW archives and are—with the consent of the interlocutors—accessible to the public. As such, our interviews can have new lives, and the potential to serve new purposes among feminists in Beirut. And that was one of our primary intentions, to have feminist frameworks and discourse circulate more widely to contribute to the feminists organizing in Lebanon.

....

Deema Kaedbey is the cofounder of the Knowledge Workshop, a feminist organization in Beirut. She is also coeditor of the feminist webspace, *Sawt al Niswa*. With a PhD in women's, gender, and sexuality studies, her own work explores queer feminist frameworks that construct alternative histories of feminism in Lebanon.

Nadine Naber is a professor in the gender and women's studies program and the global Asian studies program at the University of Illinois, Chicago. She is the author of *Arab America: Gender, Cultural Politics, and Activism* (2012); *Race and Arab Americans* (2008); *Arab and Arab American Feminisms* (2010); and *The Color of Violence* (2006).

Author's Note

Nadine's research in Lebanon was funded by the Knowledge is Power Project on Gender and Sexuality in Beirut at the American University of Beirut.

Notes

1   Here, we draw upon Maylei Blackwell's analysis of "third world women's" activism in the United States in the 1960s and 1970s. Blackwell uses the term "multiple insurgencies" to analyze forms of feminist activism that have "gone often ignored because they occurred *between* and sometimes in contestation to various social movements." Blackwell names "feminist subjects who were multiply insurgent, those who struggled on numerous fronts to confront multiple oppressions" (Blackwell 2015: 281).

Works Cited

Atallah, Sami. 2015. "Garbage Crisis: Setting the Record Straight." *The Lebanese Center for Policy Studies Featured Analysis*, August. https://www.lcps-lebanon.org/featured Article.php?id=48.

Blackwell, Maylei. 2015. "Triple Jeopardy: The Third World Women's Alliance and the Transnational Roots of Women-of-Color Feminisms." In *Provocations: A Transnational Reader in the History of Feminist Thought*, edited by Susan Bordo, M. Cristina Alcalde, and Ellen Rosenman, 280–91. Berkeley, CA: University of California Press.

CSKC (Civil Society Knowledge Cenre). n. d. "Social Movement Responding to the Lebanese Social Crisis." *Civil Society Knowledge Centre*. Accessed June 11, 2019. https://civilsociety-centre.org/party/social-movement-responding-lebanese -garbage-crisis.

Mavropoulos, Antonis. 2017. "Lebanon Waste Crisis: How it All Started." *Wasteless Future*, January 12. https://wastelessfuture.com/lebanese-waste-crisis-how-it-all -started/.

Moghnie, Lamia, and Stephanie Gaspais. 2015. "What's Feminism Got to Do with It? Is There a Need for Feminism in the Current Protests in Lebanon?" *Sawt al Niswa*, September 9. http://sawtalniswa.org/article/509.

Stanlie James

Remarks for a Roundtable on Transnational Feminism

National Women's Studies Association, Baltimore,
Maryland, November 16–19, 2017

Abstract: In 1977 a collective of Black Lesbian Feminists published the Combahee River Collective Statement, a manifesto that defined and described the
interlocking oppressions that they and other women of color were experiencing and the deleterious impact of these oppressions upon their lives.
They committed themselves to a lifelong collective process and nonhierarchical distribution of power as they struggle(d) to envision and create a just
society. Twenty-nine years after the appearance of the Combahee River Collective Statement, over one hundred African Feminists met in Accra, Ghana
to formulate their own manifesto and ultimately adopt the Charter of Feminist Principles for African Feminists, which was first published in 2007
simultaneously in English and French. This paper reviews both statements
and acknowledges their critical contributions to the evolution of Transnational Feminisms.

The 2017 National Women's Studies Association (NWSA) annual conference in Baltimore, Maryland celebrated the fortieth anniversary of the
Combahee River Collective Statement (CRC [1977] 2009). Honoring this
iconic statement as the conference theme provided an important opportunity for the NWSA membership to reflect upon the inspirational/
aspirational nature of this critically important feminist document. Combahee, a collective of Black Lesbian Feminists, began meeting together in

MERIDIANS · feminism, race, transnationalism   18:2 October 2019
DOI: 10.1215/15366936-7775630 © 2019 Smith College

1974. Their statement was first published in 1977 and included four major topics:

1. The genesis of contemporary black feminism
2. What we believe, i.e. the specific province of our politics
3. The problems of organizing black feminists, including a brief history of our collective and
4. Black feminist issues and practice. (CRC [1977] 2009: 3)

Many of the observations of this intrepid band of Black Feminists have left an indelible imprint on my intellect, serving as a guide to the philosophical scaffolding of my work. I am certain that this is the case for many others as well. For within that document we began, yet again, to define the terminology that has ushered our struggles from the twentieth into the twenty-first century. The statement formulated a concept of identity politics, describing it as the interlocking oppressions that would later become known as intersectionality. Its authors identified and recognized the danger of privilege that continues to haunt the twenty-first century and extracts a critical psychological toll on Black women. They observed that as Black women they "do not have racial, sexual, heterosexual or class privilege to rely upon, nor do we have even the minimal access to resources and power that groups who possess any of these types of privilege have."[1] Within this statement we were instructed about the dangers of sexual politics under patriarchy and about their belief that the sexual politics within patriarchy was as pervasive in the lives of Black women as were the politics of class and race. They also called out racism that was affecting the white women's movement. We were provided with a name for something that many of us experienced but did not know how to describe or explain— "smart-ugly."[2] Being identified as smart and ugly from an early age fortified the insidious personal degradation that some of us suffered in our communities and from our families. Indeed, we were continuously reminded that we "are all damaged people merely by virtue of being Black women."[3] But from those menial positions, the women of the Combahee River Collective inspired and exhorted us to "use our position at the bottom . . . to make a clear leap into revolutionary action." Because if the improbable, the unthinkable were to happen, that Black women were actually free, "it would mean that everyone else would have to be free since our freedom would necessitate the destruction of all the systems of oppression" (CRC [1977] 2009: 8).

It must also be acknowledged that Combahee held an unshakeable belief in a "collective process and a nonhierarchical distribution of power within our own group and in our vision of a revolutionary society." As dedicated Black lesbian feminists, they avowed their commitment to "a lifetime of work and struggle" (CRC [1977] 2009: 11).

My comments in this NWSA roundtable session on Transnational Feminism sought to juxtapose the Combahee River Collective Statement, briefly summarized above, with another equally important but less well-known manifesto, the African Charter of Feminist Principles. Both groups represent important forms of transnational feminism. Combahee's early engagement with what has come to be known as transnational feminism was through exploring potential relationships and constructing alliances with other women of color in the United States. The African feminists continue to forge alliances with their counterparts in countries all over the continent of Africa and throughout the diaspora, even as they continue to interact with feminists throughout the world, particularly through United Nations activities.

In November of 2006, in Accra, Ghana, some twenty-nine years after the 1977 appearance of the Combahee River Collective Statement, over one hundred African feminist activists from across the continent and the diaspora gathered for a historic four-day meeting.

> The space was crafted as an autonomous space in which African feminists from all walks of life at different levels of engagement within the feminist movement such as mobilizing at local levels for women's empowerment to academia, could reflect on a collective basis and chart ways to strengthen and grow the feminist movement on the continent. (AFF [2007] 2016: 2)

A critical outcome of this forum was the formulation and adoption of the Charter of Feminist Principles for African Feminists. First published in 2007 simultaneously in English and French, the Charter was inherently transnational. It included an introduction and a preamble entitled "Naming Ourselves as Feminists." This was followed by five critical sections: "Our Understanding of Feminism and Patriarchy"; "Our Identity as African Feminists"; "Individual Ethics"; "Institutional Ethics"; and "Feminist Leadership." Crafted to help them refine and affirm their commitment to feminist principles and politics, and to guide their analyses and practices, this Charter set out the collective values that they felt were key to their work and their lives as feminists. It sought not only to name the changes that they wanted to see in their communities but also *how* those changes were to be achieved. It went even further to spell out their individual and collective responsibilities to the movement and to each other within the movement. With this charter, they

> Reaffirm our commitment to dismantling patriarchy in all its manifestations in Africa. We remind ourselves of our duty to defend and respect the rights of all women, without qualification. We commit to protecting the legacy of our feminist ancestors who made numerous sacrifices, in order that we can exercise greater autonomy. (AFF [2007] 2016: 2)

Thus, they viewed their charter as an accountability mechanism for feminist organizing.

Similar to the Combahee Collective Statement, these African women proudly define and publicly name themselves as feminists. In so doing, they were quite clear that the work of fighting for women's rights was, and is, deeply political as was the very process of naming themselves. They asserted that by naming themselves as feminists, they were politicizing the struggle for women's rights, questioning the legitimacy of the structures that keep women subjugated, and developing the tools for transformative analysis and action.

They named their multiple and varied identities as African Feminists, stating:

> We are African women when we live here in Africa and even when we live elsewhere, our focus is on the lives of African women on the continent. Our feminist identity is not qualified with "Ifs," "Buts," or "Howevers." We are Feminists. Full stop. (AFF [2007] 2016: 3)

While the Combahee Statement calls out the challenges of the racism and sexism African American women were experiencing and also notes the deleterious impact of patriarchy, the African women's feminist charter foregrounds patriarchy. They state that "as African feminists our understanding of feminism places patriarchal social relations structures and systems which are embedded in other oppressive and exploitative structures at the center of our analysis" (AFF [2007] 2016: 4). They continue on to declare:

> Patriarchy is a system of male authority which legitimizes the oppression of women through political, social, economic, legal, cultural, religious and military institutions. Men's access to, and control over resources and

rewards within the private and public sphere derives its legitimacy from the patriarchal ideology of male dominance. (AFF [2007] 2016: 4)

They observed that "patriarchy varies in time and space, meaning that it changes over time, and varies according to class, race, ethnic, religious and global imperial relationships and structures" (AFF [2007] 2016: 5). They also insisted that patriarchy was and is "inter-related with and informs relationships of class, race, ethnic, religious and global-imperialism," so that effectively challenging patriarchy requires challenging the other systems of oppression and exploitation that frequently mutually support each other. They insist that understanding patriarchy is crucial because it "provides for [them] as feminists, a framework within which to express the totality of oppressive and exploitative relations which affect African women" (AFF [2007] 2016: 4). They go on to argue that "patriarchal ideology enables and legitimizes the structuring of every aspect of [their] lives by establishing the framework within which society defines and views men and women and constructs male supremacy" (AFF [2007] 2016: 4). Thus, they assert that their "ideological task as feminists is to understand this system and [their] political task is to end it" (AFF [2007] 2016: 4). Their uncompromising opposition to patriarchy notwithstanding, they struggle against patriarchy as a system rather than fighting individual men or women. Similarly, the Combahee statement recognizes that its authors are allies with Black men against racism even as they struggle against the sexism of Black men.

The African Feminist Charter, like the Combahee River Collective Statement, also reminds us that their "current struggles" were "inextricably linked to [their] past as a continent"—specifically in the cases of their "diverse precolonial contexts, slavery, colonization, liberation struggles, neocolonialism, globalization, etc." (AFF [2007] 2016: 5). Modern African states, they insist, "were built on the backs of African feminists who fought alongside men for the liberation of the continent." They are determined not only to construct new African states in the millennium but also to "craft new identities for African women, identities as full citizens, free from patriarchal oppression, with rights of access, ownership and control over resources and our own bodies and utilizing positive aspects of our cultures in liberating and nurturing ways" (AFF [2007] 2016: 5).

They also rightfully acknowledge, with pride, the historical and significant gains that the African Women's Movement had made over the past forty years and they boldly claimed those gains *as* African feminists because, they insisted, African feminists "led the way, from the grassroots level and up," by strategizing, organizing, networking, going on strike, and marching in protest. They had also done the research, analyzed, lobbied, built institutions, and anything else "it took for states, employers, and institutions to acknowledge women's personhood" (AFF [2007] 2016: 5).

Additionally, they firmly situated themselves within the global feminist movement against patriarchal oppression in its full manifestations. They felt that their experiences clearly linked them to women in other parts of the world with whom they claim solidarity and support. They proudly and defiantly declare, as they honored their feminist ancestors who blazed the trail, that

> It is a profound insult to claim that feminism was imported into Africa from the West. We reclaim and assert the long and rich tradition of African women's resistance to patriarchy in Africa. We henceforth claim the right to theorize for ourselves, write for ourselves, strategise for ourselves and speak for ourselves as African feminists. (AFF [2007] 2016: 5)

With that ringing declaration, the Charter of Feminist Principles for African Feminists goes on to specifically list what they are defining as their individual as well as their institutional ethics. Their individual ethics, which share an affinity with Combahee and other feminists across the world, include but are not limited to the following:

> The indivisibility, inalienability and universality of women's human
>   rights.
> The effective participation in building and strengthening progressive
>   African feminist organizing and networking to bring about transfor-
>   matory change.
> A spirit of feminist solidarity and mutual respect based on frank, hon-
>   est and open discussion of difference with each other. (AFF [2007]
>   2016: 7)

In addition to these philosophical underpinnings of their individual ethics, they go on to enumerate more specific individualized commitments of their feminism, including:

> Freedom of choice and autonomy regarding bodily integrity issues,
>   including reproductive rights, abortion, sexual identity and sexual
>   orientation.

A critical engagement with discourses of religion, culture, tradition and
domesticity with a focus on the centrality of women's rights.

The recognition and presentation of African women as the subjects not
the objects of our work, and as agents in their lives and societies.

The right to healthy, mutually respectful and fulfilling personal
relationships.

The right to express our spirituality within or outside of organized
religions.

The acknowledgment of the feminist agency of African women which has
a rich Herstory that has been largely undocumented and ignored.
(AFF [2007] 2016: 7)

This charter also focused on the institutional ethics that they were committed to following as feminist organizations, such as those listed below:

Using power and authority responsibly, and managing institutional hierarchies with respect for all concerned. We believe that feminist spaces
are created to empower and uplift women. At no time should we allow
our institutional spaces to degenerate into sites of oppression and
undermining of other women. . . .

Exercising accountable leadership in feminist organisations taking into
consideration the needs of others for self-fulfillment and professional
development. This includes creating spaces for power-sharing across-
generations.

Creating and sustaining feminist organisations to foster women's leadership. Women's organizations and networks should be led and managed by women. It is a contradiction of feminist leadership principles
to have men leading, managing and being spokespersons for women's
organizations.

Striving to inform our activism with theoretical analysis and to connect
the practice of activism to our theoretical understanding of African
feminism. . . .

Opposing the subversion and/or hijacking of autonomous feminist spaces
to serve right wing, conservative agendas. (AFF [2007] 2016: 8–9)

Further, African feminists held themselves accountable for making a
difference in the quality of women's leadership. Because they believed that
the "quality of women's leadership is even more important than the numbers of women in leadership," they were committed to such principles as
the following:

Disciplined work ethics guided by integrity and accountability at all
    times.

Expanding and strengthening a multi-generational network and pool of
    feminist leaders across the continent

Nurturing, mentoring and providing opportunities for young feminists
    in a non-matronising manner.

Crediting African women's labour, intellectual and otherwise in our
    work.

Creating time to respond in a competent, credible and reliable manner to
    other feminists in need of solidarity. . . .

Being open to giving and receiving peer reviews and constructive feed-
    back from other feminists. (AFF [2007] 2016: 10)

Amina Mama, a renowned African feminist, participated in this historic
conference in Ghana. Among Mama's many accomplishments was leading
the establishment of the African Gender Institute at the University of Cape
Town in South Africa and serving as founding editor of the continental
journal *Feminist Africa*. She is an established author and scholar who is
currently a professor and director of the Feminist Research Institute
in Gender, Sexuality and Women's Studies at the University of California,
Davis. As we renewed our acquaintance at this NWSA conference, Mama
reminded me that the participants in the African feminist conference had
pledged to return to their homes and publicize the charter and the conference through different mediums including radio, websites, and television
for example. They agreed to have the charter translated beyond English
and French into local languages so that African women would not only be
alerted to this historic event but would have access to the commitments
made with this charter by African feminists to dedicate themselves to
transforming their societies.[4]

For over forty years the Combahee River Collective Statement has served
as a touchstone, a manifesto, a living historical document that continues to
inform and inspire us. I argue that the Charter of Feminist Principles for
African Feminists is as crucially important to African women, indeed to
transnational feminists, as Combahee was and is to us. They have critically
significant ideas that can and do instruct us on how we might engage in
ongoing feminist struggles to overcome the multiple oppressions that
continue to obstruct our progress in building a better world. But even more
important, we in the United States can and must learn from feminists

across the world. African feminists (like other feminists) have much to teach us and those of us in the North (or the West) must humbly embrace reciprocity. With that in mind, I invite you to read carefully and learn from the inspirational/aspirational Charter of Feminist Principles for African Feminists as we have from the Combahee River Collective Statement.

. . . .

Stanlie James is vice provost for inclusion and community engagement at Arizona State University. She is also a professor in the School of Social Transformation. She is the coeditor of three anthologies, the most recent one *Still Brave: The Evolution of Black Women's Studies* with Frances Smith Foster and Beverly Guy-Sheftall.

Note

1   CRC (Combahee River Collective). (1977) 2009. "A Black Feminist Statement: The Combahee River Collective." In *Still Brave: The Evolution of Black Women's Studies*, edited by Stanlie M. James, Frances Smith Foster, and Beverly Guy-Sheftall, 3–11. See "The Combahee River Collective Statement" on the Yale University American Studies Department website, accessed June 2, 2019. https://americanstudies.yale.edu/sites/default/files/files/Keyword%20Coalition_Readings.pdf.

2   "Combahee River Collective Statement," Yale University American Studies.

3   "Combahee River Collective Statement," Yale University American Studies.

4   Personal conversation with Amina Mama at the NWSA Conference in Baltimore, MD, November 2017.

Works Cited

AFF (African Feminist Forum). (2007) 2016. "Charter of Feminist Principles for African Feminists." African Women's Development Fund. http://awdf.org/wp-content/uploads/AFF-Feminist-Charter-Digital-%C3%A2%C2%80%C2%93-English.pdf.

Evelyne Trouillot

Translated by Nathan H. Dize

....

Secousses

La terre a soulevé mon cœur
d'un mouvement sec et violent
elle l'a déchiré
éparpillant mille morceaux
comme larmes d'oiseaux errants
aux quatre vents de mon île
et depuis
chaque nuit
j'entends les battements
hésiter à mi-chemin
entre décombres
et étoiles

Tremors

The earth wrenched my heart
in a quick and violent gesture
ripping it apart
scattering thousands of pieces

MERIDIANS · feminism, race, transnationalism   18:2 October 2019
DOI: 10.1215/15366936-7775641 © 2019 Smith College

like the tears of wandering birds
across the four corners of my island
and since then
every night
I hear it beating
hesitating halfway
between rubble
and stars

Reprinted by permission from Evelyne Trouillot (2014), *Par la fissure de mes mots*. Paris: Éditions Bruno Doucey. Translated by Nathan H. Dize. © Éditions Bruno Doucey, 2014.

Nathan H. Dize is a PhD candidate in the Department of French and Italian at Vanderbilt University, where he specializes in Haitian literature and history. He is content curator, translator, and editor of the digital history project *A Colony in Crisis: The Saint-Domingue Grain Shortage of 1789*. He coedits the "Haiti in Translation" interview series for H-Haiti. His translation of Makenzy Orcel's *The Immortals* (*Les Immortelles*, 2011) and his translation of Louis Joseph Janvier's *Haiti for the Haitians* are forthcoming. He has published articles in the *Journal of Haitian Studies*, *Francoshpères*, *sx archipelagos*, and the *Journal of Haitian History*. He tweets @NathanHDize.

Neda Maghbouleh, Laila Omar,
Melissa A. Milkie, and Ito Peng

Listening in Arabic

Feminist Research with Syrian Refugee Mothers

Abstract: This article reflects upon three developments emergent from a
feminist approach in research with Syrian newcomer mothers in Toronto,
Canada. First, a feminist approach shapes how the authors build their
research team and facilitate internal meetings as a diverse, multigenerational group open to learning from others. Second, a feminist approach
requires that the authors center mothers' words through the critical practice of ensuring shared Arabic language and local knowledge in the research
process. The authors offer excerpts in Arabic and English from participants'
narratives to describe how giving nuance to multiple forms of expression is
key to a feminist practice of translation. Third, the authors describe how
this approach opens their project to involve a range of participatory-action
activities driven by the voices and desires of participants. The authors end
by summarizing their ethical and methodological practices in light of
inequalities at the intersection of citizenship status, class, nation, race,
and other categories of asymmetrical power. These inequalities shape the
authors' attempts to reorganize conventional participant-researcher and
student-faculty dynamics in their work together.

In November 2015, a newly elected Liberal government led by Prime Minister Justin Trudeau began rolling out an ambitious "Rapid Impact" plan to
resettle twenty-five thousand Syrian newcomers to Canada by the end of
the year. Population-level data collected by the government suggested that
resettled families would be entering with fewer resources and more severe
challenges as compared to newcomers to Canada from other conflict

MERIDIANS · feminism, race, transnationalism   18:2 October 2019
DOI: 10.1215/15366936-7789739 © 2019 Smith College

zones, or even as compared to those displaced by the Syrian war merely one year earlier (IRCC 2016). In partnership with thousands of private citizens, the Liberal plan represented a turbo-charged version of Canada's unique public-private refugee sponsorship policy, first introduced in 1979 to support newcomers from Cambodia, Vietnam, and Laos.

Like others around the world, we were following news of the Syrian crisis closely. And like others in Canada, we were involved in individual and neighborhood-based fundraising efforts. Up to this point, the three of us who are faculty had maintained separate research agendas as colleagues in sociology at the University of Toronto and our coauthor, Laila, had recently joined our graduate program to begin master's coursework. Although we studied gender, im/migration/ethnicity, family, and social policy in our own ways, we had not yet incorporated the impacts of the Syrian war and the displacement of more than five million people into our sociological practice, and our personal commitments to supporting Syrian newcomers remained confined to work outside the university setting.

This changed when the federal Ministry of Immigration, Refugees and Citizenship (IRCC) and the Social Sciences and Humanities Research Council (SSHRC) announced a joint call for proposals to address the "Targeted Research: Syrian Refugee Arrival, Resettlement, and Integration" program.[1] The program aimed to "support research and mobilize knowledge in a timely way on key issues and events—such as *education, employment, skills development, social integration and security*—in the early days of the [Syrian] migration and resettlement process" (SSHRC 2016, emphasis added). Informed by feminist standpoint theory and practices, we knew that an important explanatory and critical lens into Canada's unique refugee regime was possible if the observations, insights, and narratives of newcomer *women*—and, in particular, *mothers*—were centered. We came together to draft a grant proposal for a one-year pilot study to shed light on mothers' wellness and mental health as they worked to resettle their children and families in their first year in Toronto. This would be achieved chiefly through two waves of interviews: one, within the first months of mothers' arrivals to Canada, and the second was targeted to take place just before "Month Thirteen," which represented the end of government or public-private sponsorship of the family. Our pilot project was funded by IRCC-SSHRC in August 2016 and an expanded version of our project is newly funded through 2023 by SSHRC and the Ontario Ministry of

Research, Innovation, and Science.[2] What follows below are our collective reflections on the developments that emerged from the pilot project.

Why Women? A Feminist Approach to Migration and Transnationalism

The 2016 Rapid Impact call for proposals from IRCC-SSHRC and its androcentric focus on "key issues and events" like skills development and security is characteristic of mainstream scholarly and policy-oriented perspectives on migration, and in particular, the forced migration of Syrians and other racialized populations into Europe and North America.[3] Gender was not prioritized or flagged as a phenomenon of interest to IRCC-SSHRC, nor was it suggested as a variable in a more superficial "add and stir" approach. Despite this, we proposed a project centered on the accounts of newcomer *women* in order to better understand some of the core migration and resettlement-related issues identified by IRCC-SSHRC. We based our decision to focus on women on two factors. First, the vast majority of newcomers to Canada via Rapid Impact were women and children. This gave us a unique window to understand resettlement issues from a gender perspective. Second, we were informed by feminist epistemological logic, as elaborated by Patricia Hill Collins (1991), Chandra Mohanty (1991), Sandra Harding (1993), and Ella Shohat (2001) that high-quality, critical research findings about dominant groups and their institutional beliefs and practices are generated by centering and listening to marginalized populations. In this way, primary mechanisms typically overlooked and undertheorized in traditionally macro-level analyses of processes like globalization and migration are in fact *only* revealed in black feminist, third world feminist, and transnational feminist research streams (Herr 2014).

Thus, in the case of the Rapid Impact call for proposals, we were compelled to ask how—across a migration process structured by nation-states and their relational and symbolic positions vis-à-vis one another (for example: Canada as benevolent safe harbor; Syria as conflict zone) and as interpolated by transnational actors such as the United Nations/UN High Commissioner for Refugees—centering Syrian women's perspectives could offer "situated knowledge" (Haraway 1988) and key sightlines into these institutions and regimes. By focusing on what Mohanty has termed the "epistemic advantage" of standpoint third world feminism, we could generate different questions about resettlement in Canada from those posited by the call for proposals. For example, government data offering a population-level profile of the first Rapid Impact Syrian refugees painted a relatively grim picture about the resources and challenges they were poised to navigate in Canada. Literacy levels of these newcomers—not only in English and French, but also in their native Arabic—were low, and they would be arriving to Canada with significant, unaddressed medical and dental needs (IRCC 2016). But centering women, and mothers in particular, required that we think differently about these challenges. As low-income, mostly rural women, these mothers had already navigated complex local and transnational processes on behalf of their families, despite barriers to basic medical care and education. As survivors of war, and at great risk to their lives, they had shepherded their children through step migration and refugee camps. What resources had these women drawn on to forge strong selves and families? What lessons did their particular experiences, strategies, and insights bring to bear on scholarship and policy generated by Canadian stakeholders?

Our choice to center newcomer *mothers* was duly informed by the work of feminist sociologists like Ginetta E. B. Candelario (2009), Kimberly Hoang (2013), Pierrette Hondagneu-Sotelo (2000), and Rhacel Parreñas (2009). Each has argued for a feminist approach to studying large-scale phenomena like international migration, racial ideologies, and social policy through the shifting relations of transnational mothers. Parreñas has articulated an especially strong stance on centering women and their mothering processes: "As a feminist, I believe that we can still study gender even by solely focusing on women. This is because when we speak about women's gendered experiences, we are always already referring to men" (Parreñas 2009: 4). From these scholars' contributions, we were confident that centering Syrian newcomer mothers would not only yield beneficial insights on how they themselves were faring, but also about the linked fates of their partners and children. In the pages that follow, we discuss three fundamental ways that the project's feminist approach shaped our project.

Three Ways a Feminist Stance Shaped the Project

Assembling a Team and the Internal Organization of Our Meetings

A first, fundamental shaping of the project as a feminist one meant empirically centering the accounts of Syrian newcomer mothers through assembling a team to empower their stories. This meant that our project was, as a matter of course, situated within ethical and methodological obligations related to language and translation. In order to do justice to mothers' narratives, the project would require cultural and linguistic expertise, which in turn required us to spend our grant monies entirely on participant recruitment and Arabic-language fieldworker costs. In practical terms, women's long-form personal narratives would need to be elicited through collaborative, iterative, face-to-face work that could only be done in Arabic. Their narratives then needed to be translated into English for circulation among ourselves and the scholarly and governmental bodies that had funded the work and for political and epistemic transfer to feminist academics and activists who do *and* do not speak Arabic.

Perhaps unsurprisingly, given these significant start-up costs and methodological challenges, ours was one of a small handful of funded proposals that aimed to engage directly with Arabic-speaking refugees in their native language.[4] Bringing mothers' direct, original insights into the national conversation on Canadian resettlement was a politically and intellectually important motivation for our work. As recently urged in this journal, "Translation is politically and theoretically indispensable to forging feminist, pro-social justice, antiracist, postcolonial/decolonial, and anti-imperial political alliances and epistemologies" (Alvarez, Caldwell, and Lao-Montes 2016: v). But the research process also required another kind of feminist translation that was more difficult to achieve: social interactions and tangible resources that would be of use to the newcomer mothers and their families. In this way, participatory-action research (Whyte 1991; Fals Borda 2001) was an ideal but ultimately unattainable practice in most cases. We describe in the final section of this essay how we integrated aspects of participatory-action research with a small number of research participants, but in general, our approach resembled what Hondagneu-Sotelo has termed "advocacy research" (Hondagneu-Sotelo 1993: 56). The only outcome we could modestly anticipate in an exploratory pilot study like ours was that results from our conversations with mothers could shed light on gaps, inequities, and possibilities for social action and change within resettlement processes.

As described above, at an early stage in the planning process it became clear that we would need to build a research team with key parameters in mind. Here, insights from the literature on Black feminisms, and in particular, Collins's pathbreaking theorization of domination as "interlocking systems of oppression" (Collins 1991: 222) required that we reorganize our epistemological assumptions and sociological practice with interlocutors. As mothers and scholars based in Canada, we had to critically examine the idea of expertise and dispense with routine ideas about who would supervise, analyze, or know best in our partnership with newcomer participants, or with student research assistants. Neither Neda, Melissa, nor Ito spoke Arabic or had spent significant time in the Levant, although we had each come to Canada through a different migratory path. Neda was born and raised in the United States to parents who emigrated from Iran and now lives in Canada as a permanent resident while maintaining Iranian and U.S. citizenship. Melissa's grandmother emigrated from Damascus, Syria and her grandfather from Bishmizzine, Lebanon to the United States. She was born and lived in the United States before coming to Canada recently as a senior scholar. Ito was born in Taiwan and raised in Japan before she immigrated with her family to Canada as a teenager. She completed high school and undergraduate studies in Canada before leaving to the United Kingdom for her graduate studies, and spent the subsequent thirteen years working in Japan and the United Kingdom before returning to Canada as a senior scholar.

Given these privileges, which have shaped our experiences as mothers, women, and scholars in Canada, Mohanty's 1991 critique of essentialist notions of gender circulated by first world feminists and her formulation of third world feminism led us to consider how gender might operate as "political rather than biological or locational grounds for alliance" (quoted in McDowell 1993: 313). At the same time, key readings on Muslim feminisms have shown that projects like ours, which might fall under a global feminist banner, are regularly suffused with stereotypes about victimized Muslim women in need of saving from patriarchs in "Islamland" (Abu-Lughod 2002: 68; Mahmood 2005; Rinaldo 2013). By critically reflecting on our identities as women academics based in Canada, we had to acknowledge that despite being multilingual and from different racialized, national, and religious backgrounds, and despite our professional training and credentials, the insights and skills we could bring to this scholarly endeavor were lacking in significant ways. We certainly were not the experts on the Rapid Impact resettlement process that was being constructed, and in some cases, improvised in real time by the Canadian state. Crucially, we lacked cultural understandings that limited our ability to productively engage and interpret our interlocutors' narratives. And in a broader climate defined by geopolitical violence against Muslim women and communities, our project risked reproducing uncritical, homogenizing, and Orientalist ideas about gender and power, particularly in the context of mothers' forced migration and resettlement.[5] We understood that we needed to seek partnership and guidance from others with different sightlines and knowledge.

Through referrals from colleagues and leaders in grassroots, Syrian-led resettlement efforts in the Toronto area, we expanded our research team in two ways. First, we recruited four early-career women scholars as paid research assistants (RAs). Each scholar was already enrolled in a graduate program at the University of Toronto and all are recent newcomers to Canada with backgrounds from different parts of the South West Asia and North Africa (SWANA) region: for example, Laila, our coauthor on this essay and a UNESCO Youth Forum participant, was born and raised in Egypt and moved to Canada in 2013 after having experienced the effects of the Arab Spring in Cairo.[6] The others are Rula Kahil (Education; Lebanon), Rasha Elendari (Archaeology; Syria), and Jessica Radin (Religious Studies; United States). Each RA possessed native or native-level fluency in Arabic and experience in SWANA-region refugee camp settings and Canadian resettlement efforts. Their inclusion on the team was not only essential for building trust and understanding with the newcomers with whom we had proposed to conduct research, but also to ensure that in advance of our outreach, discussions and negotiations among the team would anticipate and address, to the extent possible, issues that would complicate our research.

To begin, Ito, Melissa, and Neda consulted closely with Laila, Rula, Rasha, and Jessica in biweekly internal meetings held before we applied for research ethics board approval from our university (a rigorous, fraught process that could be the subject of its own reflexive essay). In these meetings, we intensely vetted research design- and content-related matters against the RAs' local knowledge as recent newcomers and cultural insiders. This included soliciting and incorporating their critiques on drafts of our interview instrument, consent process and materials, appropriate forms of honoraria, and various health-related supports and resources that we were ethically and professionally bound to offer to participants. Following ethics approval, the meetings became a place for RAs to discuss what they found profound, curious, or puzzling from their interviews with mothers, and for all of us to collectively learn from the patterns that emerged out of mothers' narratives. Moreover, the meetings became a space for our group to process the arduous and moving emotional journeys of the respondents, and occasionally of the team members as well. The more that we moved in, out, and across various methodological and substantive material in our team meetings, identities that cut across our team like mother/daughter, Arab/not-Arab, Muslim/not-Muslim were salient.

Second, following the incorporation of graduate student RAs, we had institutional capacity to bring three more early-career scholars onto the team: Mohammed Ali Kala (an undergraduate student recently arrived from Syria as part of the Rapid Impact program); Anmul Shafiq (an undergraduate student who moved as a teenager to Canada from Libya); and Mohamed Afify (an undergraduate student, born in Toronto to parents from Egypt). They sought out our project as a way of extending their involvements in post-2015 resettlement efforts and we were enriched by their work as researchers and our copresenters at scholarly conferences.

The meetings, which continued throughout the course of the year-long pilot, were an intentional convening of our expanding, multigenerational team. The inclusion of Syrian and Arab-heritaged researchers was one modest effort to address what critical migration scholars and sociologists like Rawan Arar have described as the importance of "bearing witness" to refugee experiences through "varied perspectives" (Arar 2017). In Arar's case, the perspective of Jordanian humanitarian workers offers a vital counter to research on the "Syrian refugee crisis" generated by and for Western audiences. We extend from Arar's case to incorporate the perspectives of seven early-career researchers who share what she describes as "geographical, cultural, linguistic, and religious commonalities" with project participants (Arar 2017). This organizational approach, inspired by feminist and critical research practices, created spaces for the most junior members of the team to be powerful contributors.

In the next sections of this essay, we describe several of the major, recurring challenges related to the research process discussed in our meetings. Notably, although the project initially focused on the stressors mothers experienced in integrating children into schools and communities, our interview guide began with each mother narrating her migration journey and our analytic foci broadened in turn. These stories were extensive, deep, and often eclipsed the focus on children's integration. Moreover, the other stressors in mothers' lives influencing their mental health went beyond children, and thus their stories and the thematic scope of our second wave of questions widened.

SHARED IDENTITIES AND THE CHALLENGE OF TRAUMA IN RESEARCH
WITH SYRIAN NEWCOMER MOTHERS

In preparation for "entering the field" it was important for our research team to initiate conversations about best practices.[7] Karen Jacobsen and Loren Landau (2003) and Dina Birman (2006) discuss several important ethical and methodological rules for conducting interviews with members of a displaced population, which may not necessarily be applicable to members of other groups. First, the RAs helped remind us that researchers need to be aware that members of such populations are very often in a vulnerable position and have spent numerous days filing forms, answering questions, having their backgrounds investigated or confirmed, and so on. Often interviewees have not been properly briefed on what the goals of a research project are and how they can contribute to it, which we too noted in our own participant/interviewer interactions in Wave 1: participants were sometimes reluctant to move forward with the interview and sought information about the benefits of participation or reassurance about why the interview would be audio recorded. In the case of the mothers with whom we worked, many remained concerned about the authoritarian regimes under which they lived, and believed they may be arrested or harmed by authorities if they expressed their opinions (Yu and Lieu 1986). This lack of trust in or fear of government (which we likely represented to some) was observed during some interviews, either because participants explicitly expressed fear or because of the reactions some questions produced.

To counterbalance some of the challenges in eliciting mothers' narratives, or even in recruiting them to the project in the first place, we noticed that RAs inductively drew on their own identities as entry points in their interactions with the refugee mothers.[8] By talking about her own experiences as a mother and newcomer to Canada, for example, Rula was able to quickly build rapport, which allowed for the interviews to run smoothly and helped the participants be more at ease when sharing their stories. Below, Rula shares a small detail about her own everyday resettlement practice that elicited recognition and further elaboration from a participant:

> **P1:** It is a personal matter. . . . You miss your family; you miss your life. So you start to think about it. Sometimes, I forget about it. But other times, I remember. *One word* can remind you . . . that you lost all this. So you get depressed. . . . Then life goes on. And you see your

kids. . . . You see that you are [working on] securing their future.
That is what makes up for this [pain].

Rula: So when you feel this way, what do you usually do?

P1: I listen to music! [*laughing*]

Rula: Sometimes, when I listen to music, it reminds me even more [of my
hometown].

P1: Sometimes, you choose the music that puts you even more in this sad
mood. [*laughing*]

In order to make the interview process as comfortable as possible, and to encourage participants to share their stories, Rula and the other RAs intuitively shared information about themselves, being sincere about their own experiences and vulnerabilities. Of course, it was also crucial that interviewers asked open-ended questions and gave participants the time to express themselves. The RAs also had to be very sensitive, empathetic, and reactive to participants' answers—a dynamic that was sometimes the subject of debate among team members. Was there an appropriate amount of empathy to show that would honor the interaction between participant and interviewer without harming interpersonal trust or stalling the research process? Were there strategies that RAs could or even should use to manage their own emotional reactions? Best practices in qualitative research generally hold that interviewers should ask questions and wait for the interviewee to answer before interjecting or reacting, in order to avoid influencing his or her answer in any way. However, in the case of this project, it was difficult for interviewers to simply remain silent while listening to participants express suffering and trauma. The following excerpt from Rula's first interview with a participant—where the interview was temporarily suspended—was discussed at length by the team at one of our meetings:

Rula: So what do you miss most in your country?

P3: My parents. [*begins crying*]

Rula: Of course. . . . And I'm sure they miss you too. Do you call them?
[*Pause. Still crying* (00:03)]

Rula: I'm sorry . . .
[*Silence* (00:10)]

Rula: I should have told you that some of the questions might elicit some
pain.[9]

[*Silence* (00:14) *Sighs*]
Rula: Do you talk with them?
P3: *Alhamdulillah.* Yes, I do.

The mothers in our study wept most often in interviews as soon as the subject of their own mothers and fathers came up. Due in significant part to the exclusion of most non-nuclear families in Syrian resettlement in Canada, they had been separated from parents and other extended kin who were central in helping to raise their children in Syria.[10] As suggested by the excerpt above, it is extremely challenging for the interviewer to stick to the questionnaire and remain silent when sitting across from a participant who recalls tragic experiences and appears to suffer from trauma. We felt it crucial for our interviewers to at once demonstrate patience and wait for participants to speak while remaining responsive to their answers. In our team meeting, Rula described that in the moment she felt pressure to stick to the interview guide and ultimately felt guilty about having steered the participant back to the questionnaire. Collectively, and based in relevant literature, we agreed that project participants should not be pushed and for interviewers to be empowered to make dynamic and trauma-informed determinations about how to shift or let go of the conversation, if need be.

Another issue that arose in team meetings was the need for interviewers to pay attention to how they formulated questions so that they were culturally sensitive to the mothers' senses of self and dignity. For example, the interviewers were quickly reminded that the topic of marital relationships was a very sensitive one and that gendered power dynamics may in fact intervene in a mother's participation or nonparticipation in the study. In the case of one participant, her husband was vocally resistant to the idea of her participation in the project, even joking to interviewer Jessica: "I do everything with the kids—you should be interviewing me!" Jessica found that she needed to suspend the typical protocol in favor of talking with both husband and wife in order to put them both at ease before returning to the interview.[11]

Gendered interactions like this were, in some cases, a strain on trust and may have constrained or negatively shaped an interviewer's ability to elicit mothers' full narratives or disclosures. In other cases, it may have established further rapport between the women, as we saw in some interviews, where both participant and interviewer would later share a good-humored, private giggle in homosocial space. To wit, we noticed that the physical space where the interview was conducted influenced the content and tenor of the conversation. Half of our participants were involved in English courses organized by a local resettlement agency and the interviews with these mothers were conducted on-site, in the break room of the facility. The other half were recruited through chain-referral sampling, with interviews conducted either in mothers' own kitchens and living rooms or, in a few cases, neighborhood cafes.

All of these features help explain how our Wave 1 interviews could be characterized as mothers processing war- and migration-related trauma and loss, with most also offering broad reflections on their lives before resettlement in Canada. These initial interviews thus became a space for participants to speak, weep, mourn, and share their thoughts and sometimes laughter with a fellow Arabic speaker. When mothers were approached to participate in a second round of interviews, the majority of mothers agreed to continue on with us and resumed their interviews with a degree of rapport and trust built in Wave 1. In Wave 2, however, three hard realities of Canadian resettlement became more apparent in the mothers' narratives: household financial constraints and mothers' emergent desires to contribute financially, especially in light of their husbands' unemployment; their children's difficulties at school; and the challenges of learning English.

Centering Mothers' Words through Shared Arabic Language and Knowledge

A second way that a feminist approach shaped our project involved centering mothers' language, and by extension, grappling with the politics of translation. Giving nuance to multiple forms of expression is key to a feminist practice of translation. Thus, following the completion of our Arabic interviews, the next major phase of the project revolved around transcribing and simultaneously translating interviews from Arabic to English. This process presented several methodological challenges that are necessary to discuss in relation to the difficulty of conducting sociological work across diverse cultural and linguistic field settings. If, as in the humanities, we are to think about translation as an "art form," it is also crucial to acknowledge how translators make decisions about what and how to translate, which words to keep in the original language and why, and how to keep the voice of the participant "alive" in two languages, all the while attempting to remain faithful to the original text (in this case, the mothers' audio-recorded narratives). Keeping alive mothers' meanings through translation was a central value and goal of our project.

TRANSLATION AS "ART FORM" VERSUS "ACCOUNT"

In conventional presentations of language, the "invisibility" of a translator and her additional efforts to make the translated text "flow," seem "natural," or "not translated" are understood as necessary. Commonly, "invisibility" is understood as "fluency." In the translation of literary texts, "a fluent translation is written in English that is current ('modern') instead of archaic, widely used instead of specialized ('organization'), and standard instead of colloquial ('slangy'). Foreign words ('pidgin') are avoided." (Venuti 1995: 4). However, technical or social-scientific translations cannot and do not necessarily follow the same rules. In other words, for technical and social-scientific texts, focusing on an "account" may be more fruitful and is, in fact, pro forma in qualitative sociological research.

If we transfer the idea of an account to the translation of narrative interviews in sociology, ensuring flow may not be appropriate for qualitative research, though it may be for literary work. More specifically, because our interviews were two-way, verbal interactions, there were many pauses, interjections, instances of weeping, and audible interruptions by small children and others in the background. In other words, our feminist centering allowed us to see the interview process itself as a naturalistic setting that cannot be rigorously planned or entirely managed by the interviewer. Therefore, the translator and transcriber roles in this case may be to simply accurately convey the content of the interviews and the interactions therein rather than assuring invisibility.

Nonetheless, any translator faces the issue of losing some idioms, expressions, and ideas in translation. Some expressions, for example, are embedded in deep cultural context and cannot be translated literally. Moreover, figurative language can also be challenging because it is related to sounds and images that are also cultural. As we are socialized throughout our lives to associate certain images to specific situations, language plays an enormous role in perception and nonverbal communication. These issues are even more complicated when translating dialects and colloquial talk, as in our case. Translating Syrian dialects (with all of their specific images, cultural expressions, and so on) presented its own suite of challenges beyond those we had already anticipated in translating from Modern Standard Arabic (MSA) to English.

We noticed that between Wave 1 and Wave 2 interviews, mothers' facility with English had evolved, and mothers increasingly code-switched between Arabic and English. This presented us with intriguing sociolinguistic material to ponder. For example, in Wave 2, as mothers' concerns turned to the hard realities of resettlement, they also sometimes expressed criticisms of the compulsory English programs they attended. In the excerpt below, presented in original Arabic and translated into English, a participant was critical of how English was taught in her government-funded LINC (Language Instruction for Newcomers to Canada) course and, revealingly, by whom. Her critique, though voiced in Arabic, was peppered with terminology she reproduced in English:

السنة الجاية لازم رابع. بس أنا ما بحس حالي لازم تحطني رابع. لسة أنا بدي... يعني بتحسيها هي بدا تطلع... بدا تاخد اجازة.. بتحسي تدريسها مش قدير. يعني حاطين الانسات اللي بالESL هيك مثل فض عتب...ملل. مش عم بيعطوا بقلب و رب. عن جد. مش بقلب و رب. يعني بتيجي بتعيد الكلام... بتقلك مثلا كلمة صعبة: "use dictionary" Okay ليش أنا بفهم dictionary حتى use dictionary-ا ؟ أنا لغتي منيحة... أنا use dictionary...level 6, 7 عم افهم الموضوع حتى استحمل dictionary ؟ بتفضلها بتبهدل مثلا...(...)

يعني هلا في ناس صارلها ٧ سنين، ٨ سنين بـlevel 2 او 3... يا اختي نحنا كلنا صرلنا سنة! مثل المثل... جايين ناكل الEnglish عشان بدنا نعمل، مس بدنا نقعد. أنا بستغرب في واحدة صارلها عشر سنين... لك level 1 ! معقول انت عشر سنين؟ لازم كنت أنا أبلغ كندا! والaccent... أكبر غلط... بيحطولنا انسات مش كنديين. طب ليش؟ (...) شو عم بتحطيلي صينية؟ هديك المرة عم تنقلنا املا... نحنا دارسين بيلادنا "that"... "that" شو هي "dat"؟! عم بتنقلنا الاملاء... "dat". شلون بدك تكتبي "dat"؟ اتهجيها يا الله... "dat"... يا الله شو هي "dat" كتبت "d-o-t"... "dat"... على اللفظ اللي عم بتقوله. "dat". هي "that". طب ليش؟ ما هي عم بتأسسنا. اذا الaccent تبعيتا زبالة... شو بدا تعلمنا؟ قلتلهم نحنا عم نتعلم English عندي الaccent الهندي. لما بيحكوا الكنديين بنفهم عليهم. الaccent اللي عم تحكيها... هدا أكبر غلط (...). مهما كان... بنت البلد غير.

P: Next year, I have to go to level four. But I don't feel like I can go to level four. I still want to [learn]. . . . You [impersonal] feel like she wants to leave . . . like she wants to take a break. . . . You feel like she's not professional; like those who teach ESL classes do it out of boredom, to keep themselves busy. They don't do their job wholeheartedly. Really. Not wholeheartedly. She comes and repeats everything and if there's a word that's hard to understand, she says *"use dictionary."* Okay, but do I even understand what's in the *dictionary* so I can *use dictionary*?! Is my language level that high that I can use the *dictionary*? Am I in *level six, seven* . . . do I understand what's going on so that I can use the dictionary? She keeps offending us. . . . Now, some people have been in *level two or three* for seven to eight years. But we've been here for a year! A year! And like they say, we want to "eat" the English language [as in, learn it as fast as we can] because we want to work, not just stay inactive. I am surprised, there is a woman who has been in level one for ten years now. Is that possible? Ten years in *level one?* And the *accident* [accent]. . . . The biggest mistake they make is assigning instructors that are not Canadian. Why? . . . How do you assign a Chinese instructor? Last time, she was dictating us words. We learned in our country, "*that*" . . . "*that*." She was dictating us. . . . She says "*dat*." What's "*dat*!" How do you write "*dat*!" Spell it! I wrote "*d-e-t*" as she was saying it. "*Dat*" is "*that*." Why? She's supposed to be teaching us the fundamentals, and her accent is awful! How are we going to learn? I tell them, we're learning Indian English. The Indian accent. When the Canadians speak, we understand them. . . . The accent she [the instructor] speaks . . . that's the biggest mistake. Whatever it is, *bent al balad* [literally "the country's daughter"—meaning someone born here] would be different.

The example above showcases some of the nuances of translating a passage from Arabic to English when participants toggle between languages. All interviews were conducted in colloquial Arabic—more precisely a mix of Syrian, Lebanese, Kurdish, and Iraqi Arabic—which means that the interviews contain images and figurative language that do not exist in MSA. For instance, the local expression *nakol* (to eat something) is typically used for books, referring to the idea of consuming all the knowledge that exists and thus becoming more knowledgeable in a field. This is why, in the above excerpt, the participant says, "*nakol el* English"—meaning she is *eager* to learn English and improve her proficiency as much as she can so that she can start working right away.

The excerpt also introduces some of the complicated dynamics of eliciting and then transcribing narratives where a participant may express racism against nonwhite Canadians in her criticism of resettlement services. With regard to the participant's choice of words, *Ebn* (son) or *Bent* (daughter) *al balad* (literally "son/daughter of the country") is another local expression typically used to refer to someone who was born in and is ostensibly familiar with a country. In this specific context, *bent al balad* does not refer to the Indigenous peoples of Canada, but someone who is a "native" speaker of English, who exhibits "correct" pronunciation. The mother in the excerpt above explains that native English speakers (expressed principally as Canadian-born and, perhaps, white-presenting

Canadians) would be preferable, as she believes they could teach English with a "Canadian" accent more efficiently and accurately. This is why she says "a native Canadian would be *different*," in comparison to a "Chinese" or "(East) Indian" instructor whom she describes as possessing an alternative accent. Expressing herself in Arabic and English plays a major role for the mother in retaining authority, ensuring that the transmission of certain ideas is even more accurate when communicating with a fellow Arabic speaker.

Finally, the italicized words were the ones expressed by the participant in English in the original interview. We were fascinated to note which words or expressions were in English (as opposed to Arabic) and how language became ever more flexible in these interactions. For example, when the participant above repeats what her instructor says in class, she repeats it in the same language that it was originally expressed in (*use dictionary*). In this case, the participant criticizes her instructor by mimicking exactly her use of English. We use italics to call attention to mothers' code-switching and their choice to directly quote the English speakers with whom they interact, giving readers a sense of the layering of language in the original interaction.

WORDS AND EXPRESSIONS FOR VALIDATING PARTICIPANTS

As described above, interviewers must have cultural and linguistic knowledge to produce an accurate translation. In our case, certain words were used by mothers in a different way from their literal meanings. For example, the word *mufawada* was often used by participants who were sponsored as Government-Assisted Refugees (GARs). This word literally means "negotiation"; it is typically used by newcomers to refer to the United Nations High Commissioner for Refugees (UNHCR), the agency that helped them arrive to Canada. The term *ajaneb* is another example: literally "foreigners," it is usually used to refer to non-Arabs who live in Arabic-speaking countries but do not speak the Arabic language. The use of this word during the interviews was particularly interesting to us, since in this case the interviewee (a newcomer mother) is the one typically considered a "foreigner" when compared to the primary reference group of long-standing permanent residents and citizens of Canada. Therefore, not knowing what this word means in this context might affect an interviewer's understanding of the issues raised by the interviewee. In other words, interviewers and transcribers need to be aware of these specificities; otherwise it becomes hard to provide a full translation of the meanings attached.

In other cases, interviewers must rely on their own interpretations, especially when the same word is used in different ways. The tone becomes important to take into account; it is the interviewer's job to be able to pick up on what the tone conveys. Most principally, religious expression is common in the broader SWANA region and linked to the individual and social act of thanking and praising God to acknowledge God's presence and power. Religious expressions like *inshallah* (ان شاء الله ["if God wills"]) and *Alhamdulillah* (الحمد لله ["thank God"]) constantly appeared in our interviews. As Zubay writes, "When we say thanks in English . . . our gratitude is directed at our peer, another mortal. But in Arabic, the phrase *Alhamdulillah* [is] for gratitude that can only be directed toward the Creator. . . . All praise and glory be to God" (Zubay 2010–11: 13). Nonetheless, there are critical nuances to how mothers deployed *Alhamdulillah* in our research:

(1) to literally thank God for a specific blessing, (2) as a sarcastic way of talking about an unpleasant situation, and (3) as a way to avoid answering an interviewer's question.

For instance, when one participant was asked about her current relationship with her husband, she seemed hesitant or unsure how to respond. In this case, her solution was to avoid answering the question:

Rula: So, this happened until you got adjusted, right?

P13: *Alhamdulillah.*

Rula: And you and him [your husband] now, are you OK? Are you facing any difficulties?

P13: [*a bit hesitant*] *Alhamdulillah.*

In the interaction above, the participant's use of *Alhamdulillah* without any additional elaboration was a strategy she used to avoid answering the interviewer's question. In its most basic translation ("thank God"), the term makes some contextual sense as an affirmative, or positive response to two linked queries about adjustments and difficulties. But for an interviewer or translator who is familiar with the intricacies of Arabic and the cultural dynamics underlying everyday terms like *Alhamdulillah*, an alternative, and in this case, more ambiguous meaning becomes more clear. In combination with the participant's terse, hesitant demeanor, here

Alhamdulillah suggests the participant is seeking a socially-sanctioned way to avoid the question. At other times, *Alhamdulillah* was used in a sarcastic way to describe an unpleasant or unfortunate situation:

> **Rula**: And the prices went up?
>
> **P6**: Too much. I'm telling you, no one would rent this room [in the basement] for 5,000 JOD [Jordanian dinar]. I rented it for 25,000 [JOD] . . . I told my husband, "*Alhamdulillah*, I am being buried alive." [*laughs*]

Here, the participant describes her experience living in Jordan before traveling to Canada, explaining that her only housing option was to rent a room, rather than an apartment or a house, and for an unusually high price. She is specific in the way she describes her situation, comparing living in a room in the *basement* to being "buried alive." Taking her description literally, a researcher unfamiliar with the participant's cultural context might be perplexed by the juxtaposition of *Alhamdulillah* and the idea of being "buried alive." However, an interviewer and translator aware of the contextual uses of this expression understands that in this case, it is used in an ironic, skeptical manner to reflect on one's unfortunate situation while still praising God. As in the first example, the tone and attitude of the participant suggests nuance in her use of *Alhamdulillah*, and confirms its multiple meanings to the researcher or reader.

In other instances, *Alhamdulillah* is used in its literal and broader meaning, as a statement of gratitude to God for everything one possesses, and of acceptance for the situation one is in, no matter how distressing and difficult it is. It is a way of acknowledging that God has a plan for everything and that one trusts God's plans. The example below confirms this idea:

> **P15**: Yes, I had a house with four bedrooms . . . but during the war, everything . . . from the pressure, everything breaks. They fix things and they break again, and they fix again.
>
> **Rula**: OK. . . . It was hard.
>
> **P15**: *Alhamdulillah*. . . .
>
> **P15**: Yes, they [my sons] want to leave [Syria] but it's not possible.
>
> **Rula**: I see. . . . How do you feel when you think about the fact that they cannot leave?
>
> **P15**: Sometimes I don't like hearing their voice, because we would start crying. . . . What can I do? It's too much for me [*crying*]. *Alhamdulillah*.

In this interaction, the participant says *Alhamdulillah* twice, after describing two unhappy situations. First, she explains difficulties in the war and how everything in her house would "break." Later on, she talks about how hard it is to keep in touch with family who live in Syria or other parts of the world, suggesting that a simple phone call reminds her of the difficult situation they are in. Nonetheless, she expresses gratitude to God and communicates her trust in God's plans, hence the use of *Alhamdulillah* after describing each struggle she has faced. In this case, praising God and showing gratitude in the face of hardship may be a type of coping mechanism to minimize stress and a felt sense of hopelessness.

Giving nuance to multiple forms of expression is key to a feminist practice of translation. As such, the central role of shared Arabic language and local knowledge in our research process cannot be overstated. Throughout the process, the interpretive expertise of RAs was crucial both in situ with participants and in the collective Arabic to English translations RAs crafted together. Their collaboration and unique knowledge facilitated a fuller understanding of the multiple meanings of mothers' words and the communication of emotion by participants more generally.

Participatory-Action Activities and Newcomer Mothers' Emergent Power

The third way a feminist approach shaped the research was through the activities of the forty-one mothers who joined our project. Their participation took several forms across the pilot year, all of which involved mothers' ongoing consent: (1) as research interlocutors, they made ongoing decisions to either continue or drop out through the course of the study; (2) two participants joined us in scholarly partnership as our copanelists at a major Canadian academic conference; and (3) once the pilot study came to a close, several other participants were commissioned to help us convene two community-building celebrations for local Syrian newcomer families, our university, and partner agencies.

The key action item in our collaboration with the newcomer mothers was to ensure that their participation in the study was completely voluntary, bearing in mind that they would perhaps feel compelled to participate due to felt pressure from their relationships with our partner agencies or even fellow mothers. In general, our interview data showed a shift in mothers' sense of control about their destinies in Toronto across the first several months of their resettlement. In Wave 1, most mothers described a felt sense of relief that they had safely relocated their families away from the conflict. But their initial sense of relief was also paired with new worries that came from their displacement to Canada, which was not the preferred choice of destination for many. By the time of Wave 2, however, we noticed evidence of a new sense of control emerging among the interlocutors. Only two mothers decided to leave the study. We believe that, for those participants who stayed, the research interviews were affirming experiences that confirmed they were valued and that they mattered.

In some cases, our collaboration with mothers also extended past the end of formal interviews. For example, we were granted funds through our university to organize celebrations at the close of the academic year, offering our research participants a respite from some of their everyday responsibilities by providing an afternoon off with home-style Syrian food, music, dancing, and childcare/activities for their families. We were delighted, as well, to bring our children with us, in contravention of the traditional participant-researcher boundaries and roles. For those mothers recruited through enrollment in English courses, we held the event in a beautiful, newly renovated common space between a library branch and a branch of our main partner agency, a resettlement organization. The site was easily accessible by public transit, with free parking, and is a year-round, cost-free social and recreational facility we wanted families and children to experience so that they might access those resources again. For the mothers recruited via referral sampling, the celebration was held on campus in a warm meeting space at Victoria College at the University of Toronto with live music provided by a popular musical group composed of local Syrian newcomers. We provided funds to families to cover travel costs to and from the event. To cater both events, we contracted with four participants who had indicated to us a desire to start catering businesses from their homes; we also contracted with a fifth participant to bake sweet and savory Syrian snacks for a participatory-action-inspired conference panel we later convened. It was a small act of reciprocity to put funds into mothers' wallets as they built catering experience, and to show gratitude for their participation in the study as well as their labor and skill.

Apart from the dynamics of mothers' participation, and the modest supports we attempted to reciprocate, we had to think more critically about if and how we might harness the research we had produced together to destabilize taken-for-granted power dynamics and inequalities in our profession. One way we tried this out for the first time was to field a

conference panel about our project with two research participants at our
national sociology meeting. The mothers' participation, insights, and
contributions—on the panel and particularly during a dynamic Q&A with
professional sociologists and graduate students—drew on feminist praxis
to reimagine how scholarly conference panels are typically organized.

From the interviews themselves Rula and Rasha indicated that two
interlocutors seemed especially keen to be more involved in the research
and knowledge production process. One mother, Alia, had a degree in
social work and was a practicing social worker before the war.[13] She had
directly asked Rasha if there was a way for her to bring her scholarly training and skills into the project. The other interlocutor, Najwa, described to
Rula a strong interest in social science issues and a longing to attend university once her children were safe and settled. We approached Najwa and
Alia about joining us as conference panelists, and invited them to offer any
insights or comments—about their backgrounds, involvement in the
research endeavor, and experience of migration and resettlement in
Toronto—they wanted to share with the audience. They expressed special
interest in fielding questions in an open Q&A format with the audience.
Because very few of the conference attendees spoke Arabic, Rula served as a
real-time translator for Najwa; Alia was comfortable to communicate in
English with Rasha looped in at Alia's signal for translation assistance
when necessary.

Following a conventional fifteen-minute presentation on preliminary
findings by faculty and a presentation of similar length on project methodology by the RAs, Najwa and Alia briefly introduced themselves. We then
segued to Q&A, where a flurry of hands were raised. When asked by an
audience member what message she wanted to convey to Canadians, Alia
didn't hesitate: "*We* are the only people who can explain ourselves. Involve
newcomers in everything." Her directive resonated with the original goal
of our project as we had pitched it to the IRCC-SSHRC funding agency one
year earlier: that the Rapid Impact program and all related policy decisions
could only be assessed if the observations and insights of Syrian newcomers were centered in the analysis.

Another question posed to both mothers was asked by a well-known
feminist sociologist: "Why did you decide to participate in this study?"
Najwa (as translated in real time by Rula) described coming to Canada with
skepticism about the relationship between what she termed "Islamic cultures" and "the West." Based on her observations from media and what she
heard from fellow Syrians before resettling in Canada, Najwa felt strongly

that Canadians were hostile to "Islamic culture." She described that for her, participating in the research project was a way to test these ideas and to see if the "two cultures" could get along or if they would be at odds. She described being pleased to discover their compatibility, after a year of close-up experience and observation of how we, the members of the research team, conducted ourselves with her and her fellow participants. She described having felt from her first interview that being part of the project meant she mattered and was empowered in her new world. While we and the audience were both captivated by Najwa's savvy observations, all of us on the research team were especially humbled by the truth she revealed about our collective research endeavor: as we had been researching her, she had been researching *us* in turn.

Conclusion

In order to center the margins in a feminist approach to research, the unequal relations *between* women at the intersection of citizenship status, class, nation, race, and other categories of asymmetrical power must be addressed. Drawing from black feminist and third world/transnational feminist epistemologies, we felt that an important lens into Canada's post-2015 Rapid Impact regime was possible by centering the insights of recently arrived Syrian mothers. The interventions of feminist sociologists offered us a sharp analytic and theoretical justification to design our project as such, in spite of a mainstream academic and policy environment in migration studies that remains disinclined to incorporate the situated knowledge of women.

Once we began the project, a feminist approach further influenced the research in three ways. It enabled us to assemble and sustain a team of researchers that, in its internal organization, upended traditional power dynamics between faculty, graduate students, undergraduate students, and respondents. It offered us a tool kit to translate the fullness of what our Arabic-speaking respondents shared. And in opening our research to involve a range of participatory-action activities driven by respondents, the project thrived. With greater and lesser success, we attempted to put feminist epistemology to practice in ways we hadn't in our previous research endeavors. The message offered here is not unique or innovative; simply put, we are encouraged that the small adjustments we made based in feminist praxis yielded a project more expansive and inclusive than first imagined. Whether by copresenting with participants at an academic conference, bringing our families and children together over food and music, or in the primary act of bearing witness to mothers' narratives of war and resettlement, our own identities as mothers, daughters, and sociologists based in Canada continue to evolve as we learn to listen in Arabic.

Neda Maghbouleh is assistant professor of sociology at the University of Toronto. She studies anti-immigrant and anti-Muslim racism to learn how MENA (Middle Eastern/North African) refugees and immigrants forge identities in North America. She authored *The Limits of Whiteness: Iranian Americans and the Everyday Politics of Race* (2017).

Laila Omar is a sociology PhD student at the University of Toronto, and recipient of the Canada Graduate Doctoral Scholarship. Her research draws on the study of refugee and immigrant integration and qualitative methods to better understand the integration process of mothers and youth from the MENA region in Canada.

Melissa Milkie is professor of sociology at the University of Toronto. Author of *Changing Rhythms of American Family Life* (2006), her research centers on links among gender, work, parenting strains, and well-being. With a unique focus on gendered culture, she identifies cultural forces linked to mothering and fathering across time and region.

Ito Peng is professor and Canada Research Chair in global social policy at the University of Toronto, Department of Sociology and Munk School of Global Affairs and Public Policy. Her writing focuses on social policy, the political economy of care, family, gender, and employment and migration policies in the Asia Pacific.

Notes

1. We are grateful to the editors and reviewers at *Meridians* for their deep engagement and feedback on an earlier draft of this essay. The research described here was supported by the Social Sciences and Humanities Research Council of Canada and the Ministry of Immigration, Refugees and Citizenship.
2. Information about the expansion of our pilot study into a 2018–23 project with mothers and teenagers titled RISE (Refugee Integration, Stress, and Equity) is available at www.riseteam.ca.
3. For a comprehensive, critical overview of the sociology of refugee migration, including problematization of terms like *refugee* and *crisis* and erasures of South-South migration, see FitzGerald and Arar 2018.
4. This observation is based on our personal and professional communications with colleagues across Canada funded by SSHRC-IRCC. For the full list of funded projects see http://www.sshrc-crsh.gc.ca/results-resultats/recipients-recipiendaires/2016/syrian_refugee-refugie_syrien-eng.aspx.
5. We thank an anonymous reviewer for asking us to engage this important issue.

6   We use SWANA to refer to the region commonly known as the Middle East. See Culcasi 2011 for a feminist geopolitical analysis of the "Western-imperialist" Middle East category.

7   See Chughtai and Myers 2017 for their anthropological and hermeneutical theorization of "entering the field" as "a fusion of horizons where a fieldworker is 'thrown'" (795).

8   For "public mothering" as an entry point to trust and rapport in the field, see Candelario 2009: 29–31.

9   All interviews began with a review of the verbal consent form, including a participant's consent to be asked difficult or upsetting questions. In the case of Participant 3, although Rula had followed the protocol, once she began crying, Rula's immediate reaction was to doubt whether she had in fact explained that "some of the questions might elicit some pain" (review of audio recording, November 10, 2016).

10   For more on the privileging of male-led, heterosexual nuclear families and the burdens placed on refugees in Canadian immigration policy, see Staver 2010.

11   We share this anecdote to convey the complexity of conducting research with women when men seek to place themselves at the center of analysis. Contra anti-Muslim racist and Islamophobic thinking, this phenomenon does not originate with, nor is it limited to Muslim or SWANA societies. Interactions like these are part and parcel of the "patriarchal bargain" found in Canada, the Global North and West (see Joseph 2000; Kandiyoti 1988; Moghadam 2004).

12   Pseudonyms used in line with University of Toronto Research Ethics Board protocol.

Works Cited

Abu-Lughod, Lila. 2002. "Do Muslim Women Really Need Saving?" *American Anthropologist* 104, no. 3: 783–90.

Alvarez, Sonia E., Kia Lilly Caldwell, and Agustín Lao-Montes. 2016. "Translations across Black Feminist Diasporas." *Meridians: Feminism, Race, Transnationalism* 14, no. 2: v–ix.

Arar, Rawan. 2017. *Bearing Witness to the Refugee Crisis: Western Audiences and Jordanian Humanitarian Workers*. Washington, DC: Middle East Institute.

Birman, Dina. 2006. "Ethical Issues in Research with Immigrants and Refugees." In *The Handbook of Ethical Research with Ethnocultural Populations and Communities*, edited by Joseph E. Trimble and Celia B. Fisher, 155–78. Thousand Oaks, CA: Sage.

Candelario, Ginetta E. B. 2009. *Black behind the Ears*. Durham, NC: Duke University Press.

Chughtai, Hameed, and Michael D. Myers. 2017. "Entering the Field in Qualitative Field Research: A Rite of Passage into a Complex Practice World." *Information Systems Journal* 27, no. 6: 795–817.

Collins, Patricia Hill. 1991. *Black Feminist Thought: Knowledge, Consciousness, and the Politics of Empowerment*. New York: Routledge.

Culcasi, Karen. 2011. "Mapping the Middle East from Within: (Counter-) Cartographies of an Imperialist Construction." *Antipode* 44, no. 4: 1099–118.

Fals Borda, Orlando. 2001. "Participatory (Action) Research in Social Theory: Origins and Challenges." In *Handbook of Action Research:Participative Inquiry and Practice*, edited by Peter Reason and Hilary Bradbury, 27–37. Thousand Oaks, CA: Sage.

FitzGerald, David Scott, and Rawan Arar. 2018. "The Sociology of Refugee Migration." *Annual Review of Sociology* 44: 387–406.

Haraway, Donna. 1988. "Situated Knowledges: The Science Question in Feminism and the Privilege of Partial Perspective." *Feminist Studies* 14, no 3: 575–99.

Harding, Sandra. 1993. "Rethinking Standpoint Epistemology: What Is 'Strong Objectivity?'" In *Feminist Epistemologies*, edited by Linda Alcoff and Elizabeth Potter, 49–82. New York: Routledge.

Herr, Ranjoo Seodu. 2014. "Reclaiming Third World Feminism; or, Why Transnational Feminism Needs Third World Feminism." *Meridians: Feminism, Race, Transnationalism* 12, no. 1: 1–30.

Hoang, Kimberly Kay. 2013. "Transnational Gender Vertigo." *Contexts*, May 20. https://contexts.org/articles/transnational-gender-vertigo/.

Hondagneu-Sotelo, Pierrette. 1993. "Why Advocacy Research? Reflections on Research and Activism with Immigrant Women." *American Sociologist* 24, no. 1: 56–68.

Hondagneu-Sotelo, Pierrette. 2000. "Feminism and Migration." *Annals of the American Academy of Political and Social Science* 571, no. 1: 107–20.

IRCC (Immigration, Refugees and Citizenship Canada). 2016. "Rapid Impact Evaluation of the Syrian Refugee Initiative," December 21. https://www.canada.ca/en/immigration-refugees-citizenship/corporate/reports-statistics/evaluations/rapid-impact-evaluation-syrian-refugee-initiative.html#toc1–4.

Jacobsen, Karen, and Loren B. Landau. 2003. "The Dual Imperative in Refugee Research: Some Methodological and Ethical Considerations in Social Science Research on Forced Migration." *Disasters* 27, no. 3: 185–206.

Joseph, Suad, ed. 2000. *Gender and Citizenship in the Middle East*. Syracuse, NY: Syracuse University Press.

Kandiyoti, Deniz. 1988. "Bargaining with Patriarchy." *Gender and Society* 2, no. 3: 274–90.

Mahmood, Saba. 2005. *Politics of Piety: The Islamic Revival and the Feminist Subject*. Princeton, NJ: Princeton University Press.

McDowell, Linda. 1993. "Space, Place, and Gender Relations," part 2, "Feminist Empiricism and the Geography of Social Relations." *Progress in Human Geography* 17, no. 3: 305–18.

Moghadam, Valentine M. 2004. "Patriarchy in Transition: Women and the Changing Family in the Middle East." *Journal of Comparative Family Studies* 35, no. 2: 137–62.

Mohanty, Chandra Talpade. 1991. "Under Western Eyes: Feminist Scholarship and Colonial Discourses." In *Third World Women and the Politics of Feminism*, edited by Chandra Talpade Mohanty, Ann Russo, and Lourdes Torres, 51–79. Bloomington: Indiana University Press.

Parreñas, Rhacel Salazar. 2009. "Inserting Feminism in Transnational Migration Studies." *Migration Online*, May. http://lastradainternational.org/lsidocs /RParrenas_InsertingFeminisminTransnational MigrationStudies.pdf.

Rinaldo, Rachel. 2013. *Mobilizing Piety: Islam and Feminism in Indonesia*. New York: Oxford University Press.

Shohat, Ella. 2001. "Area Studies, Transnationalism, and the Feminist Production of Knowledge." *Signs* 26, no. 4: 1269–72.

SSHRC (Social Sciences and Humanities Research Council). 2016. "Targeted Research: Syrian Refugee Arrival, Resettlement, and Integration." https://www .sshrc-crsh.gc.ca/funding-financement/programs-programmes/syrian_refugee -refugie_syrien-eng.aspx?pedisable=true.

Staver, Anne. 2010. "Family Reunification Policies and Diverse Family Life." Canadian Political Science Association Working Paper. https://www.cpsa-acsp.ca /papers-2010/Staver.pdf.

Venuti, Lawrence. 1995. *The Translator's Invisibility: A History of Translation*. New York: Routledge.

Whyte, William Foote, ed. 1991. *Participatory Action Research*. Thousand Oaks, CA: Sage.

Yu, E. S. and W. T. Lieu. 1986. "Methodological Problems and Policy Implications in Vietnamese Refugee Research." *International Migration Review* 20, no. 2: 483–502.

Zubay, Bryan. 2010–11. "Insh'Allah." *Mercer Street*. http://cas.nyu.edu/content/dam /nyu-as/casEWP/documents/zubayinsho6.pdf.

About the Cover Artist

....

Trinh Mai. *They Come for Me*. 2009. Joss paper and oil on canvas.
40×90 inches.

Trinh Mai's work pays respect to her Vietnamese American heritage, striving
to document personal memories and those inherited from her elders. Drawn
from intimate experiences of heartache and triumph, of struggle and perseverance, and of loss and fulfillment, Mai's artwork offers comfort and shares the
faith that has fostered her during these times. Through her work, she lives the
refugee and immigrant experience vicariously through the elders, allowing
her to interpret these stories through her own ears, eyes, heart, and hands.

As a form of study and prayer, she absorbs life's joys and hardships, rewriting them as true tales of triumph—also a reminder that out of tragedy are ever
born the blessings that we might have never been able to predict could or
would come. Her body of work speaks on the healing that occurs while we
wade through the circumstances of life, striving to find meaning and look to
the passage of time to mend our afflictions.

They Come for Me was inspired by a dream wherein Mai watches herself claim
the blessings that pour upon her from an aperture above in a dim grove of
trees. On the first panel, the blessings come. On the second, the hand reaches
out, ready to receive. On the third, we see gratitude for these gifts.

For a more in-depth experience, please visit trinhmai.com.

MERIDIANS · feminism, race, transnationalism   18:2 October 2019
DOI: 10.1215/15366936-7775740 © 2019 Smith College

2019 Paula J. Giddings Best Article Award

Abosede George *for her article* "Saving Nigerian Girls: A Critical Reflection on Girl-Saving Campaigns in the Colonial and Neoliberal Eras," *Meridians* 17:2

Abosede George is an associate professor of history at Barnard College and Columbia University in New York. She teaches courses in urban history, the history of childhood and youth in Africa, and the study of women, gender, and sexuality in African history. Her book *Making Modern Girls: A History of Girlhood, Labor, and Social Development in Colonial Lagos* (2014) received the 2015 Aidoo-Snyder Book Prize from the African Studies Association Women's Caucus, as well as Honorable Mention from the New York African Studies Association. She is currently working on the Ekopolitan Project, a digital forum dedicated to historical research on migrant communities in nineteenth- and twentieth-century Lagos, West Africa.

Abstract: This essay discusses girl-saving campaigns in Nigerian history, focusing on the two that have been most extensively documented: the girl hawker project of the early twentieth century, which climaxed with the 1943 passage of the first hawking ban in Nigeria, and the #BringBackOurGirls campaign, which started in 2014 and is still ongoing. Though separated by time and space, in order to inspire salvationist impulses in their respective audiences both campaigns have relied on a gendered notion of imperilment that centers the image of the youthful female body threatened by sexual violence from male aggressors. Yet through its reliance on certain restrictions, gendered and otherwise, the portrait of the vulnerable girl that campaigners outline inadvertently prompts disidentifications as well.

Read the article: doi.org/10.1215/15366936-7176461